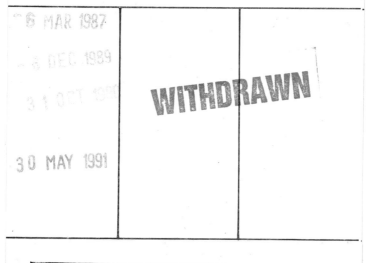

BUSINESS BEHAVIOUR
AND MANAGEMENT STRUCTURE

BUSINESS BEHAVIOUR & MANAGEMENT STRUCTURE

A.L. MINKES AND C.S. NUTTALL

CROOM HELM
London & Sydney

©1985 A.L. Minkes and C.S. Nuttall
Croom Helm Ltd, Provident House, Burrell Row,
Beckenham, Kent BR3 1AT
Croom Helm Australia Pty Ltd, First Floor,
139 King Street, Sydney, NSW 2001, Australia

British Library Cataloguing in Publication Data

Minkes, A.L.
    Business behavior and management structure.
    1. Business—Decision making   2. Management
    —Decision making
    I. Title   II. Nuttall, C.S.
    658.4'012   HF5500

ISBN 0-7099-1795-3

Printed and bound in Great Britain
by Billing & Sons Limited, Worcester.

CONTENTS

Preface

For RUTH and JENNY

PREFACE

A book of this kind calls for more than the usual acknowledgements. It was only possible to write it because of the willingness of a number of busy executives to give their time and consideration to the two authors. To them is owed a first debt of gratitude and beyond them to the many industrialists who over the years at the Industrial Seminar at Birmingham University, took part in discussions from which the authors' interest in business strategy originally emerged. The University itself, with its encouragement of exchange of ideas and knowledge between the business and academic worlds, made the study possible. The late Professor Philip Sargant Florence was chairman of the Industrial Seminar and his boundless interest and enthusiasm were an inspiration.

Ruth Minkes and Jenny Nuttall contributed their advice and tolerance to two disputatious authors; Margaret Sheridan, Linda Williamson, and Jody Chan their skill and patience in typing successive drafts.

The book was mainly written during the authors' time at the University of Birmingham and partly during periods spent by one of them (ALM) visiting The Chinese University of Hong Kong. It faithfully presents the words of the businessmen who contributed to the discussions. For the selection of material, its analysis and interpretation, the authors are, of course, solely responsible.

ALM

CSN

PART ONE

MANAGERIAL INITIATIVE AND CONTROL

1 INTRODUCTION

This book sets out to examine some aspects of strategy formulation and the exercise of managerial initiative in a small number of British business enterprises. It employs as its medium, a form of reportage or commentary on the ideas, perceptions and actions of leading executives in those enterprises and in their subsidiaries and divisions. Its aim is, therefore, a specific one: it seeks to add to the evidence and insights which are needed for a better understanding of business behaviour. This, rather than establishing general propositions, is the primary purpose though some propositions are clearly suggested.

The main questions which led to this study have claimed increasing attention in recent decades, from academics and practitioners alike. What is business strategy? How does it emerge in the large and complex modern corporation with its network of hierarchical and lateral forms? The modern enterprise has been described as a system of governance: where in such a system is to be found the elusive but glittering spark of entrepreneurship?

These questions lead in turn towards other themes, particularly those of managerial initiative and control in large companies and the relationship between the centre and the constituent parts of decentralised organisations. The critical reality which is explored in the case study material which forms the greater part of this book is the way that the senior directors and executives see this relationship. This reality is as significant as the objective formal structures, rules and procedures, perhaps more significant. When, for example, Sir Adrian Cadbury describes the centre of the business as the only part able to take 'a wide enough view,' he is in effect specifying limits to decentralisation. Similarly, when he says that the centre and he himself can lay down only a few broad guidelines for senior management, he is indicating what he conceives as limits to control. In Thomas Tilling, both Sir Patrick Meaney as the chief executive of the group and Mr. Gordon Yardley at the head of the subsidiary company, Newey and Eyre, speak independently of 'trust' as the basis of the relationship between group and subsidiary. This expressed a genuine sense of the reality of the business relationship within the group.

Managerial perception, in other words, is a statement about reality. There is a real business environment outside and an organisational structure of persons inside, to which in the last analysis that perception has to correspond if the company is to survive. But neither the external nor internal environments are simply 'givens': they are shaped by the ways in which management sees and interprets them.

In the chapters which follow, therefore, the authors have been at pains to allow the businessmen to speak for themselves. Mr. Pountain, chief executive of Tarmac, remarked that it had been a useful experience to be able to stand back from current considerations and to think more extendedly and analytically about the strategy and corporate structure of his company. The authors may claim, perhaps, that their book presents businessmen in reflective mood but focusing their attention on pressing topics of their business enterprises.

Few investigators and research workers can be wholly 'barefoot empiricists' since it requires some conceptual framework even to begin asking questions of the businessmen. The initial approach was very much influenced by the development of behavioural and organisational theories of the firm and by the concept of decision-making as processual. It encompassed the view that decision-makers work in a world in which knowledge is incomplete, imperfect, and dispersed — in the world at large and within their own boundaries. They were envisaged as doing so in large businesses which were rather like constitutional systems of government in which the process of strategy formation was diffused throughout the organisation.

At the same time, in research of this character, an eclectic pragmatism is an essential ingredient and most of all, a willingness to allow the discussion to 'run' along courses dictated by the experience of the businessmen. Despite the greatly increased volume of work on organisation behaviour and empirical studies of business behaviour, surprisingly little is really known about decision-making in organisations. The means by which business strategy is formulated and the relationship between strategy and corporate structure, exhaustively explored by Chandler and others, still remain a battleground of debate. It is important, therefore, to add to the debate the element of managerial perception of managerial decision-making.

The basic methodology of the book is, therefore, to present case material interspersed with commentary. This material does not comprise case studies in quite the sense of the conventional workbook: it may better be described, perhaps, as case evidence. Its origin is an interesting example of the way in which ideas can be stimulated and research generated by exchange between industrialists and academics.

Over a period of about twenty years, from the mid-1950s to the mid-1970s, the University of Birmingham conducted the Birmingham Industrial Seminar. The chairman was the late Professor Philip Sargant Florence. The seminar provided an occasion in which senior and middle managers in West Midlands industry and academic staff from a number of faculties in the University met for the purpose of discussing with the chief executive or a board director the development and organisation of his company.[1] The seminar was held on ten occasions every year and was attended by about sixty people, of whom two thirds were from industry.

The visitor from the company which was the subject of the evening's discussion, whether chairman or a main board director, submitted to the seminar in advance of the meeting a paper in which he described the development of his company, and this was the springboard for the ensuing discussion. Thus, over the two decades of its existence, the seminar had the advantage of acquaintance and conversation with some of the leading businessmen in the large companies in the UK. Some companies (Esso and Tarmac were examples) accepted an invitation to the seminar for a second or even a third time, and were represented over the years by the same chairman or chief executive.

In the course of time a body of papers was collected which traced the shifting interests, the attitudes and the problems which had engrossed the attention of the leaders of British industry who came to the seminar. These papers were a record of a changing period in industry and business, changes brought about in the increase of size and complexity of companies, in the external forces acting on them, in the sophistication of policy-making and in the developments in their management practice and purpose. The spread of the interests of the seminar and the unique nature of the contributions were good reasons for making a review of the collection of papers.

As a first step in the review it was decided to try to bring the map of changes up to date for a selected number of companies. Five of these companies are considered in detail in this book. The chief executives were asked to consider a range of questions about company matters of the type broadly defined above, and to do so in the course of informal conversation.

Part One is offered as a contribution to the study of the changes in management practice which have occurred over recent years. The statements which are made there by way of quotation have been extracted from recorded conversations of discussion with men in key positions in the companies, and it is only that part of the discussion which bears on the question of management that appears here. Its direction is concerned with the way in which decisions are made, with the identification of the sources of change in policy or organisation and with the responsibility shown and the initiative exercised by managers at various levels. The parts of these discussions which deal with questions of policy, strategy, acquisition or with the action of market or environmental forces on the companies are the subject of Part Two of the book.

For these purposes, permission was asked of companies to pursue the questions at various points in the management hierarchy. The companies and the names of those who contributed to the discussions in Part One are:

Thomas Tilling[2]

Managing director and chief executive:	Sir Patrick Meaney
Newey & Eyre managing director and chief executive:	Gordon Yardley
Regional director (Midlands):	Peter Hickman
Branch manager (Birmingham):	Bob Wingate

Manganese Bronze

Vice-chairman and chief executive:	The late John Neville
BSA Guns managing director:	Alf Scott

Cadbury Schweppes

Chairman and chief executive:	Sir Adrian Cadbury
Managing director of Cadbury Typhoo: (the food division of Cadbury Schweppes)	Tony Slipper
Manager-development manager Cadbury Typhoo:	Michael Jolly

Tube Investments

Joint managing director:	Richard Bagnall
Director — commercial analysis: (TI group secretariat)	Charles Duff

In Part Two, there are two further contributors from these companies, and Tarmac was substituted for Tube Investments as follows:

Thomas Tilling

Newey & Eyre commercial director	Jon Brockett

Manganese Bronze

Chairman and chief executive	R.D. Poore

Tarmac

Former chairman and chief executive	R.G. Martin
Deputy chairman and chief executive	Eric Pountain[3]
Assistant managing director	Bryan Baker
Group finance director	Graham Odgers

Each of the two Parts is self-contained although, inevitably, there is overlap between them because the themes of strategy, initiative and control, are so closely intertwined. Because they differ in length and in content, the study of Tarmac, for example, being in two parts, there is some difference in the format in which they are presented. In both cases there is a general survey of the companies and an overall analysis: whereas in the first part, the dialogues form one chapter, in the second a chapter is devoted to each company. The basic treatment is, however, much the same.

The findings of this study are set down in the running commentary on each of the firms and the main ideas are summed-up in Chapters 4 and 11. Any attempt to establish general propositions about firms has been cautiously limited, but there is no doubt that there are recurring themes in one case after another. Different in important respects though these enterprises are from one another, some threads in the tapestry of their behaviour are commonly to be traced.

One such thread is the pre-occupation with the relationship between the centre and the separate parts of the organisation. In virtually every case it is recognised that the making of strategy cannot be located in one individual or one part of the business. It is a more generalised or diffused activity. But in all cases, there is a clear sense of the particular role of the centre in the determination of the parameters of policy and the choice of strategic options. Indeed, even where levels of management below the top play a significant part in strategic decision-making, the options to be considered are set by the values and decisions of the centre.

A second thread or element is to be found in the importance of propinquity and serendipity: ideas emerge not simply from elaborate planning processes, but from informal exchanges between executives who are used to working together. The unexpected and the benefits of chance can to some extent be catered for: executives whose offices are along the same corridor and who exact no penalties for talking shop, can persistently push ideas to and fro. This is an important means of maintaining and developing the flow of innovative thinking within large enterprises. In turn, this may be enhanced by personal contact between top executives at the centre and other levels of management in divisions and subsidiaries.

This leads to a third conclusion which might easily be missed in the emphasis which is inevitably given to the place of the organisation and the heavy overlay of bureaucratic forms which are associated with great size. This conclusion is that entrepreneurship and the entrepreneur are not dead nor are they merely located in the ramifications of organisation. Individuals at the head of large enterprises play a powerful part in the setting of values, the selection of the limited number of options which the organisation at any one time will consider, and in determining the focus of attention among its members. These, it has been noted above, are essentially the prerogative of the centre: but the centre is no abstraction since it is the place in which the most senior executives of the organisation are based. The interplay of individual imagination and leadership with the rules and procedures of organisational form is one of the most inviting problems for continued research.

One striking characteristic of the various relationships discussed by the business executives is the blend of formal structure and informal conventions of behaviour in the development and implementation of strategy. Another, even more striking, is the inseparability of strategic choice of product-market scope and the creation of corporate structure. It is no doubt convenient to distinguish, as Ansoff[4] has done, between strategic and administrative decisions. But there is certainly a level of administrative decision which is as much a strategic pre-occupation of top management as is the choice of products and markets.

In making business choices, the decision-makers in large enterprises are neither narrowly confined to their existing last nor, on the other hand, do they view the whole world of possibilities. The ultimate outcomes in decision-processes are themselves the consequences of cascades of individual decisions through time which set the framework within which the firm considers its opportunities. The number of guidelines and options which can be dealt with is limited, as Adrian Cadbury points out, and there are the further boundaries set by the general outlook of the senior executives. Examples of this are to be found in R.G. Martin's emphasis on the need for what he termed 'compatibility' in acquisitions or in Sir Patrick Meaney's attitude towards excessive size in individual locations.

Professor Penrose[5] has written that a firm may be regarded as a pool of assets and that the disposition of those assets at any one time may be regarded as an incident in the changing history of the business. The evidence which follows in the chapters of this book shows that the nature of the assets, including managerial views and expertise, governs the flexibility of choice. It also shows how in the firms considered, changes were made both in response to problems and as part of the entrepreneurial impulse towards innovation.

Notes

1. There were occasional variations to this rule. Some meetings were devoted to trade union matters, when the visitor would be a general secretary of a trade union. Occasionally a paper was submitted by a member of the University staff.

2. Since acquired by another company. The interviews took place, and this study deals, with periods prior to the acquisition.

3. Subsequently chairman. For details of this and other changes, see Chapter 10, note 1.

4. Ansoff H.I. *Corporate Strategy*
McGraw-Hill, New York, 1965.
See below, Chapter 11, note 6.

5. Penrose E.T. *The Theory of the Growth of the Firm*
Oxford University Press, Oxford, 1959.
See below, Chapter 7, note 6.

2 THE MANAGEMENTS

This chapter is intended to bring together and contrast the present management behaviour of the four companies as shown by the discussion of the views which are presented in Chapter 3. Tube Investments is a large international engineering company. Manganese Bronze, in the same area of manufacture, is a small-to-medium company and home-based. Both companies have diversified, the smaller company being more diversified, in the sense of unrelatedness of the separate parts. Thomas Tilling is probably one of the few true conglomerates anywhere — a pioneer in this field in the UK. Cadbury Schweppes is a food-and-drinks manufacturing company, with an international base but remaining, in the main, undiversified. In size, range, market and business experience, the four companies differ. But they have all been subject to the same environmental forces, the same social and political pressures, to which they all have had to respond. There are some marked similarities in the recent changes in management practice of these companies which may have to be attributed to the strength of the external forces acting upon them.

It has been a marked emphasis in management practice, certainly since the Second World War, that greater freedom is given to managers at the middle and lower levels. There is a general realisation of the need for autonomy at the point of operational decision-making and this has brought about a change in business behaviour and attitude which can be observed in practice and confirmed in discussion in any large company. Most companies now recognise that increased autonomy means more decentralisation of company organisation, so that there is a change in form which accompanies the change in attitude. Altogether this seems to be understood as a change from the experience of business as it was even fifteen or twenty years ago.

The new administrative and organisational form which is being evolved is a main subject of the discussions on which Chapter 2 is based. Some change of form was forced on companies as the way of managing complexity. Size itself is a cause of complexity but, even more, there is the complexity which is due to the almost unavoidable increase in operational diversity which comes with size. Since the

Second World War most large companies, in obedience to strategic necessity, have expanded either by integration or by acquisition or by merger, and in doing so have added new lines of business. They have had to rethink their management style and reorganise their management structure in relation to the degree of the increase in the range of activities which resulted from the expansion. The following sub-sections could be seen as a set of case studies of the way in which the four companies have modified their management practice to contend with the new problems of managing complexity.

The world of the modern corporation is a changing one in which firms may respond to exogenous and endogenous pressures. To that extent, this study of individual firms deals with ideas and situations in them in particular periods. Organisation |and the degree of autonomy will be influenced by economic and other conditions: a period of constraint, for example, will affect the balance between control at the centre and autonomy of subsidiaries or divisions. The general concept of the business corporation as a system of governance is, however, unimpaired by such variations in behaviour and structure.

Research into business practice always meets the element of obsolescence. An important direction for research is to try to identify the features within the constitutional framework of the corporation which enable it to perceive and respond to changing conditions.

Thomas Tilling

Not many companies who favour growth welcome the management problems which follow an increase in diversity. Those who do welcome it, and make a specialism of managing diversity, adopt a style of management in which the special skills of each part of the diversified whole are given free play. In Thomas Tilling a conglomerate, an industrial holding company as they term it, which was built up in the 1950s and 1960s, the change in style could be dated quite sharply from 1948, when Tilling, under the threat of nationalisation, voluntarily sold its transport assets. Faced with the demise of their traditional business, Tilling decided to form a company with an entirely new look. The Tilling directors realised 'that a very real need existed for a company which was prepared to invest substantial sums in privately owned companies and which would allow the existing management to continue to run the business as before'. They adopted the concept, which was original, of building up, by acquisition, a new group of companies which were not related in the type of business which they served.[1] This group of diversified companies would be united at the centre by the high level of business skills which could be applied by the centre throughout the diversified range.

Group management at Tilling was therefore from the beginning in the business of managing diversification, a field in which they could claim to be pioneers in the UK. The organisational principle of the group was firmly rooted in decentralisation and its business principle depended on the differentiation of the skills which were employed by management at the centre and by management in the subsidiary companies. The companies under their boards would be operationally independent, and would be linked directly to the centre by the presence of a member of the board – in the case of Tilling, the board member has always been a Tilling director or an experienced senior executive who joins the company board as the non-executive, part-time chairman. The Tilling centre puts complete trust in the responsibility of the management of the companies and in their professional business judgement, and itself carries out a persuasive, supportive role, 'supporting the creative role of the company management' as Sir Patrick Meaney says, 'as being in charge of their own destiny'. Success for the group as a whole is dependent on the ways in which its small but very able centre management can contribute something extra to the performance of the companies, how it can modify the profile of the group through time by assisting growth points in the companies and by the choice of new fields or new companies for acquisition.

Meaney does not doubt that business is becoming more complex nor does he suggest that the increasing complexity of business does not create problems for management. Legislation, social pressures, political pressures have all made business, like life, infinitely more complex and more difficult. But, to him, Tilling's diversified base 'adds not one whit to the complexity'. 'It is as easy', he says, 'to run a diverse group as a specialist group'. The advantages which Tilling find in their system of management are that they have greater freedom in investment, and in turn can leave the subsidiaries to manage with greater agility, free from the pressures on big business.

What I do believe [says Meaney], is that as long as you have the right philosophy the centre will not interfere with the operations and, therefore, the trades, and that at the centre you have an overall business and investment view, which is much sharper and better informed than a general body of shareholders will ever be, and if you chose your men in the companies correctly, and allow them freedom, that managing diversification is, frankly, less onerous and not more onerous than managing specialisation.[2]

The centre is small. Of the 44 000-45 000 people in the group there are less than a hundred in the centre. As a discipline in the real practice of decentralisation, Tilling make sure that, despite the enormous temptation from time to time to build up consulting services, economic investigation teams and so on, this number at the centre does not increase.

At the centre there is a small intelligence unit of four people which is guided in the direction which is required by a committee of the managing director and the financial and legal directors. This committee of three is a sort of pre-vetting directorate, an informed bureau, which has in its range the strategic view of a company in big business. For example, when the Tilling subsidiary Newey & Eyre made a proposal that they should expand into the North American market, they had the support of Tilling, who had already expressed themselves ready to invest in America. Support from the centre was assured and this meant that Newey & Eyre could move in their chosen direction free from many of the administrative and legal problems and the financial risks which arise in a new international venture.

The main instrument for contact, liaison and support and for the agreement of minds between the centre and the company is the chairman appointed to the company by Tilling. He usually has an assistant who is a group executive. These central, group executives have different disciplines — engineering, accountancy, science, economics and so on. They are all practised by having gained experience and training in acquisitions over the years. Several of the central executive staff can conduct an organisation investigation and, if necessary, can carry out negotiations.

When a company discerns an acquisition opportunity it would examine it thoroughly at the company board under the chairman and, at that point, Tilling may attach a member of the central team to the company's investigating team — an accountant, a technician or whatever is required — to assist. If the acquisition is approved at company level, it has to come to the consideration of the centre. For it is a firm rule that acquisitions must be approved by the Tilling board. Although proposals and arguments put forward by a company are sympathetically received, Tilling would want to know, for example, that the yield meets their requirements, that it is well managed, that there is not too high a goodwill content and that there is a growth pattern. The company has to produce a full paper with certain appendices on future prospects, fund requirements and so on, and it has to convince the executive directors' committee (see Chapter 3) that the acquisition would meet their criteria. If Tilling withheld approval it would be for clear, general business reasons — not because Tilling had ceased to respect the company's judgement or its opinions on its products, activities and management. The company would be presented with a carefully prepared case for the dissent of the centre and it would be given every opportunity to plead its case further. 'We normally give chapter and verse', says Meaney.

> The Tilling chairman would go back to his managing director, and if necessary and if it was important enough, they would come and see me and would talk around it. And so far we have managed to persuade our MDs — even our most ambitious ones — that if something was not acceptable to us that it was not just a whim of ours, it was that there really were flaws in the argument. Now, here and there, we have allowed ourselves to be persuaded; and I am not suggesting at all that we are infallible; but in a number of cases over the years, a company's acquisition judgement has been proved wrong. And this has been a great help — in a negative way, I confess — in believing that we really do know about acquisition evaluations.

Tilling have developed monetary and budgetary controls and the management techniques required for maintaining them, as far as is necessary to ensure financial discipline. In the behavioural field, since 1972 or so, they have a rule, which they now firmly practise, that they would not invest in any location or plant that had more than five hundred people employed in it. Meaney himself would prefer not to go above three hundred employees. Personnel problems are just as important as any other problem in business development, and although it may be in certain circumstances that multi-businesses could have more complex personnel problems than single business companies, Meaney thinks it probable that at present the reverse is true. One of the most significant management changes in the last decade, he says, is due to the realisation that a company which buys and manages different and separate businesses, and which does not have to commit its investment to large organisational structures, has advantages in personnel management over single-industry companies, which are generally highly capital-intensive and must obey the economic laws of mass production and who often have to increase plant size.

There is no doubt whatever, [says Meaney], that if there has been a significant business management change in the last decade it is that if you can manage your investment economics so as to have small units you stand a better chance of getting a more effective and efficient performance with much better employee communications and, therefore, better industrial relations.

Manganese Bronze

Manganese Bronze is a much smaller company than Thomas Tilling and the relations between the centre and the companies are more intimate. There are about 2500 people employed in the group. There are twelve subsidiary companies geographically dispersed over the UK, with a small centre in London which consists of the executive vice-chairman, another full-time executive and the necessary office.

The Tilling group was formed from the beginning on a plan which gave the particular Tilling character to the group and the separate companies. But Manganese Bronze, as Neville says, 'has grown up by accident. This is not something that has been carefully planned at all. It has merely arisen by opportunist activities by the board'.[3] This difference is magnified by the difference in size, and it shows in the styles and the forms of management of the two companies.

When Gordon Yardley, the managing director of the Tilling subsidiary Newey & Eyre, is at the Tilling headquarters at Crewe House in London, '.... (and it is not all that often), when I am, and it is generally known that I am there, very often someone will buzz or make it known to Philip Bulpitt [Tilling chairman of Newey & Eyre at the time], so that whilst I am in, would I mind (and very often Pat Meaney would be told that I am there), if I dropped in and had a few minutes' chat'. But if the managing director of a Manganese Bronze subsidiary went to the group's London headquarters at 1 Love Lane, it would be specifically to see the chief executive, John Neville. Again, as an example of difference, the part-time chairman of the Manganese Bronze subsidiaries is the chief executive himself. So he meets the managing directors of the companies regularly, and telephone contact between them would have the ease of people who are frequently in conversation. It will be apparent from the dialogues quoted in Chapter 3 that in the smaller group the contact between the centre and the companies is closer and more frequent and that the personality of the chief executive is more easily impressed on the character of the group.

But despite these differences, the remarkable fact is that the philosophy which underlies management in the two companies is the same and that there are ways in which the constitutional character of Manganese Bronze resembles that of Tilling. Management progression in the companies in both groups is normally within the company. It does not lead to a place in management at the group centre. The managers at the companies are experienced in the trades — electrical distribution, insurance, guns and rifles — and in their dialogue with the centre they bring to the table their experience and understanding of the trades which are practised in their companies. The contribution of the centre is to discuss any proposal which they bring forward with sympathy and respect for the company management and their business judgement, but to examine it meticulously as a business possibility. There is no sign that the differentiation of the roles of the two levels of management is a chord of friction. They contribute different skills in a way which complement each other. It may be that if management progression led as a rule from company to group, the responsibilities of the two levels would not be quite so clear.

In both companies the influence of the centre is to widen the range of policy consideration. In both cases a company, as a member of the group, can think on a larger scale. But because of the difference in size there are differences in the way the influence is exerted and felt. The subsidiaries of Tilling are big enough to weigh strategic possibilities for themselves and an important function of the group centre is that it offers a point of review, giving a second opinion if that is required. The composition of the Tilling main board, which is half non-executive, could be seen as a confirmation of this character. Meaney emphasizes that the role of the centre is to 'support' the companies. Neville never uses that word. Though the centre in Manganese Bronze also supports the companies, there is this distinction, that its primary role is leadership. The much closer dialogue between the chief executive and the company boards is intended and used to widen the business sense of the participants. The role of the centre is to lead the companies on the path of business discovery.[4]

Neville gives great emphasis in Manganese Bronze to the understanding that companies and the centre both contribute to the development of policy. There is a combined source of ideas, for these do not come from one or the other in isolation. Between the two levels there is an interplay which, if it is to be productive, must be cultivated. He described a typical centralised structure as represented by the form of a triangle. 'Inside that triangle are all their mainstream activities – every executive working his way up – at the top of the triangle is the board'. But Manganese Bronze could not function in that way. 'We have to run each one of these businesses as a separate entity'. The sort of interplay of ideas between the different levels of management which Neville looks for assumes a decentralised structure. Interplay of ideas is, in fact, the essence of decentralisation.

Proposals for discussion with the centre are introduced, in both cases again, at the company board. These proposals have to be within group requirements on, for example, the expected return, the financial limits agreed and so on, and they have to be fully supported. At Tilling the phrase used in this connection is 'a full paper', and at Manganese Bronze it was 'a supporting paper . . . . some reasoned argument'. What both companies require is a dialogue with equals. The people at the companies must be able to conduct a discussion with the experienced businessmen at the centre. If this were not so, the subsidiary company would have no independent voice and the centre would be deprived of the essential part of trade and business knowledge which is required to consider policy and to make decisions.

A distinction of Manganese Bronze, natural to a company which emphasises group leadership, is the importance which John Neville attaches to training as a responsibility of the centre. The responsibilities of a director could be very onerous, but not enough is done to train the managers, who come up through industry and who in time might become directors of companies, to fulfil these responsibilities. Training has another, more immediate, purpose apart from developing future directors. John Neville insists that he wants managers who are trained to acquire an informed understanding of the character of the company and its policies and problems in order to contribute fully as managers in their present position. 'I regard it as part of my job', he says, 'to try to make them think about what they are doing, what the business is doing and why we're doing what we are doing instead of something else'. A useful discussion between group level and company level has to be instructed, animated and inspired on both sides. An interesting confirmation of the problem to which Neville was addressing himself here came from a remark by the commercial director (Tilling) Newey & Eyre. 'Britain is sorely pressed', said Jon Brockett, 'to find good quality senior management', although, as he had just said, he found it relatively easy to recruit fairly good middle management.

BSA Guns is a subsidiary company of Manganese Bronze. Its

managing director, Alf Scott, appreciated the freedom in operational decision-making and the adaptability in production of a small subsidiary company which enjoys a degree of constitutional autonomy: 'We can get a design change done almost immediately – without a meeting at the House of Lords.' The constitutional character of the group comes through quite clearly when the views of the managing directors of the group and of the subsidiary are placed side by side. A further assessment on this matter will be made separately in Chapter 4 of this study in the light of the 'evidence' of the discussions of Chapter 3, but as a preliminary it may be useful to compare the 'legal' authority of the management of BSA Guns vis-à-vis the group with its authority in practice. In a typical operational decision, Alf Scott said, 'we don't involve the chairman of the board, it's not his concern – but the working directors of BSA Guns'. The BSA directors would never discuss such a matter with the group. But there was no question of the legal authority of the group if they chose to exert it: 'Oh, they own us, absolutely'.

Cadbury Schweppes

Cadbury Schweppes is a company which is still mainly in the confectionery and drinks business. From its comparatively restricted base of product development it has expanded its organisation globally. One of the strategic imperatives of which the company is always aware is to adhere to an uncompromising definition of the product.[5]

Cadbury Schweppes has a policy-organisational problem which is peculiar to the quartet of companies which are considered here, and which is probably not very common in British industry as a whole. The company has developed the range of products which it markets worldwide under its own brand names, but the distribution of its products internationally is in the hands of foreign companies, part-owned, often with a minority holding, for whom the Cadbury Schweppes franchise may be only part of the total business. These foreign subsidiaries may be public companies with local shareholders, under whose responsibility the company board formulates its strategic plans independent of the international company. For Cadbury Schweppes, therefore, there arises in these cases the problem of reconciling the requirement of Cadbury Schweppes for global uniformity with the demands of the part-owned subsidiary for strategic independence. 'If you want growth', said Sir Adrian Cadbury, bringing forward the point which has been discussed with Tilling and Manganese

Bronze, 'you must be encouraging them [the subsidiaries] to be putting their own ideas forward, to have their own long-range plans, and all the rest of it, but that has also to be fitted in with your own ideas of what the company as a whole should become . . .'

This is the problem which every group centre has to resolve, and the difference between the form in which it appears in Cadbury Schweppes or in, for example, Manganese Bronze is not so acute as it seems. The Malaysian company which markets Cadbury products in that country (Cadbury Confectionery Malaysia SB), although it has a degree of independence by right (by virtue of part-local ownership), which BSA Guns does not have, has no more relative power to upset main group strategy. The counterpart of BSA Guns' statement about its position in the group ('they own us, absolutely') would be a statement by Cadbury Confectionery Malaysia SB: 'They own the trademarks'. How far the right to pursue an independent policy on matters of group concern is conceded in both groups is something for internal negotiation and accommodation. Power can be devolved, but the devolution is not a right but an agreed convention. This does not mean that such agreements are settled according to the whims of individual group managements. But the pressures towards devolution have become too strong to be disregarded, and devolution is becoming systematised in the new organisational forms. Meaney said that the only successful style of management is one which recognises this change. Without that recognition, Neville said, the whole concept of running a company like his collapses. For Cadbury, the same recognition was always in mind: 'Could we say?' is the response to a proposal, looking at it on both sides or 'How far can we say?'

In the Cadbury Schweppes group in the UK there is not the same separation of the subsidiaries by the type of business as in the two companies which have just been considered. The UK subsidiaries in Cadbury Schweppes are almost entirely business-related as within the food and drinks range of manufacture, and they all use the same channels of distribution. Nevertheless there may be advantages in promoting the development of an independent view within separate parts of a large company like Cadbury Schweppes. Businesses are often amalgamated, Sir Adrian Cadbury said, as an administrative convenience, because they are related, but the cost could be that the initiative of management at the operational points is stifled. 'Size is a problem,' he said, 'and we should not attempt to put small units into larger ones . . .' An example which he offered was the Cadbury Schweppes coffee company, Kenco, a relatively small UK business, which has been maintained as a separate and undivisionalised company in spite of the pressures to administer it along with related food-and-drinks businesses as a whole. Management initiative, the 'entrepreneurial possibilities', are much greater, he said, for Kenco when it is left on its own. He was quite clear that the entrepreneurial possibilities are present in the work of any manager. It is everybody's job to keep them in mind. In this and in his insistence on the need of a dialogue between higher and lower levels of management he was confirming the view which has been stated earlier in relation to John Neville and Manganese Bronze.

Interesting also is the representation of the typical organisational structure as a pyramid. Neville, when speaking about Manganese Bronze, drew a triangle on paper to represent a centralised structure and explained, with some pictorial detail, why a multi-product group could not be managed in that way. His group, like the Tilling group, is managed on the organisational principle of decentralisation. The obvious logic of Cadbury Schweppes' interrelated activities might lead the company to a form of centralised structure. But, as indicated above, organisational control does not have to bow to the obvious. It is the part of enterprise in higher management – 'top management' in the phrase which comes out from the dialogue in Chapter 3 – to penetrate below the crust. There is always a pressure to 'tidy it up', so it requires an act of perception, and it may require an exercise of extrepreneurial will, to resist this pressure.

Sir Adrian Cadbury spoke of the company as a place where 'what you have are ideas and opportunities' and where what you have to do is to 'avoid trapping those ideas within the traditional pyramid type organisation . . . '. What top management is trying to do all the time, he said, is 'to get around the inevitable barriers of an organisation'. He went on to say: 'There is no way to avoid some sort of bureaucracy – but also you have to loosen the organisation.' He used a number of phrases to convey what he had in mind. This loosening of the organisation must be a deliberate aim. You can have project teams, venture groups, planning groups, it does not matter what, so long as you are experimenting with means to set up a forum of ideas, some way of 'kicking ideas around'. Ideas can come from almost anywhere. 'So it is really a question of whether you can devise an organisational system which takes advantage of the inputs of individuals and turn them into a business proposition'.

In all this he was elaborating on the mechanics of decentralisation of decision-making, and on the development, transmission and discussion of ideas. A practical example of decentralisation within the pyramid was given by Tony Slipper, managing director of Cadbury Typhoo (the Food division of Cadbury Schweppes). He described the way in which his division is trying to operate within products groups who are given full responsibility for their products, cutting across functional barriers so that business, not administration, is given priority. At the same time the products groups could not be allowed to become self-contained or to be isolated from each other in their thinking. Here Tony Slipper's views on policy development are very close to those of John Neville.

In Chapter 3 there is, relating to Cadbury Schweppes, an additional brief but informative dialogue with a middle manager in a key position in relation to its subject. Michael Jolly had for some time been manager-development manager of Cadbury Typhoo and he was able to draw upon his experience in his work to present a view of the attitudes to the changes in management style in recent years of managers in the middle and lower levels.

If management action has the three attributes of decision, communication and participation, changes in management style will be partly the result of changes in the relative degree of importance which is given to the three. But the management chain has two ends, and changes in style are also partly the result of changes in responses all along the chain. Most of the discussion of this section, following the interests of the dialogue on which it is based, has been concerned with the attributes of management and only occasionally with the personal responses of the people involved. It is with these responses that this section of the Cadbury Schweppes dialogue almost entirely deals. The chief executive perceives a change in the character of the people lower down the management scale. Previously, it was possible to give orders, to 'command', but now you have to 'persuade'. '. . . The new generation are not only independent of mind, but also certainly you will not get the best of them if you simply tell them to do things . . .' (Meaney). The view lower down is of a change in the character of the people higher up. 'Historically, it seems to me, the boss was never wrong. Now it is becoming more acceptable that the boss may not be the man who is in the best position to make the total decision'. The two views do not conflict. Jolly, without saying so, implies that the impulse of change may be extra-institutional — that there is a sociological change impinging on the firm. Meaney is absolutely clear and emphatic on this, and does not suggest that the general social attitude does not affect the leaders. Jolly's position is complementary to the main run of discussion of this section in that it offers a glimpse at the shop-floor of management.

His observations about the open style of management which was being instituted in the last few years in parts of the company, and his phrase that 'you are conditioning people to expect a style . . . ' raise an interesting question. When a system like this has been installed and working — a system in which people are beginning to be more involved in the decision process — everything which is done tends to reinforce itself. Having done it for a while, it becomes a thing to be done in the future. In this way — without judging the merits of such a development — each point builds up another one, and the way the firm is actually run is discreetly changed. The point on which the questioning was focusing in this stage of the discussion with Jolly was that what actually happens in a firm is not always the result of formal action but may be due to an accretion of modes of action which are informal and whose strength depends mainly on custom. This is a matter which is discussed more fully separately in Chapter 4 where it is described as the power of the conventions of behaviour.

Jolly's remarks here were significant because they show how the conventions of behaviour appear as extra-statutory happenings — 'on the side' — which develop, in use, a continual, quasi-constitutional sanction. This is why he said that changes in management style and attitude occur as part of a 'process of evolution'. The words suggest that the motivation of the change may not be discernible. With attention fixed on the company and its management structure, the source of change may be obscured simply because it follows a pattern which is being set outside the firm.

Tube Investments

The same pressures towards devolution and delegation were felt at Tube Investments, and the company is organised in a way which emphasised the advantages of small manufacturing sites and small independent management units. But the dialogue with Tube Investments approached the subject from a different direction, which saw the importance of total size of a manufacturing company. 'There is a critical mass", said Charles Duff, 'you've got to be really very big in order to survive at all'.

Yet Drynamels, the company in the TI group which has been made a case study in what follows, has some one hundred and fifty employees, and seems to have no disadvantage in management compared with larger companies in the same business. Many other subsidiary companies in the large, multi-business groups like TI can be quite small and manage effectively. BSA Guns in the Manganese Bronze group, with about three hundred employees, is another business of the specialised type which offers few economies of scale. Cadbury Schweppes' Kenco, a small business with a 'compact management unit', can be left on its own 'to run itself'. Tony Slipper's mention of his product groups of product teams seems a deliberate attempt to develop a cross-matrix form of organisation, which is being set up at a level within the division.[6] This confirms the possibility of effective management at lower levels and with smaller units.

On the other hand, Charles Duff's view that 'you've got to be really big to survive' is unquestionably borne out in the recent history of big business. There is a place for the very small and the very big, but there is an uncertain zone in between. In Duff's words, the big firm has to achieve a 'critical mass' to be secure. All our firms subscribe to this philosophy and they have either expanded recently or they are expanding at the moment. Tilling want their subsidiaries to be big enough to have some influence in their markets. What brought attention to Drynamels in the first place, and occasioned its study in these pages, was the suggestion that the company was too small to withstand the challenge of bigger manufacturers in the future.

There is an aspect of size, therefore, which seems to put many business units of a certain size in need of a protective umbrella. The narrative with Tube Investments offers some discussion of this. In indicating that size has an importance reaching beyond effective unit management, Duff distinguished between the concerns of centre management and the concerns of management at all the lower echelons. Tube Investments had been asked to say what would be meant by following a policy which had strategic implications. In particular, would it be satisfactory (in the case of TI) to define 'strategy' as being concerned with a firm's decisions about its 'product-market mix'? The answer was informative about the range of consideration which weighs with TI centre management. 'Strategy in our terms', Duff said, 'does not mean that: what you are discussing is what we call tactics. It is, in fact, what we would delegate down to divisional management. We would be concerned with the mix of activities over the group as a whole'.

The distinction which Duff made, and which Bagnall went on to elaborate, was clear enough, though the domain of strategy is not often put at quite so lofty a level. Group management, in this view, though it maintains its interest in the management of resources does it in conjunction with the divisions and with the lower management echelons to which division may, from time to time, delegate responsibility. But the considerations to which the strategic centre uniquely responds are the macroeconomic factors – the position of the UK, the environment, the export-import balance and movements in the terms of trade.

The realm of strategic concern, as has been said earlier, is not part of the present discussion but will be given separate treatment when those implications of policy-making are considered. But, in presenting the TI view in discussions at the time, the questions which are raised point to changes in the way in which responsibility is routed and in the path through management, looking down from the top, which is followed in policy-making. In that, they have an importance for management which should be mentioned here and which, indeed, comes through in the dialogue and the case study in Chapter 3.

There is a downward shift in the level at which responsibility rests. An increasingly important concern of the centre of a large international company is to watch over its legal interests abroad and to ensure that it, for its part, fulfils its obligations under the codes of practice which prevail in each country. Acquisitions of foreign companies and the movement of currency rates become important strands of concern for the strategic centre, which develops considerable skill in handling the problems which arise. This applies both to the conglomerate centre and the centre of the traditional, divisionalised and more centralised company. A great part of the responsibility for the management of operational resources is committed to the level below the top, to the autonomous subsidiaries of the one type or the divisions of the other, and these in turn delegate their former responsibilities to the level below them. Looking at it from the bottom up, there has been a movement towards enlarging the area of responsibility of each level of management and its scope in decision-making. A manager at each level finds, as many managers mentioned in this study said, that he is being given more of a business to run.

Some Lines of Approach

To a certain degree it could be said that in developing the philosophy of autonomy the conglomerates and those companies which were following them in their business style were making a virtue out of necessity. But they were also consciously moving closer to the social climate of the modern world. All four companies, with their different nuances, showed themselves quick to recognize that the new social climate of the 1960s and the 1970s would be bound to change business behaviour. Some of the businessmen who are quoted (Meaney in particular) were very explicit about this. They are aware that there cannot be one character in personal relations in society and another for so important a part of society as business.[7]

At the same time as the social imperative of autonomy in industry was being fulfilled in management it was, by chance, being matched by an economic imperative in production. The tendency towards small production units was quite distinct from the tendency towards greater autonomy, but the development of one was reinforced by the existence of the other. In the broken terrain of business activity, all managers, even the most junior, had to be trusted to act with responsibility and initiative. A branch manager is seen as running his own business, and his chief executive says 'that is the way we like it'. This quotation is from a section from the dialogue with (Tilling) Newey & Eyre. But exactly the same phrase is used in Manganese Bronze: 'The companies in the group have the responsibility of running their own businesses, and control from the centre falls very short of usurping this responsibility'. A company which is geographically dispersed has to rely more on manager quality over a larger range of management, unless it tightens control to an extent which it may now find unacceptable. The devolution of decision power throughout the large company is so widely recognised|that it can be regarded as a new element in its constitution.

The range of independence of a manager in decision-making is a sensitive area of personal relations in management. It could be that as the circle of the manager's responsibilities and the circle of his influence spreads it might touch increasingly on the responsibilities of others. Whether this is more a source of conflict or of understanding with his colleagues depends ultimately on the degree of management maturity which resides in a company and which is one of its important hidden investments. In these four companies the policy has been to safeguard that investment by the cultivation of goodwill, understanding and trust. One of the directors in Newey & Eyre sees that as his main task. The Drynamels case study in TI and the sub-case studies of Domestic Appliances in Newey & Eyre, of the new product proposal of Manganese Bronze and of Kenco in Cadbury Schweppes provide in their different ways a commentary on this problem.[8]

In the studies of Chapter 3 there is a recognition that the traffic of managerial action has begun to flow more diffusely, and that one part of the entrepreneurial task has been to construct the guiding channels. The old channels may not serve any more, for many of the changes in managerial style are irreversible. There is a chemistry of group behaviour. Once the cake has been baked it cannot be reconstituted into its ingredients. The final comments of this study on these changes and on the new forms which are needed to accommodate them are provided in Chapter 4. Who is responsible for setting the new forms? Who 'participates' in this entrepreneurial task of reconstruction?

The size and complexity of modern firms makes it as important as ever to maintain a strong centre. Means have to be developed as required, to centralise ultimate financial control and the consideration of broad policy. But in operations — 'in action', as one company put it — the rule is towards more decentralisation. Perhaps one of the least-charted changes in company organisation in large corporations in the past two decades is the extension of decentralisation. 'Our philosophy of autonomy means only one thing and that is decentralisation' (Meaney). 'If you control [the management of your companies] in some way in a centralised concept you will remove all motivation' (Neville). One symptom of the change is that as the group grows, head office becomes more specialised and more highly competent in business but, in relative terms, smaller.[9]

Finally, it is evident that experience in the management of operations is no substitute for a continuous career education in the essential business skills. The junior and middle manager's experience in operational management may well be partial. If so, he may have to enlarge his view to comprehend company purposes and problems and undergo training to raise the ceiling of his business performance and refine his business sense. How this is done may be unique to each company. But what is common to all is that the whole pattern of increased devolution offers a training which was not available to a young manager before. The developing form of more autonomy, responsibility and initiative, reaching farther down, is itself a school for the practice of business skills.

Notes

1. This has been the experience of a large number of conglomerates which have been built up on both sides of the Atlantic since the War. 'They generally start as very small companies which are the vehicles for rapid growth by acquisi-

tion of unrelated firms. This could be called true conglomerate diversification.'
Jon Didrichsen (1972), 'The development of diversified and conglomerate firms
in the United States, 1920-1970.' *Business History Review,* XLVI, p. 217. No
attempt is made in this study to define the term 'diversification'. Gort defines
it as 'an increase in the number of industries in which a firm is active', which
limits diversification to Tilling of the four firms considered here. But Manganese
Bronze and Tube Investments describe themselves as diversified companies,
who have been consistently pursuing a strategy of diversification by acquisition
for many years. The motives of firms may differ – they may follow a synergistic
theory of acquisition or a 'bargain' theory. In the first case a firm is less likely
to diversify outside its industry. Michael Gort (1966). 'Diversification, mergers,
and profits,' in W.W. Albert and J.E. Segall (Eds.): *The Corporate Merger.*

2. This may appear to run counter to common assumptions. But Sir Patrick's
emphasis is supported in a quite different way by B.R. Scott (1973). 'The
industrial state: old myths and new realities.' *Harvard Business Review* (March/
April). He shows that diversification is not enough in itself to compel structural
reorganisation. In all European countries diversification preceded divisionalisation by many years, sometimes by 20-30 years. A critical element is competitive
pressure. Without competition, diversification can be managed by any type of
structure.

3. 'Du Pont could have had no *detailed* long-term strategy. Their new
products and markets were often accidental throw-offs from research activities,
and therefore investments in new products were frequently the result of
unintended commitments which Du Pont had 'backed into'.' Didrichsen, op.
cit., p.211. John Neville said that he had tried investment based on internal
research but concluded that it was uneconomic for a company of the size of
Manganese Bronze to rely much on that.

4. Cf. the US conglomerate Textron, originally in the textile busness.
'Textron depends on a formula of guiding, coaching and counselling subunits.
The Group vice-presidents in the firm serve an important function as internal
management consultants.' Didrichsen, op. cit., p. 218.

5. As the two following paragraphs indicate, the choice of strategy has
repercussions on the management. Cadbury Schweppes' strategy here is similar
to Coca Cola's, in exploiting its existing product. In contrast, Kellogg's strategy
is the opposite to that which is described for Cadbury Schweppes. Kellogg chose
to 'fragment the market' for their products by introducing modifications of their
products for specific markets. J.R. Morrison (1970), 'Three strategies for successful growth', in *The Arts of Top Management,* McKinsey & Co. Ltd, p. 5.

6. There may be the problem that long-range planning is run by the central
office, and so it takes account of corporate objectives; but short-term objectives
are left to lower levels, and therefore they have a tendency to sub-optimise. J.R.
Galbraith and D.A. Nathanson (1978), *Strategy Implementation: The Role of
Structure and Process* p. 127. Texas Instruments designed a new structure, putting
a semigrid through each level in which each manager added to his old product
responsibilities a new responsibility which always had a time-duration, i.e. a
strategic or tactical responsibility. 'The planning and the doing are linked, since
the same people operate in both modes.' Cf. also Sir Adrian Cadbury's observations in Chapter 3.

7. Cf. P. Drucker: *Management: Tasks, Responsibilities, Practices,* pp. 343 et
seq. There is a recognition by management of the pressure of 'present social
circumstances', not only on management practice, but also on the style of leadership, on consumer service and public relations. An illustration is in the 'Profile of
Irving Shapiro' (*Fortune,* January 1974, p. 79), who became chairman of du
Pont in December 1973. He saw the new issues as environmental control, fair-

employment policies and a transformation of the company from a 'private family fiefdom' to a 'professionally managed public corporation'.

8. 'It is universal that middle management – and especially young middle management – should always feel discontented. They always look ahead and see no opportunities for promotion coming, and they complain that they are not consulted and don't know what is going on.' H. Benson and R.L. Allan (1980). 'How much stress is too much?' *Harvard Business Review* (September/October), p. 91. This article has something to say about the stress, and the uncertainties, which middle managers feel. 'The chief executives clearly remember the stress of their middle management years.'

9. There was no intention, in the case discussions, to attach a measure or index to the term 'decentralisation'. In all four companies, decentralisation means the sharing of control in some way, but the ways are not identical. Manganese Bronze is more vertically decentralised than Tube Investments, which shows greater horizontal decentralisation. Tilling's decentralisation has gone further and in both senses: cf. T.L. Whistler, 'Organisational aspects of corporate growth,' in Albert and Segall, op. cit. In the light of Sir Patrick Meaney's passing observation in Chapter 3, on the change in management style in ICI in the 1960s, it may be noted that some of the methods of exercising indirect control which Paul Chambers instituted at ICI conformed closely to Tilling practice, e.g. 'by reviewing divisional or subsidiary budgets twice a year and having the final say on top executive appointments.' See M.J. Gort (1969), 'The British company that found a way out,' in H. Igor Ansoff (Ed.): *Business Strategy*, Penguin, Harmondsworth p. 336. When in the 1950s Arthur Cockfield at Boots helped to introduce a concept of management that allowed more autonomy and devolution he acted under the influence of Chambers, who had been Cockfield's chief at the Inland Revenue. S. Chapman, 'Strategy and Structure at Boots the Chemists,' in L. Hannah (Ed.); *Management Strategy and Business Development*, p. 102.

3 DIALOGUE WITH THE COMPANIES

Thomas Tilling — Newey & Eyre

One company studied was Newey & Eyre, a member of the Thomas Tilling group, and the largest British firm of electrical distributors. This made it possible to describe the style of management in Tilling and follow it through the chain of management in Newey & Eyre to the level of branch management. After a brief introduction on Newey & Eyre, there will be a description of the relations between it and the Tilling centre. Following that there will be a description of the relations between the higher management of the member-company, which can be defined for this purpose as the level at which company policy is formulated, and the lower management, the operating management, through which policy is executed. The purpose of the ensuing discussion is to examine how the Tilling style of management, particularly its philosophy of management autonomy, is worked out in practice.

The name 'Newey & Eyre Limited' first appeared in 1928. Half a century later, the company had become the largest electrical wholesaling organisation in the UK. By 1981 it had expanded its activities into the United States, where it was, through its subsidiaries, the fifth largest electrical wholesaler, and where, in the words of the chief executive, 'the prospect for growth is very considerable.'

A company history, reviewing this progress of fifty years, says that the achievement was due to three factors. 'It's a story of resilience and resolution during the difficult war years and vision and planned growth since Newey & Eyre became a member of the Thomas Tilling group of companies in 1952 . . . [and] it's also a story of people. Of some of the most loyal and dedicated people that have ever served the wholesaling industry. Personalities of rare character and quality.'

When Newey & Eyre put itself under the umbrella of Thomas Tilling they joined a company which was pioneering a style of management which harmonised with their own. This style can be described as one where all levels of management are allowed the greatest freedom of action within the guidelines of company policy.

Management of the Conglomerate. In 1964 P.H.D. Ryder, then managing director of Thomas Tilling, said, that one of the most important points in the published philosophy which guided the relations between the group centre and the companies who are members of the group was: 'To preserve the freedom of the boards of our member companies to manage their businesses in their own way, subject always to our guidance and supervision, particularly on matters of policy and finance'. Almost sixteen years later, when Sir Patrick Meaney was managing director, he was asked: 'What has happened to the style of management and the philosophy which guides Thomas Tilling since the time of Mr. Ryder's paper?' He answered: 'The philosophy is basically unchanged, in that the main platform is still autonomy'. The philosophy of autonomy means decentralisation, and its practice may be shown through an examination of the management structure.

The Tilling board consists of twelve directors, half of it part-time or non-executive, including the chairman, and half of it executive, including the managing director as chief executive. 'It is an effective board', says Patrick Meaney, 'and I would be sorry to see it grow (however much Tilling grows)'. The board meets once a month.

This structure is not mirrored in the directorates of the companies in the group. Each of the twenty-four operating companies has a chairman who is appointed by Tilling from its headquarters' staff, but the rest of the directors of the operating companies are full-time executive directors of that company. These Tilling chairmen are experienced businessmen. Some are Tilling directors and some are senior executives. They number five at present, and each one acts as chairman of about four principal operating companies in the group.

The Tilling chairmen are important instruments of liaison between group headquarters and the companies. The company chairmen plus the two functional directors (a financial director and a legal director) and the company secretary form the executive directors' committee (the EDC). This sits regularly for two days a month, before the monthly Tilling board meeting. It is chaired by the chief executive, Patrick Meaney, who described its meetings.

On those two days we review the operations of all the companies in the group, we review their acquisition plans and their investment plans, and the use of funds, and the possibilities of any changes in policy or plans. In addition we have a quarterly think-tank, which is a meeting out of town for a day or two when we really 'toss ideas around': we may take a particular subject for half a day and the rest of the time is a matter of coming up with whatever anybody has to say — what's wrong with the group, what's right with the group, where should we be heading, why we may not be doing well in certain areas and so on.

The companies form their plans under the guidance of their company chairmen.

They meet each month and they have to produce their plans and they also have to produce, at a later date, details of the annual budget .... Once they have produced this it becomes the monitor for the ensuing year, and if we have a perfect world, which we do not, the chairman goes in every month and he sits down at the board meeting, and he goes through the performance against the budget, and listens to the reports of operations, and if it is up to budget, or beyond it on profits (or below it on costs), he pats them on the head and has a glass of sherry and comes away. But that is not really what happens. There is a great personal liaison; we insist that our role in the companies is a supportive one. The chairman and his colleagues do not go there in the manner of a government inspector saying: 'What's this, and why that?' Naturally they enquire into it, and they want the facts. But their role is a supportive one. If the company is going off the guidelines, then they aim, hopefully, to persuade, and direct and aid the manager to get it back. But suppose that everything is going according to plan — the chairmen come back, and I sit down with them at the executive directors' committee monthly meetings and they report on their companies against their budgets and they give me special details to note, and so forth. When the plans come through, we obviously collate all the company plans — there have been guidelines as to what we think should be the real growth rate, what we are assuming will be inflation in certain countries, what interest rates might do and what fluctuations exist, these being culled from the obvious sources: and although we are not always accurate, they are, at least, a starter. So we say to our companies 'These are guidelines. If you think that you know better, in certain figures appertaining to your particular trade: if you are a wholesaler, for example, and don't think that the national rate will come through to your figures because of your rapid turnover of funds: well, OK, you adopt what you think is practicable; but then you will have to live with them.' In other words, we are all the time supporting their creative role as being in charge of their destiny. When the plan comes here, we, of course, know what we want to see as a growth rate; we place much significance on earnings per share, very closely followed by profit volume increase, and the return we can get on every pound note in the business – whether it is capital or borrowed.

Freedom of Action at Higher Levels. In 1964 Peter Ryder emphasised (and Patrick Meaney, as has been said, confirmed) the freedom which is given to member-companies of the Tilling group to manage their businesses in their own way. In 1980, Gordon Yardley, chief executive of Newey & Eyre, was asked how far this freedom went in practice. How much is delegated from Tilling to you, what reporting back is required, what can you do on your own and what controls are exercised?

'The Tilling concept', says Gordon Yardley, 'starts with 100% trust in the chief executive of the company that they are invested in. I suppose that must be the real and ultimate parameter. Once your confidence goes at Tilling level, that becomes a constraint. But there are no other real constraints'. This trust and confidence that Tilling place in the leading people in the member-companies goes not only for

the people at chief executive level at the subsidiaries but also for the people who make up the board. The responsibility of appointing a director to the Newey & Eyre board rests with me – otherwise you are not the chief executive. Having said that, that man will be known to my chairman before he is appointed. So, if he comes within the team which is already there, it is an easy one. If he is not within the team and I go outside, I would as a matter of form, expose that man to my chairman before he came on the board. Every main board appointment within the Tilling group is reported also to the Tilling board. So that there is an identity equation between the Tilling board and the key executives in running individual companies.

There are no formal checks which Tilling have developed in seeing that the chief executives and their teams are optimising in their performance rather than just doing well enough to pass muster. 'I am not aware that they have any such checks. It is the responsibility of the Tilling chairman, who is non-executive, to know sufficient about the business in which his company operates, to be able to determine that for himself. How he does that is, I suggest, a matter of feel and judgment'.

Being a member-company of a large and diversified group is bound to affect the judgement of Newey & Eyre's chief executive and his board. For example, Tilling specialise in managing diversity. But is that strategically inhibiting for Newey & Eyre, who do not venture beyond their business of distribution? The company has grown to an extent that it might have entertained the strategic alternative of diversification in its own right.

It is in the context of working within Tilling, [says Gordon Yardley], that I would not move away from sticking to my last. If we were a public company in our own right, I would think that diversification would be part of the strategy which I would develop. I think so — notwithstanding that my own discipline and that of my colleagues is within distribution. One of the options would be to consider either diversifying within distribution or diversifying in itself. It would be difficult within the Tilling concept, where they manage by diversity, to have further management by diversity within the framework. I don't think it would work — given the ground rules, as a member of the Tilling group. Their strength is in managing diversity and I would say that my strength is sticking to distribution .... That is in no way inhibiting. That fact that I can pursue distribution with blinkers on and think entirely about distribution — and primarily electrical distribution — is because I operate within the framework of Thomas Tilling. If I were on my own, with £300 million of turnover in distribution in itself and I were a public company, I would think very hard indeed whether I wanted to be any more heavily committed to distribution .... I can concentrate as it is, on the game which I really know, which is distribution.

The Tilling group works in some fifteen or sixteen marketing areas in each of which it aims to establish a substantial presence. The Tilling concept is that each of its member-companies, like Newey & Eyre, should be large enough in its field of business to have some influence in its market. Given these ground rules, diversification within the member-companies would not, as Gordon Yardley states, work. So Newey & Eyre's strategy is 'to stick to what we know' and even in diversifying within distribution, which would be in the rules, to diversify in 'complementary areas'. This is not in any way inhibiting, partly because of the strength which the member-companies derive from membership of the larger group and also because, in the case of Newey & Eyre, the company is in a market which is expanding so fast that there is no necessity to move away from it and into another. 'We should have to run out of steam in the areas we're in. And, in fact, we could open six more branches per annum for the next five years'.

Tilling is a diversified company, a conglomerate, whose member-companies practise their specialisations within their own areas of competence. The management skills of the member companies, like Newey & Eyre, are quite different to the management skills which have been developed in the group. Tilling, having decided that it was a diversified company and that it was to be managed as such, went on to point out that

> we practised this in the sense that, if we have four engineering companies, we don't have the same chairman in the four, we quite deliberately see that they have four different chairmen, and that one has the chair of a textile or an insurance company or whatever as well; and we have a mild tradition on the directors' table, if one of our colleagues becomes frightfully technical about products, we metaphorically shuffle our feet. Because our job is managing diversi-fication.

The Management of Newey & Eyre

Newey & Eyre operate through branches, each of which is under the control of a branch manager. In 1981 the company had 96 branches of various sizes in the UK, of which the largest had an annual turnover of over £6 million. In an interview with Bob Wingate, manager of the Birmingham branch, the question was put: 'How is freedom of action regarded at branch level?' He replied:

> As a branch manager I could say that we are completely autonomous .... There is very little interference from head office, from the centre. If anything, it is a guidance, and a service to us as a branch .... Of course, we have to keep within company regulations. We have a guideline in the Branch Administration Manual which sets out the broad policy of the company. Most of it is common sense. As a company we have a name to live up to, the leading company in the wholesale electrical set-up and we try to act on it — rationally, sensibly.

It was found useful to get an example of how freedom demonstrates itself in action. When does it become necessary to refer a decision to higher authority? What would happen if there was a conflict of ideas between a manager and his area director? The branch manager has responsibility for some millions of pounds of stock and the profit or loss which accrues from trading in it. With his responsibility and his freedom of action which the company allows him he would not be expected to be inhibited in perceiving entrepreneurial possibilities within his range or in acting on them. He has perhaps 12 000 items which he carries in stock, and the way in which he handles this stock measures his performance as a manager.

An example arose when Bob Wingate took into stock a corrosive-proof light-fitting which nobody in Birmingham stocked.

> My sales manager and I were looking at the daily orders and we thought, all of a sudden, that we seem to be getting an increasing number, an increasing demand, for corrosive-proof fittings. Normally it was taking about six weeks to obtain these fittings, so we wondered if we could increase our market share by getting them ex stock. We approached three companies and one of them was a leading company which had a very good name and the fitting was excellent. From there on all I had to do was to negotiate a price and I got an extra discount cover really to finance the stock. I knew that I had to turn those fittings over a number of times to get them to a commercial level, and make the correct gross margin also to increase sales.

When he was asked whether he was really free to take that decision and to act on it without referring to higher authority, he answered categorically: 'No reference at all, no reference'. But he added that if there was an 'awful lot of money committed I would not do it without reference simply because it is not my money'. The branch manager is judged on his sales and his profitability, so that in the end, his freedom of action partly depends on his success in decision-making.

Bob Wingate was then asked what happens when he is asked by his immediate superior, the area director, to promote an idea or a type of business in his branch. Would he feel bound to accept or to acquiesce?

> Before I generally decide, [he said], I will have a word with my sales manager. If the area director says that he wants an instant decision, then I have the type of relationship [with my sales manager] in which I basically know what the sales manager would

think, and I would make that decision, Yes or No. But I would not take anything up if I thought that there would be an adverse reaction — because we are committing the company's money and if everybody along the line was not convinced that it was right, then the decision would obviously be wrong. Because it would not be sold, it would not happen. Unless everybody in the chain of command is happy that that decision is right, it is a wrong decision — in my opinion.

Gordon Yardley, chief executive of Newey & Eyre, recalled that recently

I spent a day in Scotland, visiting three of our branches with an Australian wholesaler. I didn't just turn out on the spot, I went through the courtesy of asking the boss if I could go on his patch — the man who runs the business in Scotland . . . . The Australian chap with whom I was, asked a question: 'What constraints are there on our branch managers, the man who operates a trading unit?' First of all, we look on him as Tilling look on Newey & Eyre, we put a lot of trust and faith in the man who heads that unit. He has freedom to buy and sell, to hire and fire staff. So he is running it virtually as his own business. In fact, my Australian friend, Ron Cohen, having been to Edinburgh and listened to our man, as he walked out he said: 'That man, Ian Miller, the manager there, could be talking about his own business.' That's the way we like it. We like the man to think that's his own business. The assets are being entrusted to him.

These examples could be multiplied. The company obviously aims to work out the philosophy of autonomy in reality and let it penetrate right down the management structure. Whatever success it has in doing so is because higher management is absolutely convinced of its importance, and makes sure that this conviction is communicated down the line. Patrick Meaney broadens and amplifies this in this way:

At the time when Peter Ryder gave his paper this [philosophy] was unusual, and the pundits, management consultants and experts then thought that our style was loose and lacking in proper controls and the organisational measures and desired disciplines of management methods of the time. Now, fifteen years later, when we look at the philosophies which we adopted, we see that they are practised by the more specialised, larger and well-organised companies — like ICI, which fifteen years ago was heavily divisionalised and entirely structured in formal corporate management style; and now you see that they have more decentralisation and autonomy in their operations, more emphasis in policy-making and on the marketing, production and engineering side, and at lower management levels than fifteen years ago. Indeed, the social, as well as the economic pressures all over the world, have meant that there is now only one successful style of management, which is leadership by persuasion and not by command. Tilling has always practised the creeds of autonomy, decentralisation and leadership by persuasion. In an organisation you should let the people in charge of the actual operations have the highest degree of authority commensurate with their responsibility and their objectives. You should be involved with them but not interfere with their operations . . . .

He adds:

. . . This philosophy has become much more commonly practised by all types of organisations: a philosophy of giving up 'commanding', and indeed, having to give it up mainly because of social circumstances — you can no longer 'command', you have to 'persuade' . . . the new generation are not only independent of mind, but also certainly you will not get the best out of them if you simply tell them to do things. You have to carry them with you in what they themselves practise and in developing their own intellect and their application to business.

The autonomy of the branch manager in this company is a fundamental feature of Newey & Eyre. It is an expression of the importance which the company attaches to persuasion. The company expects from all parts of its management an exercise of individual initiative which matches the freedom of action which it allows. In the words of the chief executive of Tilling, there is that conviction that freedom means that 'you can no longer "command", you have to "persuade".' But could the idea of branch autonomy become so enshrined that it might hinder the development of a unified company strategy? In a case of the working out of management, if one could be found, when the optimal strategy depends on unanimity, how can management be seen to be persuaded to be unanimous? Is there a danger at least, if not of a conflict between parts of management, of an intractable problem of 'achieving unanimity'?

In 1980-81 the board of Newey & Eyre decided to pursue a new strategy in one part of their distribution business, the sale of domestic appliances, which had always hitherto been entirely in the hands of their managers. The new strategy would centralise sales, and take the business in that line (less than 20% of the total business of the average branch) out of the control of some branches. It would also mean that some branches would be asked to handle much larger stocks in certain lines rather than in others, as would be decided by company policy. The effect of the change of strategy or, rather, the development of a strategy where none had needed to exist before, was that the control of this business, its distribution and its buying and selling, was being taken out of the hands of branches and put in the hands of centralised, functional, higher management.

It is clear that such a policy, crudely implemented, would at least offend the spirit of the idea of branch autonomy. But, as the manager of the Birmingham branch has been quoted as saying, autonomy must be exercised 'rationally, sensibly'. In the philosophy of Tilling-Newey & Eyre this means that changes are not best brought about by edict. This case of the handling of the domestic appliance business is worth examining to see whether the company was able to bring about agreement in practice.

One of the branch managers, who under the new policy was asked to take on stock, seems to have been concerned with the change for the very reason that it affected the idea of branch autonomy. The managing director of the Midlands region, Paul Hickman, a senior member of the company who had been through all the stages of management in the company from service manager to his present position on the main board, had the task of opening up the problem and seeking to allay the concern.

'One of the questions posed on the seminar', said Paul Hickman in an interview in which he explained the problem,

is by a manager who said that he wants an explanation of the Stratford statement (which arose from our managers' annual meeting at Stratford) on 'mandatory domestic stock' (he did not 'understand' the word 'mandatory' − it is an evil word to him) and the answer he was given is that it is not mandatory at all. It is an agreement with him to have confidence in what we are doing and to impart that confidence to him.

Who, in this case, will give that answer?

'I am down to give that answer, and Ron Douglas, the marketing man who reports to Jon Brockett [the commercial director]. So he will back my persuasive answer with his factual answer'.

It is clear that for a strategy like this to be employed agreement within the branches must be unanimous or the strategy must be forced through without agreement. Since there is a principle of branch autonomy, in the face of a strategy which requires unanimity, it is reasonable to ask whether the prime role of the regional director in such a case is to achieve it. And this is the way in which Paul Hickman looks at the problem focused by the question at the seminar:

> The commercial director says to me: 'Can you achieve that agreement?' I do it through my area directors and, if necessary, directly with my branch managers.
> Would you say that is a very important role of the line?
> Yes, very important.
> The most important?
> I could say that it could be the most important role. Yes, that is my main task.

At another time in the interview Paul Hickman emphasised that company policies have to be 'sold' down the management line 'You have to be firm in making policies but you have to get acceptance of the policies. If you have not acceptance — say, of 96 managers, you have not got acceptance by 50 managers — you would have to sit back and think about it. You would have a wrong decision'.

The commercial director, Jon Brockett, confirmed indirectly that the task of achieving agreement down the line, 'selling' company policies down the line, falls on the regional director and his area directors. He would, if necessary, set out to 'demonstrate' the advantages of the policies advocated by the board, but if he failed in that, 'then I would invoke the power of the line management to sort it out. But it does not happen much as a matter of fact'.

It is natural in a company whose business is distribution, and whose managers right up to the top have for the most part risen from the rank of salesman, that the problem of achieving agreement on policies is often stated in the vocabulary drawn from that field. Bob Wingate recognises that, in a company where he, as a manager, wants to give freedom to act to people below him he must assume that there is no difficulty about discipline.

That is the problem, [he says], and I am looking for the best way of putting it across at a meeting. It is not much use simply saying: You will do this. You say: This is what is happening – what is the best way to overcome it? You put the problem on their shoulders. A free discussion, come to your conclusions, and that is the policy made. I have already got my ideas, but I won't put them over as such. I will ask. But if it does not come to the right conclusions, when I am chairing that meeting, then I have failed. (You can be sure I won't) . . . . I think that my years as a salesman have helped – you have to be very tactful – but they know when I have come to the point. That is the manager's job. He has to sell the company's policy and discipline to his staff.

The expectations which people at one management level have of another is often a good index both of the general relations between them and of the extent to which the exercise of initiative is encouraged down the chain of management. When Paul Hickman was asked what he would regard as the most important characteristics and attitudes, seen from the level of the board, which a branch manager must have, he replied at once: 'Enthusiasm'. In following up this answer he still kept that requirement in the forefront. 'He needs that enthusiasm, the ability to delegate, and he also has to be a good administrator. He has to be a bit of an accountant, and he has to be a "wheeler and dealer". A man of many parts. Certainly man management is a prime requirement'.

Paul Hickman spoke of 'enthusiasm' in this way to put in one word his ideal of the relations between the board management and the branch management which has been developed in Newey & Eyre.

. . . Going back over the past thirty years, all our successful managers have been 'one-off' individuals, having quirks of attitude, jumping the rules and regulations quite often . . . enthusiastic enough not to give in to rules and regulations which he doesn't understand or which he does not want to accept blindly . . . I would say it is invaluable, provided that it does not become too disruptive. A person with that skill, or rather that aptitude – it is not a skill, it is an aptitude – is invaluable to the company . . . I don't think that you ever prevent the entrepreneur of whom you were talking earlier on, his spirit, coming into a business.

Turning the telescope round, the view of the management structure from the position of Bob Wingate at the level of the branch was: '. . . It is a pyramid structure which is very short. It is always difficult to decide which structure to use in a company . . . I have tried to analyse the structure of some of our competitors . . . but I think that ours is the right one'. The 'way of life' of the company, its philosophy, said Bob Wingate, has the stamp of success. 'I don't see it changing much. You have to keep analysing even what is successful about it and say that it is right, we are convinced that we are right. There is no need for change for the present but don't be too complacent because things change all the time . . .'. When he made a point about the practical relations between his level and that of higher levels he echoed a remark which has been quoted in answer to a question to the commercial director: 'We are practical people and generally there is very little disagreement'.

Manganese Bronze – BSA Guns

Management initiative in a diversified group like Manganese Bronze is rooted in, and dependent on, its own style of decentralised administration. John Neville, vice-chairman and chief executive of Manganese Bronze, speaks, at the beginning of the interviews, of 'the GKN triangle', which is the form in which he portrays the typical administrative structure of the large, modern, business corporation.

. . . Inside that triangle, [he says], are all their mainstream activities, in other words, the businesses on which they intend to build forever into the future as the management sees it at that stage. At the top of the triangle is the board. Every executive works his way up – he may be working on fasteners down here when he starts, but he may go up through castings or forgings or anything else you wish to mention, engineering components, transmissions or something of this kind. They see it as one monolithic organisation in which the executives hopefully are moving up the triangle rather than down or sideways, but they may be required to work geographically anywhere, and as far as product is concerned, almost anywhere, aiming, of course, eventually to get into the triangle at the top. So that you create one family of people and they are all working together this way, and therefore the control comes from here all the way down step by step right through all the businesses and you have the feeling of what the people at the top are doing, penetrating every business in the organisation.

He went on to explain that Manganese Bronze could not function efficiently with that centralised structure, because it has not those interrelated activities in the same way as GKN. '. . . We're not selling into one industry, nor are we engaged in a single industry. We're engaged in a lot of them, and therefore, in our case we have to run each one of these businesses as a separate entity, otherwise I don't know how you could possibly from the middle manage it all'. The companies in the group have responsibility for running their own businesses, and control from the centre falls very short of usurping this responsibility.

. . . Each one of these companies has its own board, which is quite clearly charged with the responsibility of running the business, albeit within certain guidelines . . . and the only thing they have in common is me as chairman, but obviously it doesn't have to be me, it could be anyone who is doing a similar job. And the boards have their own style — very often a very different style. Managing directors frequently manage their affairs in ways which don't strike me as right, but I think I can cross my heart and say that I don't think that I've ever said to a managing director, look, you shouldn't do it that way, you should do it this way. Because once I do, then the whole concept collapses.

As a chief executive of the group, John Neville is a 'manager of managers', which is the typical task of the managing director of a group which has undergone diversification. What is expected of him, and what he expects of himself, is the exercise of a skill which is quite different from that of the managing directors of his subordinate companies, whose job is to manage their businesses. The 'concept' is a simple one that the specialist knowledge of the products, and the buying and selling in relation to them, resides in the management teams in the companies. 'I mustn't appoint a man as a managing director and then tell him how to manage, he must do it himself. The idea behind it is clear and that is that the people who are given the responsibility for running the business must be given a free rein to do the job the way they think is best. After all, they're on the spot, they see what the problems are every day, they must develop their own management techniques, their management style'.

Nevertheless, when John Neville said that the control of management is achieved by the imposition of guidelines and rules, and that it must not curtail proper management freedom or hamper initiative, he was speaking of a control which is comprehensive enough. The fundamental tool is the submission of the company plan which the group centre demands of each company. This is not merely a financial/administrative plan, as it may appear to be superficially, because a plan which a company submits to the board discusses investment, building, plant, labour, 'right across the board'. What this means fundamentally is that the advantages which group management gives to the companies include (possibly above all) insistence on the discipline of rational consideration of all management problems.

'. . . Let's go back to how you impose the guidelines and rules', said John Neville in the interview.

. . . Every year, every company has to produce a plan for the year that will follow − the company's financial year. This must embody a complete study of the market place, and what they're going to sell and therefore, stemming from that, what their costs will be, what their requirements for plant, equipment, building, labour, right the way across the board, and what new investment will be necessary in order to carry out the plan. These plans take three months to prepare, so it's not taking an evelope and jotting down figures − last year we did £4 million sales, let's say we do £4.5 million this year, it's not that sort of exercise at all. It has to be done in depth and ultimately we have month-by-month projected profit figures. We have estimated balance sheets, we have cash flow statements and we have schedules of new investment, if appropriate. The whole picture is there . . . . These [separate plans] are summarised in this office to make sure, for example, that the financial resources available will permit these plans in total to be carried out. We also particularly watch the cash side all the time from this office: we monitor it to make sure we don't get into any difficulty. And we also determine anything which smacks of being a new project, because we do not allow any company to buy a business or sell a business, or sell a company, for example − some of them have subsidiaries − nor start a new business without our approval, of the parent company board . . . . So these are the fundamental, basic controls, and each one, each company must report on its progress, comparing the actual figures with what they forecast at the beginning of the year. So you've comparisons all the way through . . . . Other than that, of course, we exercise no control at all.

He gave some examples of the sort of freedom which the management of companies might expect and the sort of control to which they would not be submitted by the chief executive or the board.

> . . . If they decide to send a delegation to a conference in America they don't have to ask me. They're normally polite enough to do so. They don't have to consult me whether they only take two weeks holiday a year — and if they only take two I'll soon be saying something. I think it's very unhealthy for people not to have a proper holiday. But if a man takes eight weeks holiday, as long as the results are all right, that's fine. I don't want him to take three months without saying something, I think that's too much . . . . In other words, within the bounds of common sense, I hope the management of each company will do the thing their own way as long as the business is developing along intended lines. The way in which they do it, I don't want to criticise at all . . . [Of course, if the business is not developing, the chief executive would intervene with the company concerned] . . . to say 'I'm very sorry, but we've discussed it frequently, business is going back all the time, you must either start the thing going the right way, or bluntly, I'll assign somebody who will'. You have to realise that the ultimate sanction is always there.

Management Initiative and Entrepreneurial Freedom

As chairman of the boards of the subsidiary companies, John Neville has a key role to play in fostering entrepreneurial thinking within the management staff of the subsidiaries. Aware, as he has just been quoted to be, of the responsibility of the company managements to 'run the business', and recognising that this is so 'because they have the facts, they can see what is going on', he must be careful, when in the chair, not to inhibit the thinking of members of company boards. The subsidiaries are the seed-bed of a certain range of innovatory thinking, and the centre has to cultivate the selected growths. An important task of the chief executive at the board meeting is to distinguish the best run of argument and to give it momentum. So he has to 'encourage very open debate at the board meeting', and to see that ideas are reasonably argued. 'I try to discourage the meeting where the agenda is pre-ordained — where there are 27 items written down and you go laboriously through every one of these things, none of which is of any interest – and try to talk about the things that actually matter'.

He was asked whether the very existence of an agenda might be inhibiting in that, at least, someone has to determine the agenda and make a selection of the points for discussion. In his answer he outlined the development of company board discussions to the present time, and explained that the form is intended to give good ideas, wherever they may arise, more leverage. The arrangement of the agenda is the responsibility of the company secretary (who, except in the case of one company, comes from the company and not from the centre), and

it is his job to collect together the items which the other directors would like to see debated for some reason. And he sends me a copy of what is proposed before the meeting, and if I wish to change it, I do. But if people do put items on the agenda, I encourage them to write at least a brief paper to explain what it is they want to talk about, and not just make a bland statement, quite cold – 'I think we should invest in North America', for example. I mean, put cold to a meeting – I mean you just can't go on that way. You must have some reasoned argument about what the background is, why we've got to make the change and why we've got to go to North America and not Brazil or Central Africa or anywhere else you'd like to name. Therefore supporting papers are, I think, an essential element. But everyone's free to put items on the agenda if they so wish. Beyond that, I repeat, that if we are having trouble securing business we need at the prices we want, I'm apt to ask the company 'What are you going to do?' To begin with [in the early days of the expanded group], we've met with fairly stony silence because people haven't done much thinking. But I suggest that if you were to attend a board meeting, you would find that most people now would have quite a lot to say, because they've been trained a little bit – perhaps that's something they do get from the group.

He was then asked about how far the form of board meetings provides for the discussion of new ideas. Can policy considerations and strategic approaches which might be entirely novel be easily discussed? For example, somebody might say, with a supporting paper, that it is time we moved into the North American field. That is one thing. But how do ideas which have never been entertained before get generated? Where does innovation and fresh thinking come in? The question being put suggested that the forms of managerial discussion which had been outlined so far showed quite clearly how the subsidiaries, with support from the centre, generate a flow of ideas within existing activities. But this falls short of entrepreneurial change, and it was on this which he was now being asked to comment and on the mechanisms which allowed for it in managerial discussion in his group.

John Neville answered this question first with an example from his experience. A few years ago, he had been pressing one of the companies in the group (BSA Guns) to go into the manufacture of a new product which seemed to be within the broad range of their existing products. But the managing director of the company and all his colleagues were totally opposed to this proposal. Nevertheless he persisted with this, 'and eventually there were massive papers written, studies of the world market, everything we've done. I was still not really satisfied, but in the end, faced with such massive resistance, I had to give in from a practical point of view, or else get a new board I suppose, who'd do what I told them'. In fact, he said, events have proved the company board absolutely right, and if he had persisted further with his proposal, he would, he said, have put that company in serious financial difficulty.

One lesson which can be drawn is that entrepreneurial change is a team responsibility, and this may be specially important of a change in a diversified group. The initial ideas may come, or come in part, from the centre. But they have to be worked out with the subsidiaries. '. . . Your subsidiary company depends on some thinking being put before them by the parent company. And that they're entitled to expect in my opinion. It would be slightly strange if there was nothing coming at all. But they have to play their part . . . '.

Another lesson which can be drawn is that the essential element in this sort of collaboration is training. That is important because training offers the sort of encouragement which leads towards an enterprising management style and which makes the group innovatory. Many companies fail to train managers to function well at the higher levels — the

people who come up through industry, working their way steadily up the ladder until, by pressure from below they find themselves at the top, in most cases totally unconditioned to do the job of being a director of any company. The system is all wrong in the UK. Nothing is done in many companies to train people for the responsibilities they have in due course . . . . They can be very onerous . . . '.

Turning to his own company:

> All our middle management, as far as is possible, are sent on courses, to give them the technical knowledge which they have never been given before of what the jobs are all about . . . And when they get on the board, I regard it as part of my job to try and make them think about what they're doing, what the business is doing and why we're doing what we are doing instead of something else . . . and people have got to learn that they have to be able to stand up and debate it, even if they've made a mistake — it's very much better they say so. Very much better for the organisation, and colleagues then can contribute help and everyone will benefit in the end.

John Neville went on to emphasise that in a diversified company the main sources of entrepreneurial change cannot be tapped by the centre in isolation. '. . . Above all I don't think in a conglomerate, that it is likely that you would find any board of directors which would be able to identify the areas where diversification is desirable or extension of the business in this direction rather than that. I think it would be too difficult when you're remote from it, sitting in this office, for example'. Enterprising ideas are discovered all along the management line, and there will be an interplay of ideas between different management levels so long as there is open discussion.

He gave an example of policy-making which concerned the product of a sub-group of three of his companies. The sub-group was formed to put the three companies (which are engaged in powder metallurgy) under the control of one board, so that as chief executive and chairman he could concern himself only with that board. The board became the policy point with these three companies and with what they do. He used this example as an illustration of how a major change of position of the group came about through the participation of group and sub-group management.

> The original idea emerged from meetings at the sintered metal companies, where it was being expressed clearly that there was growing worry about the size of the UK market and a belief was emerging that it was going to contract. And when someone like myself said, well what are you going to do about it, initially there were no sensible answers, and I was asking the sort of question, have you thought about establishing yourself in France where, as

it so happens, we already do a lot of business, or Germany or some other country? And from there it got to the point where I debated the matter in depth with the parent company board, and pressed my own view that the first priority should be to establish ourselves in the United States, on the grounds that one single component for General Motors would be a business in its own right, if that could be obtained. But it could not be obtained by a company which was manufacturing in the UK because General Motors would not give you their business. I think you have to recognise that there's an interplay between the two levels of boards, and that new ideas don't come from a single source, but they tend to emerge if you can only get the discussion.

John Neville was asked about the concept of the management which he practises. Was it a concept which he derived from his own experience and to suit his particular blend of abilities, or was it based on a general philosophy of management? How far would he expect changes in the running of Manganese Bronze if it was put in the hands of another chief executive with a very different outlook and personality?

I would expect it to change materially. Perhaps wholly, I don't know, because I think fundamentally the answer to your question is that no two people would really agree exactly how a thing should be done. It is a function of personality, training, experience, everything you like to bring into the equation, which means that one man believes you should do it one way, and another in another. The chairman and myself when we started did not agree at all . . . . We spent the first four years arguing about everything, but gradually we established an understanding of how we were going to operate. And, as far as we're concerned, it has worked very smoothly ever since. Any successor has got to find his understanding with the chairman, if not this chairman, another chairman. I think it's very much the problem of the individual. I don't think there's any such thing as a Harvard Business School solution. With great respect to the Harvard Business School — who do a wonderful job — but I don't honestly think that you can reduce business management to a set of rules.

Here he was referring to the type of skills and the span of knowledge and experience which a managing director of a conglomerate must be able to dispose of in the centre. Melvin Anshen, writing in the Harvard Business Review (July/August 1961), describes a conglomerate as 'a structure of unrelated or accidentally related companies anchored to a central core of unusual management competence, both general and functional ... '. The type of work which John Neville has to do has arisen in response to the administrative requirements created by the diversification of his group. His experience before taking over executive direction of Manganese Bronze had been as an accountant, a stockbroker and a banker. He had worked up to the level of works manager in industry, and he had studied law to the extent that 'I'm quite happy to draft a legal agreement'. But when he spoke of the way in which he conducts relations with his subsidiary companies and their managing directors what emerged was not a pragmatic formulation but a philosophy of management which was not so removed from that which Patrick Meaney expounded at Thomas Tilling.

I know of no way in which you can motivate the management of your companies except by giving them autonomy. If you control them in some way in a centralised concept you will remove all motivation, or most of the motivation. You can't prevent it – and for example, no-one in this company gives any instructions to any subsidiary company, except myself. They know I'll throw them out on their ear if they try to do such a thing. Equally, I never communicate with anyone in a subsidiary company, except through the managing director, or if he's on holiday, whoever he's designated to act for him. But I never, for example, would ring up the chief accountant and start cross-examining him about the figures. If I want to know something, I ring up the managing director and ask him, and if he doesn't know, he'll go away, find out and come back and tell me the answer. This seems to me to be fundamental where the businesses are different. If they were all the same, if our business was making furniture, and we just happened to have fifteen companies which were all furniture manufacturers, I don't doubt that you can have a centralised staff, centralised marketing, centralised buying very likely and all the rest of the paraphernalia, and run these different companies as one organisation. But just imagine, how am I going to try to run guns and car bodies and taxi cabs as though it was one business? It just can't work.

He manages diversity in the Manganese Bronze group of companies by controlling the degree of diversity which he allows, by decentralisation of the structure of the group and by seeking participation of the management in policy-making. These three principles can be applied successfully only if management can act with a degree of autonomy within, that is, certain guiding rules. They amount to a philosophy of management whose purpose is to foster management initiative and to encourage innovatory thinking. His method of application of this philosophy has the keynote of training. One of his main contributions as chief executive of the group as he sees it is to make sure that his management is trained to function efficiently at the higher levels to which they may rise and to be able to participate at the board or director level as equals in policy discussions.

On the other side of the coin to participation in policy-making is participation in the agreement of decisions. When Sir Adrian Cadbury discussed this he used as an example the decision on the Cadbury Schweppes merger. John Neville took up this question by distinguishing between decisions which are normally within the range for a particular business or a subsidiary company and those decisions which fall outside that range. Among the latter would be all those decisions which are matters of fundamental policy to the group. The degree of participation of the two levels of management (group and company) differs between the two types of decision.

> Decision-making in practice is made if I know a decision is required because I'm asked, what decision do you wish to take? And I discuss it with the chairman. If it is completely fundamental to the group, we would not usurp the proper function of the main board. It would be improper for us to do so. But if it's a decision which we consider to be of an appropriate kind, we take the decision then and there normally .... Quite seriously, we would never expect almost any matter to wait more than a few hours unless somebody was abroad or somebody was ill, or there was some relatively, we hope, unusual circumstance ... a second-class decision taken promptly, to my mind, is infinitely preferable to a first-class decision taken in three months' time. The business is gone by then anyhow.

> But when it is a matter which lies within the range of company determination, the weight of decision-making is clearly shifted to the company.

> Normally I would not, obviously, expect to have to take any decision which involved the more normal activities of the companies day by day. Decisions, nevertheless, are needed over a wide area all the time. And it is up to the managing directors to create an

organisation which enables those decisions to be taken promptly and expeditiously at all times because the greater the delay the more difficult it is to get it right in the end . . . I would have hoped that decisions were taken at every level.

A View from a Subsidiary Company — BSA Guns

The Birmingham Small Arms Company started as a grouping together of gunmakers in the nineteenth century, but by about 1930 BSA Guns had become a 'Cinderella activity of the group, dependent on the facilities of motor cycle engineering to make the parts and put them into an assembly area and put them together. And BSA Guns from the 1930s up to 1973 was a selling company and had no manufacturing facilities at all. It depended entirely on the Birmingham Small Arms Company making parts and BSA Guns sold what it made'.

When the company was taken over by Manganese Bronze in 1973 the new parent company at once separated out the various BSA activities like car-bodies, sintered metals, powdered metals and guns from the other group activities and set up a company for each activity, with its managing director who reported to the chief executive of Manganese Bronze. The change which this made for the management of BSA Guns was that 'we now had a company to run', with its own board responsible for all its functions, but bound to the group by the presence on its board of the chief executive as chairman.

Alf Scott, managing director of BSA Guns, is sure that the people who make decisions should be near to the product and that this interest should penetrate the whole management, right to the top — because the whole management team must participate in decisions, and the top is the place, in the end, where decisions will be made or, at least, approved.

> I think that the control at the top is very important. I don't know whether it matters if you are selling soap flakes, but I certainly believe that where you are in a specialist engineering business you need people with a feel for the business, a feel for the product and a feel for the market and for what is wanted — not just engineering ability. We have had some excellent engineers [in the past at BSA] who didn't know a damned thing about motor bikes. I feel that that is where we went wrong. We had tremendously talented people from Rolls-Royce — they couldn't make a motor bike.

Alf Scott was presenting a view on a particular form of business management which indicated that the problems of controlling a specialised business within a large group are best solved by a type of conglomerate management. His experience had led him to think of the problem of management of specialisms related to the product. But, no doubt, his thinking could be applied just as well to any type of specialism of skills, to anything which differentiates one business performance from another. He was asked to define more closely what he meant when he talked about 'a feel for a motor bike'. Is that a feel about the market for motor bikes? About what a bike will do, what it can be made to do, to whom it can be made to appeal? Is it a marketing thing which is being talked about?

In his answer he returned to his experience in the rifle business.

I have been in the gun business for thirty years and one gets a feel for what will sell well and how it should be put together and how it should be made to perform and how it should be cosmetically finished to appeal to the public. Also, what the public expect to get and how you can provide them with value for money, which is probably the most important thing – that people feel they haven't been 'done'. They've bought a BSA Air Sporter and they've paid £60 for it, and we want to make them feel that they've got damned good value for that sort of thing. And those are the sort of things that I mean about a feel for the product. Knowing what you have to do to give the customer something which is going to satisfy.

The small firm, [said Alf Scott], has in some respects a tremendous advantage in that the people, generally speaking, in a smaller firm are much closer to the product. You don't have the problems of committees of finance people trying to decide whether you are going to put a new type of wheel in a motor bike. We do it with four people. We have a financial director, a manufacturing director, a sales director and myself. We say we want to do this, and we state there and then 'that's what we will do', or 'we can't afford to do it'. That's terribly important in my view – that you can make your decisions and then damned well get on with it.

He confirmed later, in answer to questions, that another advantage which the small firm has is 'adaptability' in production method, which can, it was suggested, be achieved at 'shop floor level' in a firm of the size of BSA Guns. He said that this might not present any problems even if the workforce were doubled. But after a point it would become difficult. In any case, as things are, 'We can get a design change done almost immediately, and get it down on the shop floor and start and make something slightly different', without 'a meeting at the House of Lords'.

Freedom in decision-making is needed 'at the point where decisions are made', in order to allow the development of ideas. In a conglomerate this point must be the company where the business is. In such a group as Manganese Bronze, which is managed at different levels, there are various sorts of decisions to be made, but in all matters which lie within company competence the company team is allowed to give unimpeded consideration to business possibilities. Alf Scott gave an example of a current business decision.

We are just about to bring out a new air rifle. This was conceived about two years ago by discussions, informal, sometimes over a drink, about 'It's time we did something to fill that slot in our range, and how shall we go about it?' And then we got our general thinking out, and then we got the design boys involved and said — this is what we would like to achieve: it's got to meet this specification, it's got to be in two calibres, it's got to give us this performance, and we want something better than we have got on this one and we would like to retain the features of this one. Then you start to put together the package. So you get the thing on the drawing board and you make the first one, and then you have a quick look at the cost and that it looks as though it will come in the right sort of slot in your marketing strategy, so then you move on and get your design and development moving and get your planning organised. And you get to a point where you can say — OK, we can make it, it's going to cost us so much, do we go ahead or don't we? And then that becomes a decision for, not the board of BSA Guns because we don't involve the chairman of the board. He is not involved, it's not his concern, but the executive — that is, the working directors of BSA Guns who are finance, manufacturing, marketing and myself — get together and say: 'Right, this is an opportunity'. The marketing people say we reckon we can sell 8000 at this much, and half of them will go abroad, and on that sort of basis we make the decision to go ahead, having made the decision how much it's going to cost us, what the returns are going to be in the first year, what the tooling has cost us and whether we can see a reasonable return over that period of time.

In the period of the collapse of the BSA company, Alf Scott was an executive with BSA Guns and he remembers the top management in the group as being 'tremendously remote' and 'uninterested' in any of the business that we were trying to do. 'It's a sad reflection', he said, 'on that type of management'. Was the fault that he now sees, in that earlier period before the takeover, that the information flow was inadequate?

> We didn't have any information. We were not allowed to know what the product cost ... the costings, of course, were done by a cost accountant who hadn't got any interest in the gun business at all, it was one of the bits that he had got to look after along with the motor cycle business, so that he wasn't interested in it. He did a factual costing with no understanding of the product or any thought of what the prospect might be or development might be, or how important it might be to look at the costing in a certain way in relation to what next year's sales might be ... which is totally unsatisfactory ... You know your basic cost but there's no enthusiasm, there's no interest there ... whereas at the present moment, we can look at every individual cost, we've got people there who can say, well that's really too expensive, we ought to be able to make that cheaper. And so we go back and look at a different method of manufacture or different source of supply. So that there's this great day-to-day involvement in each individual part to try to make it in the best possible way.

This is, of course, a confirmation in the actual practice of the subsidiary of the principle of autonomy on which the chief executive of the group based his philosophy of management. Alf Scott was asked whether if BSA Guns was, for example, considering adding another item to their range, he would feel obliged to discuss it with the holding company. The answer was a categorical 'No'.
'You would never discuss it with them?'
'No'.
A corollary of the principle of company autonomy is that one company does not feel competitive with another in, for example, the quest for favours of group finance or loan accommodation. One of the other subsidiaries had just built a factory for £2 million (no doubt, with finance obtained or underwritten by group headquarters), but Alf Scott's company interest did not extend beyond awareness. 'You see, I'm not concerned. It really has got nothing to do with me. I am

concerned with doing my business, with my company . . .'.

Nevertheless, autonomy is not a constitutional requirement of the group. It is a convention of the system of management which enables the companies and the group to perform well. BSA Guns aims to make a profit of 10% on turnover, 'banks' the profit with the group and draws on this account for its investment requirements. The group could refuse to sanction the use of such funds if it wishes − 'they own us, absolutely' − but it does not. Within the existing management system it could not, as Neville put it, for otherwise 'the whole concept collapses'.

Cadbury Schweppes

Before the Second World War Cadbury Brothers Limited would have been said, by their own definition, to have been a company in the chocolate business. It began thereafter to expand its range of business into other types of confectionery and then further towards a more general range of food. By the 1970s, subsequent to acquisitions and mergers (chiefly the merger which established the name of Cadbury Schweppes), the company would perhaps have preferred to define its business broadly in terms of its customers. Its business would follow the changing needs of its customers in the fields (mainly, but not only, in foods and drinks) which it serves.

In the past few years Cadbury Schweppes has decided to pursue more actively a policy of development on an international basis. Although more than half of its total sales are still made in the UK, emphasis is being put on expansion of company activities internationally in Europe, the United States, Australia, Africa and other parts. One of the two major objectives which the chairman has stated in recent annual reports is 'to build on our established position in the North American market'. The acquisition of Peter Paul Inc. (USA) in 1978 gave the company a firm base in the American market and changed the strategic balance of its operations outside the UK.

Enterprise and Management Initiative. In interviews at Bournville in 1980 Sir Adrian Cadbury, chairman of Cadbury Schweppes, accepted the opportunity to answer questions on company policy, strategic objectives and management style. When asked about the way in which entrepreneurial possibilities arise in the firm − when he was asked to attempt 'to identify and isolate that quality of entrepreneurship, especially in the large modern corporation' as the question put it to him — he drew attention to the organisational aspects of fostering management initiative:

> ... About entrepreneurship, I think what we are very clear about is that size is a problem and that we should not attempt to put small units into larger ones — usually for the sake of organisational tidiness. So, for example, we have a relatively small business in the UK, Kenco, which is a coffee business — there was a lot of pressure to tidy it up by putting it into our tea and foods division — it is obvious that if you have Typhoo Tea and a range of food drinks, that coffee fits in with this. Now we have, in fact, not done this, because by maintaining Kenco as a separate and specialised unit the entrepreneurial possibilities of finding gaps in the market — to go back to your point — is that much greater.

Later in the interview he returned to this example of policy. He emphasized that leaving the Kenco unit on its own to run itself was an organisational decision made to avoid stifling initiative.

> Now you may say that that's a negative decision. But I think it was important in terms of the actual result; because I am totally convinced if we had put it into the larger division it would have had a serious impact in the long term on the way that business develops and on its profitability. It is an example of how the structure is also important. You can stifle a business. You hope that in your organisational decisions you don't let bureaucracy, or tidy-mindedness, result in a structure which is actually inappropriate to your aims.

This was an example, he said, of policy which has to be made at the top level: '... It seems to me that it has to be a top decision, otherwise all the forces will push it the wrong way. It is always awkward to have oddments'.

Sir Adrian spoke of the problem which had been discussed in Tilling and in Manganese Bronze — the problem of combining the highest degree of independence of the subsidiaries with the necessary control of main policy from group. In Cadbury Schweppes, the difficulty might be aggravated by the policy of local shareholding which the company follows.

> If you are attempting to sell your products internationally, [he

said], if you take something like Schweppes, which is perhaps the most developed example of this ... clearly the most effective way of increasing the business is simply by improving your geographical coverage by franchising. But the franchise problem, in fact, is perhaps rather different [because of the existence of local share-holding] .... It is much less complicated if all you have are wholly owned subsidiaries, which are simply extensions of yourself ....
The problem if you have local shareholders arises when the Australian company says to you: 'Frankly we do not wish to invest in the project you have in mind, we would rather put our money into the development of hotels and casinos, where the return on our capital will be higher'. Now, that is the problem, because how can you push a decision on a board who may well say: That decision is contrary to the interests of the people whom we also represent – the local shareholders? This is the point of difference from the classic problem of centralisation and decentralisation.

This may not be merely a question of policy which arises, but of right. It is difficult, on grounds of group policy, to prevent a subsidiary in such a case from doing something else on its own. 'It is not merely a matter of "why not?" – it is saying: "What right have you to stop us?" Since we have to consider the 38% of our shareholders who are Australian, what are we going to tell them at the annual general meeting as to why we have turned down this wonderful opportunity?'
Sir Adrian explained the dilemma which Cadbury Schweppes often had to resolve – and the lines of resolution which the group favoured – by citing an issue which had arisen in its Malaysian subsidiary.

The actual issue was that the Malaysian company wanted to market compound chocolate [chocolate with substitute fats in it] and sell it under the Cadbury name, which we would not sanction. Could we say – how far can we say? – 'We do not really think that you should be manufacturing compound chocolate on the basis that the Malaysian consumer will not notice the difference in taste and will appreciate the lower price. We believe that you should stick to making straight chocolate in line with our international standards'.

In answer to questions Sir Adrian spoke generally on the entre-preneurial possibilities of managerial action.

. . . What you have are ideas and opportunities, and you are looking for ways of translating those ideas and opportunities into profitable openings for the business; what you are interested in is the linkage between them. The ideas can come from anywhere — they can come from inside and outside the business, you can buy them in from consultants, you can get them from reading commentaries, or whatever — it doesn't matter. The object of your organisation is to avoid trapping those ideas within the traditional pyramid type organisation, the hierarchical one, divided into a lattice-work of functional divisions which run vertically and status divisions which run horizontally. The challenge to an organisation is that there may be some very bright ideas coming up from the bottom right-hand corner of the pyramid and the real question is how do you get those bright ideas out of that corner and into something which is a marketable concept. What you are trying to do all the time is to get around the inevitable barriers of an organisation — there is no way to avoid some sort of bureaucracy, just to keep the business running and prevent things from happening which would be disastrous to it — but also you have to loosen the organisation up and to have project teams, venture groups, it does not matter what, but some way of forming ideas which are around into new business opportunities.

Sir Adrian put the requirement of developing ideas, not on any one person, but on anybody who could contribute ideas.

. . . I don't see this as the job of one person — I see it first of all as very much a team approach — and in the case of the people on my planning group, they all obviously have a hand in it. But the ideas can come from almost anywhere. So it is really a question of whether you can devise an organisational system which takes advantage of the inputs of individuals and turn them into a business proposition.

Sir Adrian was asked about the part which operational managers played in the development of ideas. If they are part of the planning team could it be said that the creative ideas come along from them as part of their function as operational managers? Is there any distinction which could be made between those executives who have a fundamentally creative role and others who are primarily doers of the job? 'I don't find that a rational distinction', he said. '. . . I would have thought that it is a bit of everybody's job who has any kind of management responsibility. It may or may not be put into action, but it's there'.

But, on the other hand, there may be a range of possibilities which an operational manager may not normally be expected to entertain about his own business responsibilities, which are almost beyond his proper interests, and which nevertheless must be allowed for and considered somewhere in the company. '... Almost by definition,' Sir Adrian said by way of example, 'it would be very unusual for somebody who was actually working in the confectionery business, if you like, to think up ideas which envisage the elimination of his present business. So that, those kinds of ideas have to come from outside, not necessarily from outside the company'. So a company could establish a forum, a group, in which the different lines of interest could intersect.

... What we have is a planning group, partly from the centre who are not attached to a division and therefore do not have that kind of worry, but, all the time, you are kicking ideas around with the operational people, as you said, so that you don't end up with a nice clear-cut distinction that operational managers are responsible for the future of their own divisions, full stop, while chaps at the centre are responsible for everything outside that — in fact, what you have to get is an interaction between those two groups, because if you just left it to the people in the field they would not look widely enough.

Management Initiative and Participation. The executive directors of the international main board of Cadbury Schweppes Limited are, beside the chairman and managing director, the directors of the international departments (finance, planning, personnel, marketing and technology), and the managing directors of the main operating regions (UK, the United States, etc.).

At one step below the international board are the boards of the operating regions, which are likewise composed of the heads of the main departments, and the managing directors of the divisional activities. The managing director of the UK region is Terry Organ, and he includes in his board the directors of industrial relations, administration, buying, marketing services and finance, together with the managing directors of the divisions — Confectionery, Soft Drinks, Health and Hygiene and Tea and Food.

A division in the UK is a substantial operating unit. Tony Slipper is managing director of the Tea and Food division (which trades under the title of Cadbury Typhoo), and he is responsible for the profit of roughly one-tenth of the whole of the Cadbury Schweppes group. He described management initiative and flexibility as something which is incorporated in the management framework by delegation. The UK managing director has

> full responsibility and flexibility within his region, and he delegates the same level of flexibility to me and the other managing directors. Now there are limits in a big company to which you can do this if it is going to be properly managed. In my view, it is essential to have a formal system in order to make sure that targets are being met or not. Having set these formal procedures, and the parameters mentioned earlier, then the operational units must be given total flexibility within those parameters in which to operate.

He distinguished between

> the need for a formal administrative procedure in running a group as diverse as Cadbury Schweppes, and the need for flexibility and discretion within the divisions in selling the products, dealing with the trade and developing the business. Every managing director has his own way of running a business; some are more formal than others, so it is very hard to be specific on any one style of management.

Tony Slipper described a type of decentralisation in Cadbury Typhoo on the basis of the product.

> Within my division we are now trying to operate within product groups, rather than strictly functionally. These groups should cover a range of products and would have represented on them the various senior managers from each function. By having these groups, and giving them responsibility for the development of the products within these groups, one is able to cut across functional barriers and ensure that the various businesses are given priority as opposed to just the functions within these businesses.

He was careful to indicate that the operational thinking of separate parts of the division cannot be allowed to be partitioned and enclosed, and there must always be cross-currents of ideas between different areas of the business. 'Longer-term planning in my view is about ideas being floated upwards, downwards and across the various organisations. I do not believe any one area of a business can in isolation decide what the long-term strategy of any company is to be'.

One feature of flexibility in the company is the system of participation which is being developed. The philosophy of management participation in policy formulation and decision-making was fostered in the time of Lord Watkinson as chairman and has been furthered in recent years. In 1975 Adrian Cadbury had become chairman of Cadbury Schweppes, and in his annual company report of that year he wrote about the importance of involvement and participation of people at all points in the company in the decisions which affect them. He went on to say that this

> can only be fostered by an open style of management, which accepts this outlook on people and on work. There should be no illusion about the difficulty of managing in this way and it is on supervisors and middle management that the main burden of the change falls; it is therefore essential that they should know that they have the full support and backing of their boards. What can be claimed for a positive policy of involvement is that it opens up new possibilities for settling conflict and winning commitment, not that it will automatically achieve these aims.

But the development of a system of management participation in Cadbury Schweppes has a long history and it came from motives which were quite different from those which guided the philosophy of Thomas Tilling, as described by Patrick Meaney earlier. Both Cadbury and Schweppes, when they had been separate companies, had had a history of employee concern, and, in the case of Cadbury, the company had been built on the idea of group responsibility. In 1967, Adrian Cadbury, chairman of Cadbury Brothers, as he then was, presented a paper to the Birmingham Seminar on 'The Need for Organisational Change', in which he reminded listeners that the history and background of a company exert a profound effect on its organisational structure.

> The importance of committees in our company structure, [he said], stems directly from the Quaker influence of the founders. The method by which Quakers come to decisions is to discuss a

matter through until a sense of the meeting emerges. In business terms this means a structure based on group responsibility, rather than a hierarchy of command. Such a structure has important advantages. It involves bringing into the discussion all the functions of the business that can contribute to the final decision, which should lead to better and more informed decisions. It is also useful from a training point of view both because practice is provided in the mechanics of decision-making and because of the insight into the interrelation of the activities of the company that it gives committee members. Finally, and arising from the same point, the opportunity to take part in the running of the business can be a counter to the lack of involvement, which is often said to be fault of the modern corporation.

In the interviews of 1980, Sir Adrian gave an example of the importance of participation in the agreement of decisions. He said that even in a major strategic decision like a merger (he was referring at the time to the Cadbury/Schweppes merger) a wide agreement within the company was necessary to achieve it.

It would have been impossible to have got that decision accepted without a large number of other people taking the same sort of view. It was not a decision which could have been imposed – this is the participatory end of it. I think that the world has changed even since then, and I would judge that it would be even more difficult now, without establishing an even broader basis of agreement right down the line than was necessary in 1969.

A View from the Middle Level

A change in the style of management requires acceptance by the whole stream of management and the ability in all levels and ranks to carry the change through. An executive of Cadbury Schweppes, Michael Jolly, who was then manager-development manager of Cadbury Typhoo (the Tea and Foods division of Cadbury Schweppes in the UK), was asked to say, as far as he could, what were the attitudes of people in the lower and middle levels of management to these changes. What do the senior managers and their subordinates think of the development of an 'open style of management'?

Michael Jolly thought that there was a process of evolution going on in the attitudes to changes in style.

There are two very strong arguments. One is: if you don't consult with people who have to implement decisions they are not likely to carry out that decision well. That is the participative thinking. The other is: if I have to spend time consulting with him down there, I am wasting valuable time which should be spent thinking about the next thing. The cynic would say: I would much rather be getting on with it instead of doing everything by committee. The reason why I put those two points to you is because I want to say that there are as many managers in one camp as there are in the other. Yet the reality is, I think, that the vast bulk of managers are in both camps. If a decision has to be taken which affects people at the layer just below, they would be likely to be involved to a certain extent. If you start to talk with your subordinates on a matter, or if they are consulted from above, the view goes back: let's stop talking about it, let's get on with it. But it is the case (and we had a classic example of this only the other day) that if a decision is acceptable by the people who have to implement it, then away they go — they are getting the direction they want. But if it is not acceptable there is the backlash: why did you not consult with us? Quite honestly there are a lot of people feeling their way. There are people who take the attitude: I am paid to make decisions — and they sometimes tend to be the older managers, who may be fearful of opening the discussion out in case they lose control. Then you have the others who seem to be happy to keep a nice balance .... Some of the managers who are in their fifties are now adopting a very different style of management to that which they operated in their thirties, because over that period of time they have gained confidence in themselves to operate a style in which they may be open to attack, risking people highlighting a fallacy in your argument. Historically, it seems to me, the boss was never wrong. Now it is becoming more acceptable that the boss may not be the man who is in the best position to make the total decision.

Michael Jolly gave a personal view of the state of participation and involvement by managers in the company which he based on his own experience. (In the post which he had been occupying he had 'quite a fair amount to do' with the directors of the firm and with people at the senior management level just below the directorate, and his work had made him acquainted with managers all the way down).

I could perhaps sum it up for you by saying that the actual path which we seem to be following at the moment tends to be: I the manager, will decide 'what' (because that is what I am paid to do), I will communicate to you 'why' and I will participate with you in terms of 'how'. That is how it looks (I believe) for most of the managers looking downwards. But looking at it upwards, they would say: What is the point of talking about 'how' when you have already decided 'what'? Thank you for telling us 'why' — it is better than not knowing. This may be a cynical view of people looking upwards. Of course, most managers tend to think that in decisions which are made from above, he could decide better, but that is a little bit worrrying because one must ask why he is not in the position of the decision-maker. But, of course, they do not have access to the sort of information which the manager has. And the what, the why and the how is probably the way we are running at the moment.

The expectation of involvement will rise as you go up the management levels.

But even there you have some managers who want to be involved at a much lower level. There is the management style which is in operation in any area and there is the management style which is expected by those below. If a new manager says (to take extremes): 'I'm the new boss, and this is the way I am going to operate. You will get on fine with me so long as you don't challenge me and you do things the way I want it and I shall back you all the way'. Similarly, if he says: 'I am looking to each of you for a major contribution on the methods and the way in which our area is run and this includes the methods of your operation and mine, etc. and I would like us to meet once a month to discuss among other things the broader issues of policy, I will send you the necessary information' — in other words, you are setting your staff out as a very participative manager. In both cases, you are conditioning those people to expect a style by which they will be managed. In both cases, maybe less in the former one, I think you will tend to find that is acceptable. Where sometimes you get the biggest problem between the style which is coming from above and the style which is looked upon going up is because there is a misunderstanding about what 'we thought will be the style' and the style which is. There are fewer people (but there are some, I believe) who having been asked to participate say: 'I don't really want to participate — you tell me what you want me to do and I'll go on with it'.

Tube Investments Limited

Tube Investments was first formed immediately after the First World War by the merger of four Birmingham-based companies, two of whom were tube-makers and two who were tube-users. The assets of the new company in 1919 were £1 million. In the years between the wars, TI diversified into bicycles, domestic appliances and engineering products, and in the 1950s and the 1960s it expanded greatly into steel and aluminium, and into fabricated products. It is now an internationally-based group of diversified engineering companies, and of its annual sales of over £1.2 billion its overseas external sales account for more than one-third.

At the time when the discussion with TI was held, the company was organized in six engineering divisions, a Consumer division and an Overseas division. The company structure of TI has since changed more than the structure of the other three companies who appear in this set of studies, but the constitutional basis of management, as presented here, remains the same for TI as for the others. In Chapter 2 of this study attention was directed to the sensitivity of organisational structure to exogenous and endogenous pressures and it was suggested that it should have the flexibility required to reflect economic circumstance. Though a study such as this may offer a comment or a brief analysis of a particular company structure and the reasoning which led to it, there is implicit in any discussion of company organisation the understanding that it may be modified to accommodate changes. Structure gives expression to the requirements of policy. The one changes in agreement with the other, and modifications in structure in response to circumstance do not invalidate either the analysis of a particular structure or the reasoning which led to it.

The total employment of the group in the UK is about 45 000, and most of the employees of the company work in manufacturing sites of not more than a few hundred. There is a principle of autonomy of the subsidiary companies in the group which is effective through the divisions. It is enshrined in a statement which appears at the beginning of each annual report: 'Group policy encourages maximum delegation of responsibility for operations to individual company managements and aims at close identification of employees' interests with the particular businesses or locations in which they work'.

Discussion with Directors of Tube Investments Limited. At the Birmingham Seminar in 1961, Mr. R.D. (now Sir Richard) Young, at that time assistant managing director of Tube Investments Limited, presented a paper which reviewed the growth of the company since its formation in 1919. He directed the attention of the seminar to the continual increase in the range of activities of the company in the forty-two years of its existence, and placed great emphasis on the decentralisation of the administration of the company.

This policy of decentralisation lay at the root of the formation of TI. 'At the end of its second decade', the paper says, 'TI's organisation was still that of a federation. In general, each company was responsible for getting and making its own orders, recruiting its own management and making its own name and way in the world. Little was heard of TI as such . . . '. This policy was strongly maintained in the years which followed, as the way to create a management with initiative.

This devolution of authority continues to be the mainspring of TI's administrative policy. TI keeps short its channels of communication and intends to prevent them becoming channels of authority for seeking and passing orders from above with the consequent risk of developing managers who might lose the will to initiate because of reliance on the judgement of others.

In November 1979, at an informal meeting at the university, Roy Bagnall, a managing director of TI, and Charles Duff, a director in the TI operations secretariat, were referred to the paper of 1961, and asked to comment particularly on the views presented in the paper on the centralisation and decentralisation of the company. They were asked how they now see the relations between the centre and the parts of TI, compared with eighteen years ago.

In answer to this they confirmed that in a very large diversified group like TI ('TI is a fairly vast conglomerate', said Bagnall), group headquarters looks at the general movements in trading and its finance and does not itself manage the particular business activities in detail. The oversight of the management of the companies is the domain of the divisions, who have 'tactical freedom' to do so, and who also have to safeguard the operational freedom of the companies. 'A good deal of autonomy runs at company level', said Bagnall.

It seems that |divisionalisation had the intended effect, among other things, of incorporating this autonomy of the operating companies in the constitution of the group. This it did by creating a level between them and headquarters. The divisions insulate the companies from the main board and the headquarters staff, while these in turn, have the role which has been described in the section on Manganese Bronze as typical of a conglomerate headquarters. They try to provide a point of exceptional managerial competence, offering the advice and assistance of group functional resources in areas where they are needed, they monitor capital expenditure over the group as a whole and they ensure that company activities in total conform with group financial objectives.

This has certain results for the range of possibilities which different parts of management take into account. In Chapter 4 (on strategy and entrepreneurship) these distinctions are discussed more fully. What is interesting in the present range of discussion on management initiative was the brief definition which Charles Duff offered of the general area of strategic responsibilities of the group management of TI as 'the mix of activities over the group as a whole'. He uses the phrase 'mix of activities' in order to contrast this with the 'product mix', which he says is the concern of the divisions and which he would call a tactical concern. Bagnall amplifies this by saying that 'strategy would be concerned with the aspects of the environment and the areas in which we are involved', and 'the mix between the consumer goods and the capital goods section of our industry', and the shares of the home market, the traditional export areas, and things which are 'mature businesses'. Under 'strategic' thinking also would be the attention which is paid to the way currency movements affect the pattern of trade.

Under this scheme there are three clear levels which can be distinguished where initiative should be exercised and freedom be allowed. The companies have operational freedom, the divisions have tactical freedom and the main board retains strategic control in their own hands. As in the case of Manganese Bronze, diversification and decentralisation in TI went together. Both groups had to find a way of accommodating the free run of particular knowledge with the necessity of general control, and differed only in the extent of the formality of the methods adopted for achieving it.

The difference is not one of philosophy but of circumstance. By any measure, TI is about thirty times the size of Manganese Bronze. As Neville says of Manganese Bronze, if his group, or if the number of the different companies in his group, expanded by, say, ten times, he would probably be driven to a more formal structure for Manganese Bronze. In TI, the insulating layer of the divisions was introduced for reasons of control, and particularly for the control of expenditure. But it was also introduced in order to free initiative in the companies in a way which is achieved in the much smaller group of Manganese Bronze by the mere personal presence on the company boards of the chief executive who can himself ensure the necessary control quite informally without inhibiting initiative. Bagnall puts the two reasons for divisionalisation in TI in one sentence when he says: 'Our philosophy is summarised in "centralise the policy and decentralise the action".'

How this philosophy is practised can perhaps best be seen by presenting an example. In 1977 a small but technologically progressive company in the TI group became the subject of interest to another company as a possible acquisition. Under the spur of external interest, the TI management began to give special consideration to the possibilities of the subsidiary company's development. The question which had to be resolved was whether it would be better to accede to the proposal for acquisition or whether sufficient resources were available, or could be made available, to the company, to ensure its future development as a member of the TI group. The examination of this question led to an assessment of the future of the company in which group, division and company participated and, eventually, to a plan for accelerated growth for the company. This participation and subsequent commitment of the management in the plan throughout the group makes a brief case study of the discussions which occurred in the company between 1977 and 1980, and the action which materialised| from the first approach with a proposal for acquisition to the final agreement of the ten-year growth plan.

Drynamels

Drynamels, a company grouped in the machine division of TI, manufactures industrial coatings. There are about 140 employees. In 1978 its sales were about £3 million.

Drynamels' great asset is its strength in the powder coatings market.

This is a clearly growing market with a great potential, and Drynamels have achieved a leading position in it. The process comprises the electrostatic spraying of dry powdered coatings onto the workpiece, followed by fusing and stoving. It is rapidly superseding wet-paint processes, which are wasteful of solvent and paint and hazardous through toxicity and fire risks. The market is still in a state of technical development to establish new formulations and applications but demand is growing rapidly, notably in the motor and domestic appliance industries.

In mid-June 1977, International Paint, the paint division of Courtaulds, made contact with the TI group secretariat to put forward a proposal to acquire Drynamels. On 24 June, representatives from International Paint came to see the chairman of TI, Brian Kellett, to pursue this proposal. Their interest derived, he said of this meeting, from Drynamels' market position in powder. They said they recognised that Drynamels had taken the lead but claimed that the big paint-makers were now moving seriously into this area. Berger had just acquired a large powder plant in Holland, International themselves had a plant in Germany and were just commissioning a plant in the UK about equal in capacity to Drynamels. They claimed that UK powder prices were about 20% higher than European prices but that this differential would soon disappear as all this new capacity came to bear on the UK market. They estimated that about 20% of the UK market for paints would switch to powder but this would take five to seven years because of the changes needed in user's plant. They were determined to be major participants in the powder market and felt their distribution strength would allow them to achieve this. Nevertheless they would welcome the immediate fillip that acquisition of Drynamels would provide and thought TI might decide it would be prudent to come out of the business before the challenge from the major paint-manufacturers developed fully.

Brian Kellett replied to this suggestion by saying that TI had not been seeking to sell Drynamels in recent times and had no problem in providing whatever resources might be needed to exploit its lead in powders. He enquired whether they might see any merit in a possible partnership of TI's production technology and Courtauld's distribution strengths, but they did not respond to this. He undertook to study the proposal which International Paint had made and to give them a definitive answer or talk further with them within a few weeks. He sent proposal for their views to the two managing directors of TI and to the managing director of the machine division, and to Mr.

Charles Duff, who was, as director-commercial analysis, the member of the group staff who received the initial contact.

Charles Duff made an appreciation of the proposal from which there arose, as he perceived, a logical sequence of action. Following their immediate appraisal of Drynamels as 'a profitable and self-sustaining operation with attractive growth prospects' it was becoming clear that the preliminary decision would be to consider a faster growth plan for this activity, and to seek the commitment of the managing director of Drynamels to this plan.

On the same day as the meeting between the chairman and the representatives of International Paint, Charles Duff had circulated to the joint managing directors an analysis of the powder market and an appraisal of the position of Drynamels. The three main points of the appraisal were that 'Drynamels appeared to be self-sustaining and efficient', that 'the technical content of the market effort in the powder field seems to be such that there are likely to be few economies of scale' and third, that strength of the company could be attributed chiefly to technical resources of the development chemists under the technical director. The analysis went on to ask whether the most was being made of the opportunity. It recognised that the company and the division were aware of the possibilities and that the company 'should continue to grow organically, developing new business as fast as the current technical resources permit'. If the growth was to be accelerated, it would be done largely by drawing in new customers who have been converted to the technology of dry powdered coatings.

The chairman had made it known that before he could offer an answer to the proposal which had been made by International Paint, he would want to know if the division believed that a growth opportunity existed and, if so, how it intended to accelerate Drynamels' progress. The analysis of possibilities was therefore committed to the secretariat.

The secretariat began to survey group opinions and to liaise with the machine division on the development options open to Drynamels. The planning director of the machine division, Bob Solt, sounded opinions within the division and, in July, he prepared a paper in which he reviewed the position to see whether there was any danger to Drynamels from entry into the market by the big paint-makers. This paper confirmed that it was not possible to identify any factor which would give a large paint-maker an advantage over a company of the size of Drynamels and, in particular, it observed that the specialised nature of the business 'does not offer economies of scale to a high capacity plant'. The technical staff, which had given the Drynamels organisation its lead, should be retained, by offering the opportunities and the morale lift associated with a growing company. The review concluded by advancing the idea of an accelerated growth rate from a possibility to a plan. It led to the establishment of a Drynamels expansion committee made up of company, division and group personnel, to consider the different options.

Discussions in the committee in the second half of 1977 led to the proposal for the acquisition of a company with a significant market in industrial finishing and especially in powder coatings. A systematic review of these companies identified one as the most attractive for acquisition. It was a company with a 100%-owned subsidiary in the UK and a 97.8%-owned subsidiary in Europe, and with a stable management and a good track record. But, having considered the possibility of this favourable acquisition carefully, this strategy was turned down, early in 1978, in favour of organic growth from within.

In August 1978, a planning meeting with the group managing directors, the managing director of the machine division and the directors of Drynamels articulated more precisely the terms of reference of the Drynamels expansion committee. The committee was charged with examining the existing plans in five areas in detail: the level of powder penetration of liquid paint; the allocation of R & D resources; the total organisational ability; competition; and the appropriate price/quality/market share strategies. The committee was to report its findings before the end of 1978.

The TI Drynamels target plan was therefore produced for a strategy for rapid growth in Drynamels. It circulated in February 1979 and projected growth over the decade until 1988, involving capital investment of over £5 million (inflated value), and achieving a sales turnover of £19 million per annum (current figure, about £3.1 million), and profit of £2 million (current figure, £0.32 million). To achieve this objective, three lines of information had to be followed:
(1) An assessment of the extent of growth in established powder applications in the next five years. Because the Drynamels staff were in close touch with the relevant market sectors, it would be the responsibility of Drynamels to report on this.
(2) Investigation of potential powder application would be a requirement laid on the division.
(3) The exploration of overseas markets would be a responsibility of the Drynamels expansion committee. Drynamels was excluded

from the export market by the Libert licence, but this was due to expire in 1980. Discussions were being put under way to explore the possibility of export markets in certain areas where the technology developed by Drynamels was in the lead.

In the spring of 1979 the TI group managing directors committee considered the target plan and approved it. They urged the Drynamels management to ensure that the scheme did not fail for lack of management or technical strength, and they asked Drynamels to draw fully on the advice and assistance of group functional resources in these areas.

The sequel to the Drynamels case was that TI disposed of Drynamels Limited in 1981 for reasons which are not part of this study. The case presents the way in which the consultation process operated, with particular emphasis on the features which have a bearing on management initiative and control throughout the group. The important elements of the consultation and planning process, from the initial contact by International Paint to the formulation and approval of the growth plan, was the active participation of divisional and group planning people through the Drynamels expansion committee, and the commitment of the managing director of Drynamels to faster growth.

4 IMPLICATIONS AND CONCLUSIONS

Background

In comparatively recent years business historians and writers on business organisation and policy have devoted increasing attention to problems of corporate behaviour and to the interplay between strategy, structure and markets. Among economists traditional theory was not on the whole addressed to such questions: the rigorous form of the economic theory of the firm with the assumptions that the firm's objective is unambiguously given and that all alternative means and their outcomes are known precluded examination of the processes by which objectives and strategies are, in practice, formulated. Although the term 'entrepreneur' remained in use, it had no true counterpart in the theoretical firm since no genuine decision-making function required to be exercised.

It is, of course, true that numbers of economists have analysed questions arising from the growth of the modern corporation, of the multi-divisional form of organisation and of discretionary behaviour by managers: Marris and Williamson are notable contributors in those areas. Cyert and March combined economic and organisational analysis and sought to construct a theoretical, predictive framework for the behaviour of firms conceived as coalitions and sub-coalitions with multiple objectives. More recently the work of Arrow and Leibenstein has been directed towards the economic study of firms as organisations.[1]

In the study of the processes by which decisions are made, the administrative procedures and the way in which matters come on to the 'agenda of organizations' in Arrow's phrase, the progress which has been made also owes much to business historians and organisation theorists. Chandler is one outstanding name in this area. Important contributions have also been made by such writers as Hannah and Alford in the UK. There is a large organisationally-oriented literature on corporate behaviour of which Bower and Burns are notable examples.[2]

Even allowing for this work, there is still a dearth of investigation and knowledge, empirically based, on the internal functioning of the 'black box', on the growth and decision processes of the modern business enterprise. The present study has, therefore, been concerned to add something to knowledge of this kind of by examining certain aspects of managerial initiative and control in several companies. Since the main part of the study consists of managerial self-perception it is open to the criticism that it does not necessarily reflect the reality of the power relationships within the firms. Certainly there is force in this argument, even though the present authors make no claim to presenting a general theoretical statement. Nevertheless, it seems important to acquire insights into the actual behaviour of firms, and the way in which managers themselves perceive the questions is a relevant factor in that behaviour: the reality of firms and of their environments is partly a matter of what their managements perceive it to be. The 'problem' of a business is partly what the decision-makers elect to regard as its area of interest and competence.

In this study, two further elements are relevant to this question. The first is that attention has been focused on a limited number of problems: the second is that the companies have been examined at more than one layer of management. This latter point reduces the disadvantage of securing only 'the top man's view' and at the same time casts light on the extent to which decisions, including strategic decisions, are generated at various levels in enterprises. Entrepreneurship is concerned with those decisions which govern the shape and direction of the firm, and to determine the locus of strategic decision-making, or more probably the various loci, is to identify the entrepreneurial sources within complex business corporations.

The information which has been presented here bears especially on the sources of managerial initiative and the modes of managerial control in complex business organisations. The companies considered differ in products, markets and size. In one of them, for example, diversification is explicitly confined to areas of existing managerial, technological and marketing expertise (TI): at Thomas Tilling, on the other hand, its chairman regards the very essence of the business as the management of diversity. In contrast to the widely accepted proposition that diversity and complexity are particularly difficult he clearly thought in terms of managerial synergy, and said that the main board gave rather short shrift to excessively specialist talk from its members.

Entrepreneurial Individuals and Organisational Process

The strategic decisions of firms are made by individuals within them working as individuals and as members of units or teams. In Simon's words:[3] 'Every executive makes his decisions and takes his actions with one eye on the matter before him and one eye on the effect of *this* decision on the future pattern — that is to say, upon its organizational consequences'. While that is true at all levels of organisation it is also true, of course, that in organisations there is a structure of authority, a system of hierarchy. The striking remark in Cyert and March that ultimately it is hardly more meaningful to specify profit maximisation as the firm's goal than maximising the wage of Sam Smith, assistant to the janitor, does not mean that they are equal in their capacity to generate and control its development. It is certainly clear in the firms considered in this study that the top men in it believe that they and a small group make a number of the important decisions for the enterprise as a whole, and that this belief is shared at levels below them.

This belief has four related aspects:

(1) There is the explicit view of chief executives that some decisions are made by them or by the managing director in consultation with the chairman without the need to take matters to the board of directors. Neville says this of Manganese Bronze but qualifies his remark by saying that in a fundamental matter neither he nor the chairman would usurp the function of the main board. The reverse aspect of the chief executive's authority in a diversified company with highly autonomous divisions or subsidiaries is expressed in Yardley's comment that the Tilling concept rests on trust in the chief executive of the company, i.e. of the group. A failure of that is conceived as the only real constraint. This attitude extends to other levels of management: within the subsidiaries, as well as in the context of the group, individual managers exercise some similar discretion.

(2) Even where decisions are made through layers of management, the top of the organisation sees itself in control through a variety of means. The general values and identity of the company are conceived to be determined at the centre and to bind all elements in the group: autonomy is exercised within policy guidelines. The centre has a form of overall strategic control: each subsidiary is part of a bigger business. Autonomy is subject to the ultimate sanction of top management and to financial control over what

is regarded as significant for group policy as a whole. Subsidiaries
are aware of the boundaries within which they must operate, and
will be required by the centre to set out all relevant information
about substantial projects. It is recognized that the centre is the
repository of special knowledge and skills: this is typified in the
attitude of Tillings towards decisions on acquisitions. There is
central responsibility for top-level appointments in the subsidiaries.

These factors were expressed in the references made to 'way of life'
and in such precepts as Bagnall's statement that the aim in TI was
to centralise the policy and decentralise the action. Neville was explicit
with respect to the ultimate sanction: Yardley was clear that major
diversification was a matter for Thomas Tilling as a whole and not
for Newey & Eyre: every appointment of a director is reported to the
Tilling board. The general belief about top authority is embedded,
however, in a framework of consent:

(3) Chief executives take it as part of their role to be generators of
ideas. But in no case do they regard it either as their *sole* function
or as a function *wholly reserved to them.* Thus Neville sees himself
as a 'manager of managers': his function is the acme of *general*
management, something which becomes of growing significance
in a diversified company. There is also a remarkable coincidence of
view among all the industrialists concerned that ideas, including
major ideas, originate in more than one part of the management
system. Neville's reference to an organisation as a triangle is
matched by Sir Adrian Cadbury's comments on 'the traditional
pyramid type of organisation': he remarked 'that there may be
some very bright ideas coming up from the bottom right-hand
corner of the organisation and the real question is how do you
get those bright ideas out of that corner and into something which
is a marketable concept'.

(4) In every instance there appears to be a firm belief that effective
decisions depend on acceptance within the organisation. In the
first place, chief executives are rather cautious about enforcing
a personal view on matters which lie within the specialist
competence of the autonomous unit, subsidiary or division.
Neville's example of his idea for BSA Guns is perhaps a sharply
delineated case but it is not at all atypical. Meaney puts the point
as an explicit philosophy in saying: 'In an organisation you should
let the people in charge of the actual operations have the highest
degree of authority commensurate with their responsibility and

their objectives'. In the second place, the argument is that it is necessary to carry all layers of management with the major decisions if they are to work. This is not necessarily an argument as to participation in the conventional sense, though it may be, and it does not eliminate the factor of ultimate sanction. But it seems to penetrate to quite major decisions: Sir Adrian Cadbury said that even in a major strategic decision like a merger it is necessary to have a broad base of agreement (here he referred quite explicitly to the participatory aspect). Michael Jolly, an executive of Cadbury Schweppes, speaks of the risk of 'backlash' if this consideration is ignored.[4] Third, there is a widespread conviction that ideas cannot simply be generated at the centre, a conviction which is found in Manganese Bronze as markedly as in the much larger firms of Cadbury Schweppes and TI.

Thus Neville, although he clearly sees the overall role of the centre, says that 'above all I don't think in a conglomerate that it is likely that you would find any board of directors which would be able to identify where diversification is desirable ... ': Cadbury said he could not see it as a rational distinction to divide executives between those who have a fundamentally creative role and those who are simply implementers.[5] R.D. Young drew attention 'to the risk of developing managers who might lose the will to initiate because of reliance on the judgement of others'.

The evidence of these studies, within a limited number of firms, is admittedly fragmentary, but it does contain a number of themes which recur in all instances. The character and influence of leading individuals do count: they are very important determinants or influences in the formulation of the general values of companies and in their managerial styles. They are important also because all (business) organisations have some hierarchical structure and systems of authority and control. But top management — individual or board of directors — is exercised within a framework of organisation: once the firm moves beyond a certain size and degree of complexity the place which tradition has ascribed to the single entrepreneur is better filled by a concept of entrepreneurship as something which pervades a firm and is exercised through various layers of management.

Conventions of 'Government'

The evidence also suggests that an important element in the way firms actually behave may be described as the power of the conventions of behaviour. The formal structure of a business is only one part of the reality of the decision-making process, one which no doubt becomes increasingly significant with growth in size of firm. Mr. Saxon Tate, in fact, considered the growth of formal structure as a function of size: the authors regard that as an undoubtedly substantial part of the truth, but as only one part of it. The conventions, i.e. the understood relationships, are of perhaps equal importance. As Yardley, the chief executive of Newey & Eyre, put it, about a visit he paid to three of their branches in Scotland: 'I didn't turn out on the spot, I went through the courtesy of asking the boss if I could go on his patch – the man who runs the business in Scotland . . .'.

This kind of understanding can be formulated in effect as part of the general guidelines in a company: thus, Yardley, in speaking of diversification, says: 'If we [i.e. Newey & Eyre] were a public company in our own right, I would think that diversification would be part of the strategy which I would develop'. But he also says: 'It is in the context of working within Tilling that I would not move away from sticking to my last'.

Those phrases appear almost to specify that the relationships are informal: even if this is so, of course, the borderline between formal and informal relationships may be rather inexactly drawn. In no company is it really imaginable that a major diversification by a subsidiary could fail to come to the main board: its implications for finance, for example, would suffice to make that necessary. In that sense Yardley is giving expression to the hierarchical right of the group to authorise or refuse consent to major developments. But there is also the understood aspect in that (1) the Tilling chairman is held to have a general role of 'feel and judgement' about the performance of subsidiaries without 'formal checks' to ensure 'that the chief executives and their teams are optimising in their performance rather than just doing well enough to pass muster'; (2) Yardley defines his own area of strategic thinking with an implicit recognition of what he needs to concern himself with and what properly belongs to others who can take a wider view.

A similar situation is depicted when Alf Scott at BSA Guns said that if they were considering adding another item to their product range they would not at all regard it as necessary to involve the holding company. When asked 'You would never discuss it with them?' he replied categorically 'No'. As is pointed out in this study, the autonomy which underlies Scott's attitude is not enshrined in the formal constitution of the group: it is a convention of the government of the group. This does not mean, however, that it is a casual custom. It is a condition of the successful functioning of the system, and Scott goes so far as to say that its abrogation by the group (in respect of the use of funds) would be incompatible with the management system. If this understanding were to be ruptured then, in Neville's words, 'the whole concept collapses'.

Despite the power of such conventions, however, it may be that the participants at times exaggerate their importance and particularly the extent to which decentralisation is a function of expanding enterprises. The determination of Newey & Eyre to 'stick to its last' within the framework of a conglomerate group is made the easier as well as the sensible approach, since, as Yardley puts it, to think otherwise 'We should have to run out of steam in the areas we're in. And, in fact, we could open six more branches per annum for the next five years'. In difficult periods it is *prima facie* likely that the centre will wish to exercise closer control because of considerations of cash flow etc. This point need not, of course, be regarded as specific to this group.

The Genesis of Change

Business historians, economists and organisation theorists have devoted considerable attention to the factors which generate change in an organization:

(1) Some writers have come to the conclusion that firms generally undertake major change only in the face of severe exogenous shock: strategic shift is induced by crisis. Organisational inertia, failure to grasp the significance of particular signals, e.g. changes in sales, and the self-interest and tunnel misperceptions of established interest in the enterprise all militate against radical, disequilibrating changes.

(2) Another approach has been to suggest that major changes are attempted only when 'neighbourhood solutions' have been unsuccessful. Thus, in response to decline in sales or market share, price adjustments and cost-cutting will be prescribed. It is only if, subsequently, these solutions in the neighbourhood of the perceived problem do not yield the desired results that attention may be directed towards more fundamental matters (product range, organisational competence, etc.). (See Cyert

and March, 1963).

(3) Rosegger,[6] in a paper on the investment decision in the steel industry in the United States, observed that some kinds of large-scale capital expenditures were undertaken when managers came to believe that unless something was done 'the functioning of the system' would 'be seriously impaired'. This perception arose as a result of production, marketing, financial and internal managerial pressures.

(4) Herbert Simon[7] introduced the concept of 'evoking mechanisms' in the context of particular decisions and emphasized the function of attention-focusing as a prerequisite of decision-making. The idea can be extended to wide categories of decision. Among the firms considered in this study it is interesting to observe that organisational form and autonomy were justified not only as requirements of large-scale firms but as a means of generating innovation. Autonomy ensures that responses are evoked and decisions generated by those with knowledge of operations and proximity to the market, and who are directly concerned in the success of the activity. Whether or not a business will perceive and attend to problems and whether levels of management below the top will accept decision premises is partly a matter of organisational design and deliberate attribution of responsibilities and accountabilities. The result will not necessarily come of itself: innovative response undoubtedly requires spontaneity, but in a firm, in which the visible hand has superseded the market mechanism, it has to be provided for. This is perhaps especially so in a large and complex corporation.

While no single feature can be detected as the universal generator of strategic change the symbiotic interplay between strategy and structure is assuredly evident. To economists and business historians, moreover, it is of peculiar interest to observe the relevance of political analysis (i.e. of the tools of political science) in the understanding of behaviour and change in the large and complex modern corporation. The genesis of change may be exogenous or endogenous, sudden or gradual: its unfolding throughout the large business enterprise is a complex process, political in the sense that it involves negotiation and consensus — or at the least, tacit acquiescence. The evidence is consistent also with Professor Penrose's emphasis on the nature of management as a team: the emphasis on loyalty, trust and corporate philosophy seem to be genuine realities. Yardley refers to '100% trust in the chief executive of the company they are invested in', Wingate the 'way of life of the company'. Neville speaks of entrepreneurial change as a team responsibility. It is inconceivable that in any organisation there should be no rubs or discontents, neither policy disagreements nor administrative frictions. The authors are not seeking to present an idealised picture of behaviour in organisations: indeed, progress may result from the existence of disagreements — from the effort required to resolve them. Conflict, defined as imperfect compatibility, is inherent in the idea that in business enterprises, as in other organisations, there are multiple objectives to be met — multiplicity which stems from the variety of individuals and units of which the enterprise is composed. The emphasis is, nevertheless, on loyalty and trust and the commitment which these imply, as prime movers in the progress of the business.

One feature which is hinted at in the material and which merits further exploration is the extent to which strategic decisions emerge as the result of particular almost *ad hoc* decisions taken to meet specific circumstances or even as a result of administrative procedures. This is most likely to be the case in large, non-market institutions in which rules and procedures are of particular consequence, e.g. in universities in which examinations play a significant part. But there is some evidence that such outcomes are also experienced in large business enterprises with complex systems of administration. This coincides with the view expressed by Mr. Tate on formality as a function of size and hence helps to account for the difference between Manganese Bronze and the divisionalised structure adopted by TI. How far in business the pattern conforms to non-market systems is precisely what requires further research.

There is a hint of a related problem in Cadbury's comment that 'almost by definition, it would be very unusual for somebody who was actually working in the confectionery business, if you like, to think up ideas which envisage the elimination of his present business'.

The ideas which have been considered as to the interrelationships between layers of management are closely relevant to the genesis and unfolding of change. All the comments made by the top individuals in these firms recognise the extent to which performance and direction are influenced by the perceptions and operational plans of senior-middle management. This is expressed in, say, TI, which refers to 'maximum delegation of responsibility for operations to individual company managements': it is emphasised in Cadbury's remarks about operational managers. (On the significance of middle management in relation to strategy, see e.g. Bower, 1964.)

Conclusions

As the authors have pointed out, the material presented in this study cannot constitute a comprehensive analysis. It is designed to afford some insights into the actualities of behaviour in business enterprises and it suggests some consistent patterns which are broadly in line with the work of those writers who have written about firms as complex networks of 'diffused entrepreneurship'. Even in large organisations, however, and even accepting the proposition that there is no such thing as a consensual goal (except in the most general terms), it seems to be the case that:

(1) The influence of individual leadership and management style is important: how important and how exercised will repay further examination.

(2) While objectives have to be discovered — as Lindblom[8] puts it, in the context of specific programmes of action — general philosophy and policy guidelines govern or at least greatly influence what is perceived to be possible and appropriate.

(3) Since firms are complex organisations — not the monolithic 'the firm' or 'the entrepreneur' of conventional theory — in which it is virtually inevitable that managers at various levels should exercise their own discretion, top management exercises its influence and control through organisational processes and understandings. How far this is so and how far it can be done by a personal link is probably a function of size.

(4) As a corollary of (3) it may perhaps be said that firms, at all events when they are large and complex, have 'governmental' characteristics: faced as they are with the pressures of the market and their own managers, their problem is to reconcile these characteristics with the need to generate entrepreneurial initiative. Thus the development of organisational systems will be designed to enable the centre to maintain control (e.g. of capital expenditure) and as Cadbury puts it, to get a wide enough view: '. . . If you left it to the people in the field they would not look widely enough.' But it is a further and crucial purpose of organisation in business to provide for generating of ideas: to repeat a point made earlier in this study, to provide for 'the free run of particular knowledge' while allowing for 'the necessity of general control'.

The characteristics which have been depicted in this study may very well be related to the nature of the products and to the management environment of the modern corporation in an advanced economy.

In other situations the position of the individual entrepreneur may be different: nevertheless, it seems legitimate to suppose that size and complexity will, in a wide variety of situations, generate similar pressure and produce some similar responses. Moses, it will be remembered, was counselled by his father-in-law to delegate decisions and to leave a number of them to be made within the discretion of subordinates.

Notes

1. See for example:
Marris R.   *The Economic Theory of 'Managerial' Capitalism.*
        Macmillan, New York, 1964.
Williamson O.   'The modern corporation: origins, evolution, attributes'.
        Journal of Economic Literature XIX, No. 4, December 1981.
Cyert R.M. and March J.G.   *A Behavioral Theory of the Firm.*
        Prentice-Hall, Englewood Cliffs, New Jersey, 1963.
Arrow K.J.   *The Limits of Organization.*
        W.W. Norton, New York, 1974.
Leibenstein H.   *Economic Theory and Organizational Analysis.*
        Harper and Row, New York, 1960.
2. Some examples are:
Chandler A.   *Strategy and Structure.*
        The M.I.T. Press, Cambridge, Massachusetts 1962.
        The Visible Hand.
        Harvard University Press, Cambridge, Massachusetts 1977.
Hannah L.   *The Rise of the Corporate Economy.*
        Methuen & Co. Ltd., London, 1976.
Alford B.W.E.   'The Chandler Thesis – some general observations.'
        In: *Management Strategy and Business Development.*
        L. Hannah (Ed.) Part One: 3.
        Macmillan, London, 1976.
Bower J.   'On the amoral organization'.
        In: *The Corporate Society,* R. Marris (Ed.)
        pp. 178-213.
        Macmillan, New York, 1974.
Burns T.   'On the rationale of the corporate society'.
        In: *The Corporate Society, op. cit.,* pp. 121-177.
3. Simon H.A.   *Administrative Behavior.* Introduction to the
        Second Edition P. xvii.
        The Free Press, New York, Paperback 1965.
4. In a meeting with Mr. Saxon Tate, Managing Director of Tate & Lyle, he remarked that he believed in avoiding sudden, radical changes in direction – because 'you could not carry the management with you.' This point is not dissimilar to those already made: they also bear a considerable similarity to Lindblom's proposition, developed in the context of public administration, that consensus is a (the?) criterion of a good decision.
5. Alford's idea of 'diffused entrepreneurship' similarly runs counter to the notion of a sharp distinction between executives who make policy and managers who implement it. This question arises very sharply in discussions of the

character and functions of 'middle management': B.W.E. Alford, *op. cit.*

6. Rosegger considered that given the long lead times and uncertainty in capital investment in steel, *ex ante* calculations of profitability, though relevant, could not be the determining factor in the investment decision in technological innovations.

7. Simon H.A.   'Administrative Decision Making'.
                Public Administration Review.
                Vol. XXV, No. 1, March 1965.

8. Lindblom C.E.   'The science of 'muddling through'.
                Public Administration XIX, Winter 1959.
                'Strategies for Decision-Making'.
                University of Illinois Bulletin (Department of Political
                Science: Edward J. James Lecture on Government), 1971.

The material in Chapters 2 and 3, and the paragraphs in Chapter 1 describing the seminar and interview procedure, are reproduced by kind permission of John Wiley and Sons Limited and previously appeared in *Managerial and Decision Economics,* Vol. 4, No. 1, March 1983, pp. 1-34.

PART TWO

THE MAKING OF STRATEGY

THE COMPANIES: A GENERAL SURVEY

In this second part of the study of a number of UK companies the interest is shifted from managerial initiative and control to strategy formation. The first part was concerned with the status quo and the second is a study of change. The style of management which allows freedom of action to all levels of management was established in the first part as a means of promoting operational efficiency. Here the concern is with the organisational difficulties which accompany strategic revision in a large modern business corporation whose management expects to act with a degree of autonomy. A specific difference between the two parts is that the first was concerned with the state of the separate parts of the business organisation – the branch, the factory, the foreign owned subsidiary, or the division, while the study which follows enquires into the activities of the separate units only so far as these can be seen to have strategic importance and might be expected to contribute to the movement of the whole. The differences in treatment and interests are reflected in the selection of material on which the two parts of the study are based and the perspective through which the material is presented.

The Formation of Strategy

The dialogues of Chapter 3 started from a series of questions, the purpose of which was to trace the channels through which discussion of policy flowed and the manner in which strategy was elaborated. It started from the problem of identifying the entrepreneurial function in the large and complex modern business corporation, where there appeared to be no single entrepreneurial figure or specialist entrepreneurial team with sole responsibility for the formulation of strategic ideas. The design of the discussions was to enquire into how this responsibility is shared through the hierarchy and to suggest where in the practical working of management the arc of strategic responsibility rests.

Kirzner[1] speaks of competition as an activity, not a state of affairs. The activity of business management is the subject of this study because it is this which sets the business in motion. In small firms which manufacture a single product or a few closely related products, the most conspicuous type of business activity to which the management address themselves is in their relations with the market and their consumers. This was why when attention was focused on this type of firm, economics habitually described entrepreneurial achievement as a feat of market perception. As the firms which were studied grew in size, all policy making, including policies in relation to internal organisation, came to be seen more and more as an activity, a process, which cannot be wholly encapsulated in such a phrase as 'decision-making'. In this process all management was seen as having a stake: decisions emerge — or, to use the word currently heard in board room discussion, they evolve. One part of the entrepreneurial task of higher management in a large company is to extend the activity horizon of all levels of management, for 'everyone has a creative part to play'. Everyone must be aware, as Neville said, of the state of company business, 'what we are doing, what the business is doing'.

Nevertheless, although the creative spirit — the entrepreneurial spirit — may pervade a company and although this pervasive all-level entrepreneurship may contribute to the strategic movement of the company, the evidence of the dialogues is that this is not sufficient explanation of how creative ideas arise and how strategy is formed. The study which started with an enquiry into how strategic responsibility was shared progressed into an enquiry into the part played by the top man. It became evident that, despite the obituaries which have been appearing in recent economic literature, the individual entrepreneur may be still alive and well. Mr. Hickman, of Newey & Eyre, spoke of the entrepreneur and his spirit and character and was perfectly ready to place him at the top of an organisation. Rather it was an essential for success in any company that the individual at the apex should have these qualities. It is not possible to manage otherwise because the spirit must be in 'the man at the top'.

The essential contribution which is made by the top man, said Hickman, is to initiate, and this ability he may owe to his creative insight or to his power of distilling (Poore's word) the ideas which come from lower levels. When Hickman was asked how far a chief executive can initiate and later influence the further development of strategic ideas he answered: 'I think he plays a bigger part in the initiating of ideas. The way we plan it or operate it is then discussed within the Newey & Eyre board'. When a subject is raised which has strategic implications it almost certainly becomes a matter for board discussion because a board cannot operate as such unless it is made aware at once of anything which has strategic potential. Not to do so, said Neville of Manganese Bronze, would be to 'usurp the proper function of the main board'. In the phase of development, therefore, there would be a progressively deeper involvement of the management. 'We do operate very much like a Cabinet, if you wish', said Hickman. 'We have our board meetings and my colleagues in those board meetings sit down and discuss strategy'. As much time as is needed is given to board meetings on matters which require it. They could be discussed and developed over a period of weeks or months or even a year or more. All the time when this policy is developed everybody who is on the board is really party to it and so his views would be merged into the general stream of thinking.

The companies which have been studied here have a more or less decentralised structure. Heflebower[2] has described the extreme case of decentralisation as one in which the enterprise might be looked upon as a group of teams bound together by certain common objectives and the ultimate authority of the top command. He distinguishes between decentralised management or administration and the decentralisation of the power to choose. The authority of the top command (or of the 'centre', in a diversified company) is discussed in many places in this study and, taking Heflebower's distinction, it is clear from the dialogues that the concern there was always with the decentralisation of the power to choose. The autonomy which is practised in their management by Tilling, for example, or Cadbury Schweppes, is not the same as the independence or separateness which is achieved by dividing the enterprise into project centres because, in the latter, decisions come from the top in the form of orders to be administered. What is delegated in the companies studied here is not the power to administer but to business-manage their affairs. This was the meaning which one of the chief executives conveyed when he said that he needed business-men not managers.

Probably all the top managements in this study would prefer to emphasise the responsibility rather than the authority of the centre. Authority is evident, but this modification in thought and terminology to which the top management can be supposed to submit is quite as real because it is founded on an appreciation that authority is exercised constitutionally. Newey & Eyre treated seriously the charge that decisions about reorganisation were mandatory, (as is shown later in this chapter) explaining that the change was constitutional because it lay within the bounds of strategic necessity. Meaney says of Tilling that the responsibility of the centre is to 'support' the companies and Neville for Manganese Bronze uses the word to 'guide'. The centre management in Tarmac has the responsibility to 'review' the plans which come up. Cadbury and Poore do not want control of company plans to be exercised by higher management, but they maintain the responsibility of the centre to fit them into the general strategic purpose of the company. Cadbury will not have a clutter of directives. The company has broad objectives, which are set out as guidelines. 'We are saying: these are the things which we are trying to do in the business and I am sending you my ideas on the way in which I would like us to be seen to be carrying out these guidelines'.

Higher management is responsible for freeing the channels through which managerial communication flows, or 'getting around the barriers of an organisation', as Cadbury said. When the old channels do not serve, it is an entrepreneurial task of higher management to construct new ones. The trouble which companies seem to experience is not a failure in this, nor in a failure of top management to make decisions authoritatively. When a decision has to be made at the higher levels there is always a point at which authority can be seen to be exercised. The case of Drynamels (which was a company in T.I.), shows an inexorable process of decision entirely due to the higher levels of management. Policy is certainly debated all along the line and there is an increasing tendency that the decision-making side of management should be more 'open'. But this does not mean that authority is confused or that decisions are disputed. On the contrary, even where authority is exercised constitutionally (as is usual), the danger is that authority can be the more easily exercised precipitately. It cannot be assumed (see the remarks of Brockett, or Neville, or Jolly in both parts of the book), that the average manager wants to be burdened with responsibility for difficult decisions. When a subordinate manager is consulted or is invited to offer his views he may find that the easiest path for him to follow would be to leave responsibility for guiding the consultation towards a decision with his superior and to do so before he himself is committed to a position. It is easier to support than to propose. 'I was speaking about the reluctance to be decisive', said Brockett. This suggests that the 'perpetual dialogue' between management levels may sometimes be prolonged simply because no-one wants to make a decision. There may be a shallowness of participation against which, as the dialogue shows, higher management is always on guard.

Strategic Choice

Tilling's fundamental strategic choice was its commitment to multi-market activity. On the other hand, in the Tilling subsidiary which appears in this study (Newey & Eyre), there is a strategy intent which is the opposite to that of Tilling. Newey & Eyre's strategy, Paul Hickman (a main board director) says, is orientated to a specific market because it is only by attending to the interests of the company's established distribution outlets that its strategy can be designed. Diversification, for example, whether geographical or in product or in methods of distribution would be entertained, he says, only if it serves the existing pattern of customers. Much the same could be said of the foundation of Cadbury Schweppes' strategy. Although the whole corporate organisation of Cadbury Schweppes has undergone a degree of diversification by divisionalisation in the home market and even more through its worldwide geographical expansion, the company holds to the strict limit of its strategic choice imposed by its own definition of its market. Its corporate strategy is truly a market strategy in the sense that changes in company strategy depend on changes in the perceived dispositions of their customers and their needs. In both companies their customers are commercial outlets and customer relations are personified in the firm by the 'sales rep.' through whom they are conducted. It is on his skill and experience that the success of the company is ultimately dependent.

Hickman has the idea of an entrepreneurial spirit which he sees as pervading the whole company. At one point he seems to be suggesting that this spirit has to be nourished before it can emerge, but a little later he says that 'the entrepreneurial spirit will never be prevented from entering a company' in any case. Both views are tenable and there is support for both in all the company dialogues. There is a general agreement that the entrepreneurial drive emanates from a spirit which is personal and innate; but there is also a team spirit which is due to the experience which is built up in a particular business and which has to be trained and disciplined by the company as a contribution to its strategic purpose. Hickman, Neville (Manganese Bronze) and others, (Hickman perhaps most explicitly) emphasise the importance of independent contributions, particularly at the stage of initiation. In many sections of the dialogues there is an expression of entrepreneurial performance in a large company which suggests that it is composed of particles of independent action rather than as something which is fashioned throughout as one. The thought is of discrete management actions by individuals whose view of the responsibilities which they carry in their own parts of the business embraces the possibility of frequent change. The challenge to an organisation, as it appears from the dialogues, is to put no impediment in the way of these 'unauthorised' changes. The task of top management is to allow a corporate form to evolve which can accept the composite of accumulated relatively minor changes as one of the sources of strategic change.

This was reflected in Sir Adrian Cadbury's words when he spoke of the plans of the separate units in the company as 'primary building blocks'. Fitting them into a general strategy, he said, is a matter for the top. Poore is thinking on the same lines when, commenting on the strategic process, he says that a business idea has to be fitted or designed into business use. He sees the responsibility of the centre lying both in starting the flow of creative ideas and in fitting them into the strategic envelope. Strategy is not a seamless garment conceived and worked as one, but rather it is composed of mixed strands which are woven on many looms and by many hands. The team action, if it is to be described in that way, is not a matter of 'thinking it out together' but of 'fitting it out together'.

Though companies set strategic limits which are widely different to each other it is striking how firmly, once the limits are set, their managements hold to them. The responsible board directors seem to adhere to a strategic position over years, almost as a point of doctrine and they are ready, as sections in the recorded dialogues show, to defend, rationalise and expatiate on the limits on which they stand. Often the director who did so, was answering the question: 'How would you describe the business of your company?' – a question which is always on the mind of management and which calls for a definition of business limits. Yet it is common enough when a top management changes, that these limits and the choices which flow from them are discarded and replaced by a new set. It is particularly interesting in this study that Tarmac twice (1958 and 1979) in its recent history was involved in a complete change in the top management, after which entirely new strategic positions were taken up. When a thoroughgoing strategic review follows on a management change it must be supposed that there is an important element due to the personal character of the people involved.

This could be said for choices in general and might account in part for the wide differences in strategic positions taken by companies who in respect, for example, of product, size and technological experience may be expected to pursue similar paths. These choices are subjective to the extent that they are expressions of a top management's conception of where its own management skills lie. The strategy is chosen by the top management ('otherwise you are not the chief executive' Yardley said of the similar matter of responsibility) and their choice is made on the grounds that it is the best vehicle, for them, for capitalising on the long term quasi-rents which are derived through their own management skills. It is difficult to assess the strategic position adopted by a company on purely objective criteria, because the only group of people who can correctly estimate the special skills of a top management, before the outcome is proved in action, is itself.

There is a subjective element in the choice of degree of diversification. The chief executive of Newey & Eyre said: 'Tilling's strength is in managing diversity and I would say that my strength is in sticking to distribution.' When he said that it would not make sense for Newey & Eyre to diversify since Tilling is diversified he was not saying merely that it would offend common sense for him to do something which Tilling could do but was also implying that Tilling do it better. When John Neville said that you cannot reduce business management to a set of rules, he had in mind, as his remarks in the context of his whole observation on the matter show, the importance of the subjective element in the strategic disposition of a company. 'It is a function of personality, training, experience, everything you like to bring into the equation, which means that one man believes you should do it one way, and another in another . . . Any successor has got to find his [own] understanding . . .'.

When saying this John Neville had also in mind the subjective character of all the decisions which are made by executives throughout the company. It is made clear time and time again, not only in Neville's words but in these open dialogues with directors in the other companies, that there is this subjective element in every entrepreneurial action at any level of managerial decision-making and that it is this element which autonomous management aims to release. A company wants to capitalise on the quasi-rents which accrue to it, not only in their property in their higher management but in their property in the skilled and trained managers at all levels. Hickman, as we have seen, chooses the word 'enthusiasm' to comprehend the elusive qualities of hidden entrepreneurial talent which the manager may carry within himself. Cadbury would not allow that creative ideas lie in the special province of one set of executives. Everybody, he said, who has any kind of management responsibility has a creative role. Even when circumstances might subdue it for a time, 'it is there'. The rules and regulations, the 'do's and don'ts' which Yardley mentioned, are no more than a support, a rope to hold on to. What the company is looking for are executives who regard them as such but, looking beyond, can use 'the assets which are entrusted to them', with enterprise.

Management Autonomy and Strategic Choice

Another board director of Newey & Eyre who entered into the discussion of the formation of company strategy was the commercial director, Jon Brockett. Both Hickman and Brockett distinguished between the type of responsibility which is carried by the lower and higher levels of management. Both agree that the branch manager should be entrepreneurial in action though his entrepreneurial range will be limited because his activity horizon is near. Hickman's view of the company is that it attracts people with ability, 'one-off' individuals who, such is the company's management style, can be absorbed successfully into the organisation. The limitation of the branch manager may be that his view is 'parochial'. Brockett uses the phrase 'short term' when speaking of the interests of management at the branch level — the first level of management which carries substantial responsibility. 'The branch manager', says Brockett, 'concerns himself in the main with managing his resource and he applies his time predominantly in relation to the problems of today.' This coincided with some of the things which Mr. Bob Wingate, the manager of the Birmingham branch, said in answer to a question whether a manager could be expected to see, from the branch office, the possibilities, for example, of the move into the USA market. 'Because sitting here', it was suggested, 'you can also think: well, the sort of thing which I do here could be exported'. Mr. Wingate did not think that a branch manager would think in those terms. His imagination would be concerned with what happens in his branch. But Mr. Wingate made the additional point that the experience of managing a branch eventually bears fruit when the horizon of possibilities is extended, when the strategic use of the total resource of the company is considered, say, at board level. 'You must remember', he said, 'that two or three of our board are ex-branch managers. So it is difficult to say that it did not come from here.'

What seems to emerge from the combined views of the two board directors who entered into this part of the discussion is that there must be a limitation of the autonomy of the branch manager which is due to the limitation of his horizon. This is a job limitation, not a personal limitation. His autonomy in the job cannot be allowed to go so far as to upset company strategy. In searching for a reason to explain why a manager at the lower level cannot be expected to extend the horizon of his view as far as his seniors, Jon Brockett notices the lack of professional competence which a branch manager must often feel as he carries out his diverse responsibilities – '. . . he cannot be expert on every particular area.' He goes on: 'I think – I do not know it as a fact – I certainly feel, in recent years particularly, the emergence of a professional resource at the centre here in various functions has tended to invade the branch manager's autonomy – or the autonomy which he thought he had.' The recent decision to centralise and extend the field of responsibilities of the commercial director points in the same direction. The company as a whole felt the need to add to the professional competence with which the services which go into its business as a merchant distributor are carried out and on which the board itself acts.

The Corporate Constitution

In the course of this study many questions arose in connection with the autonomy of all levels of management on the job, which was first presented by the directors in their dialogues as a philosophy of management and then verified as a fact lower down the hierarchy. How does this autonomy arise? How is it limited and how modified? What are the responsibilities of higher management in this matter? In earlier sections of the study the idea has been introduced of a corporate constitution and conventions of governance which embody the philosophy of management of a company and the practices which form its management style. It appears from the dialogues which come later that, since the overriding priority in the company is the fulfilment of its strategic objectives, the constitutional forms to which it holds are dependent on the strategies. When a strategy changes the constitutional forms may have to be modified, and since strategy is the *responsibility* of higher management (here taken to be the chief executive and the board), so is the constitution. The paragraphs which follow are devoted to an expansion of this idea.

The extent to which the management style and the constitutional machinery of a company is obedient to strategic necessity (and is therefore under the control of top management) is shown in the case of the reorganisation of the Domestic Appliances business of Newey & Eyre — a case which has been given special attention in this study. It was fortunate that the discussion of this reorganisation was carried out with two directors of the company who had very different responsibilities. An outline of the case may provide a background to the strategic threat which the company decided to counter.

Traditionally the sales of domestic appliances — a term which includes radio and television sets, cookers and washing machines as well as shelf goods like electrical goods, electric fires and so on — had been a smoothly operating sector of the company's business. The price to the ultimate customer was controlled by the manufacturers and the control safeguarded the distributor's margin. A distributor like Newey & Eyre held in stock a range of appliances according to the branch manager's market preference and the traditional independent retail outlets went to the electrical distributor expecting to be able to view a selection of products. The range of choice was part of the service which the distributor offered and the investment was justified by the profit margin. After the abandonment of retail price maintenance a 'strategic point', in Brockett's phrase, was reached. Large retail outlets appeared which bought directly from the manufacturer and sold directly to the user customer at prices which were at a substantial discount. This constituted a threat that the market position of both the traditional distributor and the traditional retailer would be undermined.

The strategy which was worked out at Newey & Eyre was a reorganisation of this business in the branches by which purchasing and marketing was centralised. Brockett in speaking about the problem and the solution which was adopted by the board is entirely concerned with the strategic necessity. 'Instead of, as currently occurs, 95 branches at their whim and fancy variously stocking domestic appliances, we say that a much more rationalised approach is required. In this area it is proposed that the autonomy of the branch manager will be removed.' He would 'demonstrate' the advantages of the new strategy but, if required, he would 'invoke the power of line management to sort it out.' Hickman, speaking in the dialogue for the regional managing directors, dwells on the need to reach agreement. This is, for him, the area of importance — 'Yes, that is my main task.' Organisational changes had to be manifestly accepted by everyone throughout the company. All the branch managers would have to feel confidence in the rightness of the new strategy and Hickman recognises the critical position which the regional managing director occupies at that stage. The seminar of branch managers which has been alluded to earlier was arranged to clear the strategy and to present the reasons. The marketing manager was there to present his factual answer to the problem to back 'my persuasive answer'.

It is possible to detect in the words of the two board directors, one with responsibility for the management down the line and the other for management of functions, differences in the emphasis in their views of the problem and the selection of the features which they regard as important. Hickman wants to preserve the state of constitutional understanding which he sees as a feature of the company's management style. His task, with a functional colleague, is to expound the new strategy to lower management and for himself to explain and agree that consequent changes in management style are not 'mandatory' but are part of the larger agreement on strategy to which all management is bound. Hickman's task is an example of the perpetual task of the entrepreneurial direction of the firm of creating an appropriate constitution or modifying the existing constitution in accord with strategic change. Although it has to be ready to modify it in changing circumstances, it still has to hold on to and defend it against arbitrary changes, because strategic and organisational change is successful only when the established constitutional forms favour it.

Since the constitutional machinery of a company, which includes its management style, stems from its strategic needs, the corporate constitution must be adaptable, not static. It exists as a form which holds the management system together and which prevents destructive opposition. But it may not be definable because it is being constantly modified and renovated as a part of the process through which consideration of every new strategy passes. Brockett, for example, recognises the branch manager's autonomy in the same way as Yardley, Hickman or Wingate, whose words have been quoted, but he makes conscious a qualification which already has been in their thoughts — '. . . or the autonomy which he thought he had.' This amendment may well be taken as a portent of constitutional departure. The strategic necessity from which it arises is 'the emergence of a professional resource at the centre', of which the company felt the need. Rights are not denied; but no right is permanent in an institution which can survive only if it is itself responsive to change.

To implement that strategy the management style of the company would have been modified in a way which was apparent throughout the company. The modification was, and had to be, a creation of top management because such modifications or amendments as these to the constitutional form of the company arise as the subject of continuous review of the current form in accordance with strategic change. Nevertheless the constitution is one of the treasures of the company. It distinguishes the particular style, the working environment — the 'way of life' as Mr. Wingate called it — of the company for all who have a part in it, and for that reason it cannot be arbitrarily changed. This is the substance of Mr. Saxon Tate's remark which has been referred to earlier, that it was important to avoid sudden, radical changes in direction because 'you could not carry the management with you'. Sir Adrian Cadbury also, it was noted earlier, said that the decision on the Cadbury Schweppes merger required a broad basis of agreement right down the line. When a proposed strategic change is thought to be potentially disruptive to management, it is not because objections are made to the introduction of a new technology, or a new product, or a new marketing or distributive or administrative technique. Such changes are usually welcomed as a challenge. It becomes a source of strife or stress when the change may threaten a dissolution of the achieved constitutional environment, the environment which is itself the creation of the people who act in it and who perceive that it is much easier to destroy a corporate environment than to create it. The constitution of a company is seen by management as something embedded in its history, an achievement over time.

The Companies

Thomas Tilling

Mr. P.H.D. Ryder, managing director of Thomas Tilling in the 1960s, and one of the 'voices' which is heard in the dialogues in Chapter 3, says that Tilling invented the industrial holding company in 1950 as a means of investing in privately-owned companies. Underlying the Tilling idea was the axiom that the companies which joined Tilling should be chosen because of the quality of their management and their ability to carry on in harmony with the new centre, the prime consideration being quality *and* continuity of management. From that axiom followed the corollaries which fitted together to make up the management style which marked Tilling — a style in which trust and persuasion were dominant and which allowed for as much flexibility in policy making and as much autonomy in action as is feasible at all management levels. These qualities shaped the character of Tilling's internal society from the early days and gave a distinction to what can be described as its constitutional form.

Tilling had willingly decided to follow a route which forced the board to face the problem of managing diversity, a problem which is 'obviously quite complex'. Ryder shows that what was needed was a balance between the requirement of autonomy in policy making in the subsidiaries (to take advantage of their special skills and experience) and the requirement of control from the centre, (without which a group strategy would be impossible). Tilling decided therefore to form a new management team with a great breadth of experience at the centre and a system of co-ordinating the work of the centre and the subsidiaries. Tilling's achievement was to set up such a system in 1950 which gave a balance between the dual roles. This system, as Sir Patrick Meaney, managing director since 1973, indicates in the interview of 1980, remained essentially the same.

The way in which the system of dual roles has worked over the years can be seen in contrast in the words of Mr. Ryder, speaking of the centre in 1964, and Mr. Gordon Yardley, managing director of the Tilling subsidiary Newey and Eyre, speaking in 1980. Ryder says that part of Tilling's published philosophy was to preserve the freedom of the subsidiary companies 'subject always to our guidance and supervision'. This is not an easy task, says Ryder. 'It is not enough for the company to show better figures than the year before; our representative must try to satisfy himself that there is not more to be done to exploit more successfully the company's resources of know-how, finance and manpower.' Yardley was asked the same question: what control would Tilling have over a subsidiary (or its chief executive), to be sure that it was optimising? What checks are there? 'I am not aware that they have any such checks,' said Yardley, who then went on to say that the chairman, appointed by Tilling, would have sufficient understanding of the business to make a general judgement of performance, 'without getting involved'. Ryder shows that any correction which the Tilling-appointed chairman, or the executive at the centre, might think desirable becomes a matter for discussion — 'consideration is given to the best method of selling the idea to the managing director and the board of the company'. Yardley emphasises that there is no formal way of applying corrections. 'It is, I suggest, a matter of feel and judgement.' Tilling, he says, hold to their philosophy of picking the right companies and the right team to manage those companies.

The system of dual roles has certain spin-off advantages. Meaney referred to the troubles which often arise in large businesses because senior people become distanced from the work force, with the consequence of poor industrial relations. The dual system sets the pattern at the top. Each level will have, Meaney says, 'a strong ingredient of management, a strong sense of identity and recognition of senior people'. It means that it is accepted that appropriate management skills are available at every level and that the task of management at every superior level is to develop and display skills appropriate to itself without treading on the toes of the level below — 'without getting involved'. That is the meaning of management autonomy as Tilling see it — that special skills must be allowed to be used unhindered. If Tilling do not explicitly define autonomy in that way, it is nevertheless the way in which they practise it. Specially it does not mean that any manager is quite free, because freedom, looking upwards, depends on the constitutional understanding that the higher levels, also, are not free in their relations to the lower.

Earlier in this chapter, the constitutional basis of the freedom which is allowed was discussed more fully in relation to Newey & Eyre and a study is made of a reorganisation of one section of the business of the company. This case of reorganisation suggests that the management style of a company is sensitive to change and the force which determines the style and controls the change is the same that controls the reorganisation, namely the top management. This is not surprising since all major change either has strategic implications in itself or arises in obedience to a strategic impulse, and strategy remains a responsibility of the top.

Cadbury Schweppes

The nature of the strategic process in Cadbury Schweppes can be described as a combination of the bundle of strategic intentions or sub-strategies which are developed in the scattered companies of the group and which then are tied by the group centre into the framework of global requirements. The responsibility of the centre is twofold. Firstly, every encouragement is given to the companies in the group, whether they are home based and fully owned or whether they are based abroad and with a shareholding in foreign hands, to develop their own plans. No restrictions are made by the centre on imaginative thinking in any part of the business. But secondly, the centre has a responsibility for ensuring that the disparate sub-strategies, which would hardly be expected to complement each other, at least do not hinder the development of a main group strategy. The task of the centre in harmonising these two different responsibilities is crucial. In exercising their strategic freedom, the companies will be reminded that the other responsibility of the centre remains, which is, in Sir Adrian's words, that the centre must maintain 'a coherent view of how you would see the company as a whole develop'.

Cadbury Schweppes global strategy is an envelope into which the sub-strategies must be fitted. Sir Adrian does not think that this global strategy is likely to be clear cut, tidy or worked out exactly as conceived, though he cites the case of the merger with Peter Paul in the USA which, 'curiously enough', had worked out 'very much according to plan'. In speaking of the 'messy world' of reality, where information is generally limited, often inaccurate and which may be confused, he seemed to find a set of strategic guidelines more appropriate to his purpose than a defined strategic goal. These guidelines are those against which decisions, wherever they arise, can be measured. They are the main things, – the two or three things, not more ('to believe that you can have more than three pretty broad objectives like that is to delude yourself'), – on which the whole company will concentrate. So the company has these broad corporate objectives within which the strategic process, the fitting together of the sub-strategies, will be worked out.

In Part One of this study of a group of industrial companies, which was concerned with managerial initiative and control, attention was paid to the peculiar policy-organisational problem of Cadbury Schweppes which was that of branded products marketed by foreign, independently owned companies. There is always the danger that the intentions of the local subsidiary company might conflict with those of the group, that the subsidiary might have its own ideas as to how the business should be developed and so frustrate the Cadbury Schweppes principle that its brands should be internationally uniform, that 'they will taste the same, they will be packaged in the identifiable form, they will be marketed in a broadly similar way'. In examining this policy problem of Cadbury Schweppes, the passage in the former study made a comparison of the position of their foreign companies with that of the subsidiary companies in Manganese Bronze and considered how far management initiative and the pursuit of an independent policy is conceded by the centre in both groups. The evidence, it was suggested, was that in both it was a matter of internal agreement and accommodation. 'Power can be devolved', it was suggested, 'but the devolution is not a right but an agreed convention. The pressures towards devolution have become too strong to be disregarded, and devolution is becoming systemised in the new constitutional forms'.

When the comparison of these two widely different companies is extended to the strategic process there appears, once again, a similarity between them. In both companies the strategic process seems to be founded on the same principles and in obedience to the same logic. In the comments in the section on Manganese Bronze which appears below, it is noticed that although the companies are said to operate on 'a free rein', the fact that they are parts of a group means that they cannot be quite free. They are constrained by the realities of group integrated behaviour, which occasionally have the force of rules, but often present something which is more a rubric of good business manners. In this way the application of appropriate business sense by the companies in either group is not impeded. The themes are proposed by the companies and they are gathered together in a group composition. The discipline which is imposed is not intended, it seems, to be one of restriction but, at best, of creation and, at least, of enlargement. The rights of managerial initiative are safeguarded by the discipline which, by putting them within bounds, makes them proper. In the context of this present study it can be seen that it is the constitutional boundary which safeguards the rights and which ensures entrepreneurial freedom appropriate to each level of management.

Manganese Bronze

John Neville, chief executive of Manganese Bronze in 1980, stressed the importance of the 'free rein' which managers must have to run their business in their own way, but spoke at the same time about the restrictions which are imposed. 'Having said that much, let's go back to how you impose the guidelines and rules.' Freedom and control are together included in the form of management in his company and the form is designed, as he makes clear in his exposition, to allow proper consideration by the companies and the centre to the problems which arise from business change. R.D. Poore who succeeded Neville as chief executive at the end of 1980 takes the same view but emphasises that the balance of freedom and control is best achieved when it is based on a firm financial discipline.

Restrictions on the companies in some matters, says Poore, frees them in all other matters. This freedom is the purpose, he says, of the discipline which is exacted by the centre. One advantage of a decentralised structure is that it avoids the problems which, for example, the Civil Service or any centralised 'monolithic' organisation often encounters, when control is achieved through departmental objectives rather than by setting 'financial yardsticks' against which the separate parts of an organisation can prove whether what they are doing is worthwhile or not. He does not think that a centralised structure will necessarily be rigid because a flexible, autonomous structure can be achieved if management throughout its compass can be held accountable to financial objectives.

It is clear in the statements of both Neville and Poore that a defined control is the essence of their system (in Neville's case it is a general planning control and in the case of Poore it is a financial control), and that the purpose of a control which is exercised constitutionally is that it leads to a higher freedom. Yet the ultimate goal of management in the company is neither control nor autonomy but responsibility.

In the case of the BSA Guns shotgun which Neville cites against himself in the interview, he has given an example which shows the importance of observing the limits of responsibility which have been agreed. There is agreement in the company on limits because without it the constitutional form which underlies the strategic process dissolves — or in words which Neville uses in another place, 'the whole concept collapses.' The case recounts how he had pressed a proposal on the management of BSA Guns to manufacture a good quality, medium price shotgun and how the company opposed it. Only their 'total and absolute' opposition to his proposal led him, he says, to withdraw his proposal, for at the crisis he was not prepared to invade the bounds of responsibility of the BSA Guns management. 'I've great respect for that board, so I did nothing of the sort', he says, and he relates, with obvious satisfaction, that events have proved the judgement of the BSA Guns management absolutely right. Poore exercises the same care in safeguarding the responsibility of the company managements. 'Of course I have ideas but I do not enforce them.' The budgets are made by the companies, he says, not by the centre, because they 'understand' that they must take responsibility for their results.

Neville's shotgun case is about the understood limits of responsibility at the two management levels and these limits are observed, it has been argued earlier in this chapter, because they assist the strategic process. But what if the judgement of the management of the subsidiary company had been proved wrong? Neville says that a subsidiary management which could not produce the results which were expected would be dismissed but the fault would be in the selection of the man and not in the system. 'I have made mistakes in appointing people – and I tell the man I've made a mistake.' But he still wants the man appointed to manage in his own way and 'I don't want to criticise that at all.'

Strategy for Poore is a main responsibility of the centre in two ways. Firstly it is a matter of putting a business idea into business use in the way he has described in his example of the automobile component which has to be made in the same country as the car. But the more important strategic responsibility of the centre is in its continuous scrutiny of the changes to which Manganese Bronze may have to adapt. When he alludes to this he is thinking forward to the future shape of the company in a way which is appropriate to the corporate level of planning. He would get some material to assist his thinking from the companies because he could not judge possible changes in the company as a whole without taking a view on the future shape of the separate units. But the future strategic profile of the company as a whole which he may want to draw could, he says, demand the liquidation of some existing activities; and thinking of that and carrying it out was 'absolutely' a special function of the centre.

> You will never get the unit managing directors to come up with suggestions that what they are doing is a waste of time. The responsibility of the centre is to ask a different question on existing products and operations to that which a subsidiary company asks. They are concerned with 'how' the operations are best managed; and the centre has always to put it into perspective by asking the question 'why'. I spend some time thinking about whether they're in the right businesses anyway.

Poore therefore distinguishes sharply between the 'corporate' level of strategic thinking and the 'business' level, to use the terms which Vancil and Lorange[3] have suggested. It is clear that Poore is contemplating a degree and a range of change which is due not to his particular management style but to the circumstances into which his company, and many others, are thrust. 'I think this is particularly important nowadays because British industry won't survive if it thinks it is going to do the same as it did for the last fifty years. We have to do something different and so I spend time thinking about that and whether we should dispose of certain activities or invest more money in others.' He, rather more than Neville, emphasises corporate strategic responsibility – the 're-entry into the "strategic game" ' as Ansoff has it, because the extent of change to which his company may be exposed would be far beyond the capacity of the main-product subsidiary companies to handle. Neville did not stress this distinction between the corporate and business levels in strategic thinking because, although he was only a business-generation earlier, the environmental pressures with which Poore is preoccupied had hardly appeared until his last year or two. As Ansoff and Leontiades[4] say:

> If the firm is in a quiescent strategic environment . . . if the political-social pressures do not threaten, if technology is not turbulent, and if strategic input sources are secure – if all these conditions are satisfied then corporate management can leave strategic responsibilities in the hands of the divisions [or the units]. To the extent to which the answer is 'no' to the respective conditions, the corporate office must begin to take on the strategic work which cannot be done at the lower levels of management.

Poore has not a 'corporate office' of the style which is suggested in the quotation above and the head office of the group is 'minimal' by choice because the decentralised decision system which Poore and Neville instituted would have made no economic sense unless the administration was also decentralised. But as the 'strategic work' of the centre is becoming more important the composition of the board may have to be reviewed because the chief executive, chairman with the board is, or should be, the strategic centre of the company – 'I don't know about that at the minute, I think it ought to be the board . . .'. The board meets about six times a year and it is mainly non-executive with a lot of experience – 'general industrial experience and particularly financial experience – and very useful indeed.' But for the future, he suggests that 'we should have on the board a young man or two young men or something like that who are interested in this kind of subject and who can make a proper analysis of the sort of things we ought to be doing.'

Tarmac

The fourth company in this set is new to this study and for that reason it is given a rather more extended treatment. The development of Tarmac's management philosophy is traced by R.G. Martin, chairman and chief executive of Tarmac Limited in the 1970s, over a period of twenty five years during which the size and scope of the company and its strategic profile were transformed. The record was up-dated in a discussion in 1983 with the present chief executive, Eric Pountain, together with the assistant managing director and the group financial director.

The first strategic departure from the old style Tarmac came in 1958 — a year which Martin describes as a 'watershed' — when the company decided to base its business on quarrying stone and other 'aggregate' and set out on its policy of aggressive acquisition. A reappraisal of corporate policy came on the agenda for discussion by higher management in 1958/9 as the result of changes in its management and of simultaneous changes in its market position. The new, younger management of 1958 set their sights on growth and their attitude was much reinforced by the rapidly rising market which they encountered almost at once. Martin describes these years as a period of unsophisticated, entrepreneurial behaviour — 'it was rather off the top of one's head in those days ... we took the market and the opportunities as we found them.' The strategy adopted, he suggests, was a reaction to pressures — the pressure of demand in an expanding market coupled with the pressure of impending shortage of supply of resources. A change of management would probably have been inevitable under those pressures if it had not occurred naturally through retirement: 'If there hadn't been a management change there would have been stresses and strains.' An example of the unsophisticated business-planning behaviour of which Martin speaks is in his description of how the expanding company achieved decentralisation by trial and error in the subsidiary companies which it acquired in those years. In the earlier acquisitions Tarmac encountered difficulties due to the changed conditions under which the new managements were asked to work, and these management problems disappeared when a new policy of decentralisation was introduced.

Martin sees a transformation of the character of entrepreneurship and strategy formation, after the 'watershed' of 1958, in which the decentralisation of the whole structure and the spreading of entrepreneurial responsibility go hand in hand. He also draws attention to the dilemma in the management of large business that a simple, logical policy of expansion could produce complex ramifications. Martin, however, prefers to regard these complexities of growth as a challenge rather than an obstacle to an entrepreneurial management. The term 'vertical integration', he says, is often used as an over-simplification of what actually occurs in this type of seemingly simple expansion because the business which is added brings in new technologies, together with new business in new markets growing from the vertically integrated activity. But the opportunities which arise from this 'concentric diversification' are often much greater than those which arise from a 'true vertical integration'. This last type of integration must be taken to mean no more than 'adding to the main features of the original markets', — the growth pattern of the original business from which a company may have been struggling to break out.

This consideration of the problems related to expansion leads Martin to a discussion of the advantages of unrelated diversification. Here he touches on areas with which the Tilling and Manganese Bronze dialogues (with Meaney and Neville) were much concerned. Central to Martin's thinking on unrelated (or conglomerate) diversification is the idea of 'compatibility'. The term is difficult to define but he uses the projected acquisition of Wolseley-Hughes to explain it, and he also tries to clarify the concept analytically by suggesting that a new business is compatible with the old if it changes some factors, but not so many that there is serious difficulty in mastering the change. In one sense he uses the term to define the limits of diversification. Unrelated diversification may be unintended. Most acquisitions, though they may be in the same industry or business as the parent company bring in some fringe activities, and through these acquisitions a company may become more sophisticated in the manner in which it deals with different activities. Experience with this unintended diversification, Martin says, may help to extend the strategic horizon of a company and give it a new perception of what it could do or may want to do. The approaches which Meaney, Neville and Poore make to a definition of the limits of diversification offer an interesting contrast to Martin's approach, but they do not contradict it. Martin is alone among them in ruling out high technology as a possible area of diversification in Tarmac, but they all agree that their range of diversification in the companies is bounded by consideration of their business experience and their business style. In this connection, it could be noted that the case of the proposed acquisition which Martin cited was strongly opposed by the management of Wolseley-Hughes because it appeared to the whole company as a change outside its established structure and style. Considerations like these always guided Tilling in their acquisitions and these come near to what Martin means when he speaks of compatibility.

Martin says that a central organisational problem of a fast growing company is the tendency to duplicate the administration of functions. Each division tends to become its own company and a decision has to be taken at some point as to which functions will be administered from the centre. 'As the divisions grow they want to do it themselves — and they usually do.' Martin resolved the problem on much the same lines as Poore and Neville at Manganese Bronze and as the executive centre at Tilling did. 'You have to retain', said Martin, 'the group financial controls at the very centre, you have to retain group publicity at the very centre, you have to retain overall strategic planning at the centre, but the rest can all be devolved if necessary.'

Another problem is the possibility of inter-divisional conflict. A seemingly intractable problem in a company in which the products of the divisions are related is disagreements about internal subsidy pricing. Martin suggests that this problem was never resolved in Tarmac in his experience probably because 'the conflicting parties did not want a resolution — they almost would have preferred to have the thing festering along and disagreeing with each other rather than have the thing settled by head office.' But in a company which divisionalises 'successfully', so that the products of the divisions are unrelated, there is also always a possibility of conflict over the allocation of scarce resources. As with the other companies in this study, the centre had no difficulty in resolving this because there was machinery to deal with it. Decisions about allocations had to be made and if the necessity was explained to the divisions, 'that was that.'

A further organisational change which growth brought was described by Martin as a development rather than as a problem and this was a change in the character of control from the top. As the quantity of data passing through the channels of communication increased, the decision process was influenced in that it became less easy to define or locate precisely at what point the leading ideas originated. The subsidiary companies passed information up and the group executive management became 'less and less immersed in the detail and away from it.' As the company got bigger there was a tendency for ideas as to what was wanted and what was decided to come from the bottom up. There is a danger that the knowledge which the top people have of the business could be reduced even to the point that they lose real control, unless organisational structure is constantly revised to modify the channels of information, the information itself, and the ways in which ideas are presented. Structural modification, Martin indicated, had an effect on the way in which decisions were reached, so it had its effect on strategic thinking.

These ideas are carried further in a discussion with the chief executive and the top management team which eventually succeeded Mr. Martin in 1979. Chapter 10 offers a 'postscript and a perspective' on Tarmac and describes a different management style, without suggesting that the past approach was inappropriate. In his concluding remarks, Martin had drawn attention to the change in outlook and the change in personalities which was becoming apparent in the company at the end of the 1970s, and the account of the subsequent life of the company which the postscript adds, provides a comment on how far the one affects the other.

The three men on the team are the executive core of the company and in their pragmatic approach to planning they are determined to avoid the 'grand strategy designs', the 'extrapolation of numbers' and the spurious precision which leads to loss of credibility. Strategy formation is not a matter of 'long-term rolling forward plans', but a week by week or even a day by day monitoring of trends. The control which the centre exercises is to watch that the performance of the operating businesses is the best possible, because if they are in fine condition they will be more likely to take the opportunities which offer, than their competitors. 'Strategy is something that develops', in the company in the context of competition. Control of performance of the operating divisions is tight but there is no question but that the divisions should themselves develop their own business in detail.

The present executive direction of Tarmac does not conceive of strategy in the same terms as, for example, Sir Patrick Meaney, or Sir Adrian Cadbury, or the corporate office at Tube investments. Tilling developed in the 1970s a strategy of balanced international investment and the centre supported the subsidiary companies in plans which contributed to it. A similar strategy can be seen in the other companies in this study. But Tarmac does not have any such corporate strategic view under its present direction, where aims are to explore and to understand the aspirations of the divisions through regular meetings and contacts and to see how far they can share in them. Their strategic aims are developed in consultation with the divisions because 'we don't think that we can see more than the people at the sharp end of the business see', and the typical action of the centre is to review divisional plans and to 'endorse' strategy. But though Tarmac's strategic perspective may be distinctive their management philosophy points, as in the case of the other companies, towards an autonomous operating divisional structure which fosters initiative. The machinery which is used is the same in all the companies: a crucial role of the centre is to control finance and to provide the cash resources — a task similar to that of a banker who requires evidence of capacity before he endorses his client's aims. As in Martin's time this role of the centre works well and there is no instance which can be recalled when a competition for limited cash resources developed between the divisions. 'It is our duty at the centre to make sure that the cash is available for legitimate projects.'

Together with the three other company studies which appear in the following chapters Tarmac presents a management/constitutional profile which is essentially the same. The same themes recur: a constitutional form which harmonises autonomy with control, an operational freedom with a financial discipline. The managements are highly professional and this professionalism is expected to penetrate below the top crust. Odgers said that the Tarmac centre, for instance, expects the divisional managements to be able to provide top-rate financial information, but he does not regard it as important for a company to follow 'the latest techniques from the business schools.' Strategy is not yet a science even in large corporations, as Gilmore[5] says, and for the medium-sized company it is likely to remain an art. In the companies in this study both the autonomy of the divisions and the control from the centre are real. In all of them, there is a basic reliance on the judgement, trust and responsibility generated by a team of experienced top executives working closely together, and the commitment of managers throughout the hierarchy.

Notes

1. Kirzner I.M.   *Competition and Entrepreneurship*
      The University of Chicago Press, Chicago, 1973.
      See, especially, Chapter 3, pps. 89-94.
2. Heflebower R.B.   'Observations on Decentralization in large Enterprises'
      Journal of Industrial Economics, Vol. IX, No. 1,
      November 1960, pps. 7-22.
3. Vancil R.F. and Lorange P.   *Strategic Planning Systems*
      Prentice-Hall, Englewood Cliffs, N.J., 1977.
      Part 1, Chapter 1, *passim.*

4. Ansoff H.I. and Leontiades J.C. 'Strategic Portfolio Management'
Journal of General Management,
Vol. 4, No. 1,
Autumn 1976, p. 29.
5. Gilmore F.F. 'Formulating Strategy in Smaller Companies'
Harvard Business Review, Vol. 49, No. 3, May-June 1971,
pp. 71-81.

6 THOMAS TILLING: AN INDUSTRIAL HOLDING COMPANY

In his 1964 paper to the Industrial Seminar at the University of Birmingham, the managing director, Mr. P.H.D. Ryder says that Tilling invented what is now known as the 'industrial holding company' as a means of investing in privately-owned companies. These were often companies which were looking for a haven which protected the owner or his family from anticipated death duties on his estate. Tilling offered them this haven in a form in which the identity of the business was not lost. Tilling, for its own part, was able to put a financial and strategic umbrella over the company which had been bought and also take the advantages which came from leaving the existing management to run the business as before.

> Tilling decided, [Ryder said], that the prime considerations when they were offered businesses in which the owner suffered from the dilemma I have just outlined, should always be quality and continuity of management, coupled with a reasonable profit record and sound prospects of expansion. The type of industry in which the company operated did not necessarily matter, and although, now that the group has taken a definite shape, we endeavour to expand our existing interests, this is still the case ... we have not so far, although I do not exclude this in the future, aimed deliberately at getting a foot into a particular industry. We have looked at each proposition on its merits, keeping an eye open, admittedly, to see that the percentage of our assets does not get right out of balance by being over-weighted in one single category of industry.

The Tilling strategy was to rely on the strength of diversification. The group would not be over-weighted in one type of business and the general range would not matter so long as acqustions were strong in quality of management and prospects of growth. When Tilling began this diversification, it aimed to build up a varied management team quite different from the specific team of the old Tilling. All the transport experts, for example, 'were, so to speak, "sold" to the

Transport Commission, together with the transport undertakings', and there was only one top executive, a solicitor, who was still in the company when Ryder was writing in 1964. 'We have deliberately set out', says Ryder, 'to create both a board of directors and a top management team of sufficient breadth and variety of knowledge and experience to enable them to tackle with some degree of success what is obviously quite a complex problem.'

Part of this complexity is due to the need to reconcile two separate requirements: insistence on autonomy of the management of the subsidiaries to take advantage of their special skills, with control from the centre without which development of a group strategy is impossible. Tilling have dealt with this problem by seeing that the group management team is represented on the board of each subsidiary company. The centre keeps contact with activities of the individual companies and exercises control when necessary by having one, (or sometimes two), of the management team from group headquarters, on the board of each main subsidiary company.

We are also represented on the board of some sub-subsidiary companies. On acquiring a company, we insist on the right to appoint our own chairman, (but we do not always take this step in the early days of a new association, because we may consider it important to preserve the identity of the company with its existing chairman). Any of the managing directors of our subsidiary companies have the right to see me whenever they want to, otherwise all communication on policy matters is through the Tilling representatives on their board.

The amount of time, however, which a Tilling representative spends each month with any one of our companies, depends on how much he is needed, or how much he thinks that he can contribute. At least, he attends a monthly board meeting, when, amongst other things, accounts which will have been circulated previously, showing figures of sales, production and estimated profit, and comparisons with budget, are discussed. The results for each company are reported each month to the Tilling board. When a project, involving sizeable capital expenditure not included in the budget, arises, the Tilling representative will normally bring the managing director of the company concerned to see me to talk about it. If I agree with the plan, it is submitted to the next Tilling board for approval.

In an operation as diverse as the Tilling group, there is always a problem of co-ordination in all parts of the organisation. At one point when the new idea was being developed, there was a danger, which the top management recognised, that the Tilling mould could be fragmented. It was seen that co-ordination between the centre and the subsidiaries was not enough and that there was a special need for co-ordination within the centre management team to provide a workable base for the future. In 1962 it was decided that the Tilling managing director could not play a part as a subsidiary chairman himself, (as he had been doing), because he was especially required to offer support, advice and perhaps direction to other members of the central executive team. He had to be free to devote his time to co-ordinating the activities of the management team and planning the development of the group. Tilling therefore set up an executive committee comprising all the members of the executive team, with the managing director as chairman, and this started to meet each month.

At this meeting the results of each company to date and current borrowings, both in relation to its budget, are considered and the group forecasts for the year are reviewed. Any other matter of policy can be added to the agenda by a member of the committee. After this meeting the deputy managing director and myself talk to the chairman, report the financial situation, and brief him as to the reports which each executive will make to the Tilling board meeting, which is held two days later.

The philosophy which Tilling developed of autonomy of the subsidiary companies in their direction and management, places a special responsibility on the general group management. There is a balance which has to be made between the two arms of this philosophy and Ryder, in an interesting passage, discusses the way in which the fulcrum is set:

Managing this group is a pretty intimate affair. Tilling representatives in their contact with the men running the individual companies, have to be friendly but firm, patient but persuasive, tactful but also tenacious. When a man sells a majority interest in his company to Tillings — I am talking about the type of man who has played the leading part in making his company successful and wants to continue to play that sort of role — he is usually a man of some considerable calibre, ability and character, and is accustomed to taking his own decisions. He is first of all attracted by the possibility of solving his own financial problems, as I said earlier, especially problems of tax, capital for development, and the perpetuation of the business, but he is also interested — as he should be — in the continuity of employment of his workpeople should anything happen to him. He could, however, solve these problems without coming to Tilling, so what probably attracts him to Tilling is point No. 4 of our published philosophy, which says: 'To preserve the freedom of the boards of our member companies to manage their businesses in their own way'. You will agree, I think, that for a Tilling representative to follow faithfully this directive, is not an easy task. It is not enough for the company to show better figures than the year before; our representative must try to satisfy himself that there is not more to be done to exploit more successfully the company's resources of know-how, finance and manpower. That is his duty and if he really believes that changes should be made, either in the policy of the company or in its management structure, he will discuss it with me and the deputy managing director at one of our regular meetings. If we agree with him, consideration is given to the best method of selling the idea to the managing director and the board of the company. We may agree to leave it to him alone or to intervene ourselves; it all depends on the circumstances of the case.

Tilling in 1980

The range of business outlined in Ryder's paper has been enlarged in recent years by taking advantage of possibilities of international investment which were inherent in the company's strategic position. In the interview in 1980, Sir Patrick Meaney emphasised that the corollary of the high degree of autonomy which is proposed for the subsidiary companies is the high degree of skills and control which has been developed at the group centre.

We have had the benefit of starting the concept of managing diversification and, as you can see from our annual report, we make a point of our skills at the centre in managing diversification . . . When the transport business was taken over and the concept of making Tilling into a diversified company arose, that concept was original — that is to say, the concepts of acquisition and diversification. Now most companies of any size have acquisition and diversification to some degree in the corporate plan. The advantage which we have, therefore, is that we started out with diversification, while many other companies which have diversified since, started as engineers or textile makers or retailers, and in our view, were applying management practices, techniques, monitoring and controls which might have been entirely appropriate to their own trade but were not necessarily appropriate or sufficiently wide ranging for managing diversified businesses.

The Growth of Tilling

The problems of expansion, Meaney said, whether by acquisition or by any other means, may not be as simple as sometimes they appear. Increase in size might well change the character of the problems which a company encounters. 'It is not a simple matter nowadays if you added another £1000mn. or so to turnover, because if you are in distribution or production or services, you have people problems, and people are clearly just as important as they are in any other side of business development.' Expansion may easily create the problem of distancing the senior people from the workforce, and Tilling's aim is to avoid the worst of this problem by the expedient of investing in small location units.

Meaney explained that on the simple concept of business just multiplying its sales, all that seems to be required is to add another dimension to the business as long as the management keeps modernising it. The pressures of mass production might then well lead automatically to setting up large organisational structures. But, he thought, there is no need to take that route. All the problems of large scale of plant or location unit can be avoided if management skills are adequate to exercise control on a large number of small units and there will be the great advantage in the quality of personnel relations.

You can still have, [said Meaney], the ideal admixture of automatic or technique type controls, paper monitoring, or whatever you like to call it; but, most importantly, you will have a strong ingredient of management, a strong sense of identity and recognition of senior people, a much better organising and developing structure for getting good industrial relations with people and, therefore, good productivity and profits.

This philosophy of small units has been worked out 'very firmly' throughout the company in a period when there has been great expansion, not only in the group as a whole but in the subsidiaries themselves. 'Some of our companies are as big as Tilling was in the days when Peter Ryder gave his paper, and some are larger. I think in those days we were making about three or four million pounds profit and some of our companies are now making ten, twelve or fourteen million pounds profits.'

Planning Structure of the Group (1982)

The structure of Thomas Tilling has been described elsewhere and this part of the present study is intended to complement that description with a discussion of the way in which planning emerges from the structure. The skeletal chart below gives the main outlines of the structure.

Planning starts with the principal operating companies.

> They form their own plans under the guidance of the company chairmen ... The companies are encouraged to think and bring the plan through and, obviously, we try to supply any planning gaps that are needed. There is a company board meeting of each principal subsidiary every month. We have certain fetishes inherited from Peter Ryder's day which we continue: one of them is that our chairmen should hold company meetings in one of the company locations — we do not advocate bringing them in to Crewe House. We work the other way round — we believe that our operating colleagues should be out with the companies.

The companies have to produce their own plan and they are also required to produce details of the annual budget and submit these to the group centre.

Strategic planning is a continuous process which is given much attention at the group executive level. The collated company plans are formulated in a preliminary way through the think-tank in their quarterly meetings — 'without any decisions being made, (it is not an executive body in that sense at all) — into what we should feed into our operating and planning cycle.' Meaney describes the way in which the numerate basis of company planning becomes, (through the

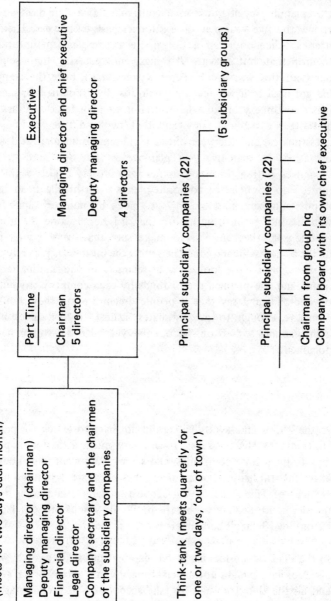

Tilling main board (meets once a month)

Part Time | Executive

Chairman
5 directors

Managing director and chief executive

Deputy managing director

4 directors

Executive director's committee (EDC)
(meets for two days each month)

Managing director (chairman)
Deputy managing director
Financial director
Legal director
Company secretary and the chairmen
of the subsidiary companies

Think-tank (meets quarterly for
one or two days, 'out of town')

Principal subsidiary companies (22)

(5 subsidiary groups)

Principal subsidiary companies (22)

Chairman from group hq
Company board with its own chief executive

continuous operation of the cycle), the foundation of group strategic thinking:

> Our planning cycle runs on a continuous five year basis and we review the five year plan on a roll over basis every year. There has been a tremendous temptation in the recent years of uncertainty to drop that, but as with all things, once you start the disciplines up, (and this was not in Peter Ryder's day), once the company has got used to it, we feel we would lose by dropping it or shortening it to three years or whatever. But we all agree that years four and five are really dreams, and that two and three are possibly guesstimates, and the year ahead is the important one for detailed operating. In that five year plan we set out our basic strategic objectives, with action programmes against every objective. Furthermore, I do not believe a corporate plan is a worthwhile dream unless it puts numbers in. I am always guided by numbers, and if you want a solid reason from me for that, it is because one of our major functions at the centre is to make sure that every pound note, dollar or deutschmark concerned with the business is properly used. So we want a close look at what seems to be the funding requirements and the planned use of funds by each company. I would go beyond that and say that if people dream dreams, they should be numerate enough to put estimates against trading, investments, cash planning and so on. So our five year plan is a comprehensive document.

Acquisitions

In the 1950s and 1960s Tilling did not have to search for possible acquisitions. As Meaney says: 'It was very much a matter of people coming to us, private companies, and saying: "We want to be bought." Though this still happens occasionally it is now rare, and it is a matter these days of Tilling identifying acquisition targets and going to the companies concerned and asking them: 'Would you like to join Tilling?' He outlined Tilling's parameters for acquisition:

> In the Plan we are looking at our earnings per share growth, we are also looking at what our financial capacities are — borrowing, gearing and all the things we have to take account of. So we look at what our survival capacities are. (We might plan a rights issue half way

through the year, for example). Then we assess what our physical capacities might be, whether we could take the increased load at the centre if we were to acquire another £100mn. worth of companies. Once we have got these parameters, as part of the planning review meetings of the executive directors' committee, we lay down our guidelines for acquisitions.

International Investment

He also outlined the Tilling international strategy for growth, whether by acquisition or by organic expansion.

When I took over as managing director, it was my main platform that we wanted to go overseas and, if we are going to be truly diversified, that we wanted to spread geographically as well as by trade. At that stage we were over 90% in the UK. My target would have been about 15% in Europe, broadly, and we shall try for about 20% to 25% in the USA. In fact, in the last six years, that is exactly what we have done.

Though the company had for many years wanted to invest in the USA, it had been deterred by the low yields available across the Atlantic.

Frankly, with all the battering which this UK economy has been taking, the investment yields and the growth rates, the new profits to be earned in Britain, are still higher than anything you could invest in in America or Europe where single figure yields obtained. The high borrowings of USA companies was a factor here, because though yields on capital employed look good, their indebtedness (until 1974/1975) was huge, way beyond the prudent levels that we would have accepted.

'Therefore', said Meaney, 'whilst we had gradually built up certain overseas interests, frankly we had never achieved what we thought that we should have.' But the oil crisis brought an enormous awareness of cash planning into USA companies and this offered Tilling an opportunity to penetrate the American company market in the way in which it sought.

As soon as the oil crisis hit, the banks started to call in their debts. As a result, a number of companies in America had to pull in their horns, and a number of them started to rethink their evaluations. One often had the case, which we have in the UK as well, but more often in America, of saying to a company: 'At your high borrowings, you would have to pay *us* to take you over.' This sounds a sort of ploy, but it was basically true; because they were highly geared, and they were not earning the rate of profit on their borrowings, but they thought that as long as they were earning on their basic capital, and could pay off the interest, that made good financial business. But the 1974/1975 crisis made them very aware of the total use of cash. We have always plugged it, and as far as we are concerned, it does not matter whether it is capital or borrowings, it is money, and you must make money work.

In the new situation in 1974/1975, having seen an opportunity of moving into America on the sort of yields and evaluations that they considered acceptable, Tilling launched a programme of acquisitions. The strategy which Tilling followed had two priorities. The prime policy for international investment was the same as they had followed for three decades in the home market, namely whenever the possibility occurred to extend existing interests by organic growth or by acquisition, that would come first. 'Whenever one of our successful companies sees an opportunity to extend its product range or its markets, or its versatility if you like, within its own markets, that has priority on the use of our funds and facilities.' So, in 1975, the primary aim was to extend the existing interests of their subsidiaries, 'providing, of course, that they are successful here, and also that their success was transferable to American markets.'

The second strategic priority was to identify *sectors* in which Tilling would aim to invest, of which they saw three which they believed might have above average growth. The first was the opposite ends of the oil and energy business — at one end was energy exploration equipment, and at the other end was the conservation business. The two others which Tilling identified were distribution and the general area of medical equipment.

'We identified energy exploration as an obvious requirement' Meaney said, 'because we could see that with the oil shortage there would be a need for exploring or re-exploring fields or wells etc., which were previously uneconomic.' He found it an ironical comment on our time that the conservation business into which Tilling moved by acquiring an insulation company, 'staggered' after the first awareness had worn off in the country, while the exploration business had been a huge success.

He recognised that the choice of distribution as a growth sector might have seemed strange, because in this country all the emphasis is on manufacturing, and distribution (or the efficiency of distribution) is often given no rating at all. But in nearly all developed countries, manufacturing, though it obviously has a vital part to play in the economy, has been declining.

Germany, [he said], is a classic case where, in spite of its economic success, manufacturing in volume terms has not grown, whereas services and distribution have. Now, one thing which we are beating the world at is distribution efficiency, whether it is retail or wholesale; and we saw that in America distribution was poor — badly organised, not managed too well, and not sufficiently penetrative in the market place. So that was another area which we wanted to go for.

The third area which Tilling listed was medical equipment which the company regarded as an ideal leg for a conglomerate.

Because, [he said], as you probably well know, even if a country is bankrupt, nations have spent more in recent years, (and I think for some time to come, will spend more), on social services and medical equipment than they can possibly afford. This still applies to America. We deliberately did not go for high technology. We went for equipment which was both for rehabilitation, (artificial legs being an obvious example — you can't cut back on artifical legs: if a chap loses his leg, he has to have an artifical leg), and at the other extreme, we went for items which reduce skill or reduce costs in clinics, hospitals or medical establishments — disposable syringes and testing and diagnostic equipment and so on.

Investment in the UK

The existence of their subsidiary companies in the UK means that the basis of Tilling's UK strategy differs from that in international markets. The implication of the autonomy which Tilling allow the subsidiaries is that the strategy of identifying sectors as in the

American market is not applicable, because the subsidiaries are already strategic units in their own trade sectors.

The extension of our existing interests is, you recall, our prime target. We have never had to make the choice, but if we had to spend something to expand our existing interests or to move into a new sector then the existing interest would always have priority. So on existing interests the companies themselves are encouraged to come up to us with their targets which they themselves identified, but at the centre we do all the thinking for new sectors. Of course, we may also indicate to our companies that they may like to consider such and such an outfit in their own sector.

Tilling do not eschew a strategy of sector analysis in the UK entirely because of the relations which they have established with their subsidiaries. There is a general case against sector analysis in the UK, which was debated in the company in the mid-1970s, when it was decided that 'we would be wasting our time if we look at trade sectors; what we should be looking at is companies.' The way in which Tilling, in practice, invest at home is to identify companies which meet the agreed acquisition criteria and financial yardsticks and then they look at whether their products and market opportunities indicate growth. The reasoning on this was indicated by Sir Patrick:

It is always tempting to identify sectors – and many a mistake has been made by us in the past, and certainly in other companies on whose boards I serve, at looking at sectors. You look at the leisure sector and, of course, it looks marvellous. Naturally, people have more time, more money, more ambition to keep fit, and so on. But in so many growth areas, or seeming growth areas, it is not always profitable. The leisure business, if you like, stands as a yardstick of something which has been enormously attractive, but in which you can't name one company which has made a 20% return on their investments.

The Centre and the Subsidiary Companies

Tilling expect the company boards to initiate and develop their own strategic plans and encourage them to do so. The main role the centre performs in relation to that is, in Meaney's word, 'supportive'.

Tilling set out the guidelines. For example, Tilling set a target for the companies of a return of 25% on funds employed. This guideline is kept in the foreground of strategic planning in the company and a project which did not shown an agreed return on funds would not normally be put up by a company to Tilling unless, in the mind of the company, there were compelling strategic reasons for doing so. But all the necessary information on expansion, acquisition and performance has to be made available by the company to the centre.

So there is the requirement on the part of the company, of agreement on plans which might lead Tilling to commit resources on behalf of the subsidiary or which might lead to a modification of Tilling's general position. Tilling retain the right of control but do not use this right in a way which inhibits creative thinking within the companies. There seems to be no need for strategic control to extend much beyond this requirement of agreement.

Gordon Yardley, the chief executive of the Tilling subsidiary, Newey & Eyre, outlined the bounds of strategic responsibility which his company observes vis-à-vis Tilling:

> Certainly if we put up a project to Tilling, I would not put it up unless I could see 25% coming from it. On the other hand, if I was a company in the Tilling group making 17% on funds at the moment — there are several — and I put up a project which shows 21% return on funds, which would have the effect of improving my 17% to something else, then I would expect that there would be a reasonable chance that Tilling would support that. But why should I, making 25% as we have had made this many years, why should we lower our standards on expectation of return on investment? Unless strategically we want to get into a particular market, and in order to get there we have to accept in the short-term lower returns because of the price down the road?

As an example of a strategic decision in which his company broke, for strategic reasons, the bounds set by the Tilling 25% return guidelines, he spoke of the entry of Newey & Eyre into the market for electronic components:

> I think that that market is a good example. The price is outstanding; but because we could not acquire a very big company, because of the p/e on the Stock Exchange, we have had to acquire several small companies, (and indeed start one company from scratch),

and we are having to face, in the short term, inadequate returns
in order to get into the business where we earn 25% and 30% yields.

Newey & Eyre's entry into the electronic components market is a
fine example not only of Tilling's flexibility despite the guidelines,
but of the insistence on the strategic responsibility of the subsidiary
company. For here there were all the ingredients of strategic consideration: the element of time, the danger which traditional business may
face unless it moves at the right moment, the early entrepreneurial
awareness of the danger, the balancing of the risks of change with the
risks of doing nothing, the resolution based on superior knowledge
and experience and the meticulous attention to detail.

If we just take that as an example of a strategic decision, we could
see that part of our traditional business in electrical wholesaling
would be at risk because of the electronicitising of mechanical
equipment. Something which has been traditionally handled in an
electro-mechanical way will now be subjected or is being subjected
to electronic processes, whether it be a micro-processor or whatever.
So our view was that unless we got ourselves into the business of
distributing electronic components we could find that a block of
our business would be lost to us. It is therefore very important
that we took the decision to get into a new market for us in order
to help protect the market which we were already in.

Paul Hickman, managing director of the Midland region of Newey
& Eyre, and a member of the main board of the company, commented
on the change of view on company policy which appears at different
levels of the hierarchy. The spread of his career in the company has
been large enough to enable him to speak with first hand understanding
of the view from the level of branch manager and below, and he is in
touch all the way through, from the lower levels to the top — 'If I
didn't, my job would be very difficult.' His thinking reflects the
balancing role of the regional managing director in the company, his
pivotal position helping to keep the different levels of the hierarchy in
touch. Sir Patrick Meaney, in a point which has been referred to earlier,
had been concerned with the problem which arises when the senior
people become distanced from the workforce, and Paul Hickman, in
his remarks on his company experience, dwelt on the same concern.
He feels that he has a foot in both camps and finds his past experience
is as valuable as his present work on the board. He recognises that the

branch manager has an entrepreneurial responsibility — 'wheeling and dealing', as a branch manager described his tactical role — and he himself, as a board member, sees his responsibility as one of communicating to the people below him, the strategic constraints, the opportunities or restrictions, under which the company finds itself operating. A spectator, considering the role of the hierarchy at this point, might see him as a medium of an exchange of ideas between the levels, a catalyst of a feed-back reaction which, at the best, could be another source of new ideas.

'It is as you said, I have to think in both directions', said Hickman, analysing his working role. 'I have to think of what is happening today and this month and this week in the branches in a trading sense and also, as a member of the board of Newey & Eyre, I have to think about the corporate plan of Newey & Eyre, the five year development plan and how I fit into the plan.'

If I may use an analogy, one is parochial and the other is broader. *Tactical* is the manager 'wheeling and dealing' as you said — he has a parochial attitude towards it for the benefit of his branch. I have to look at those factors plus how it affects other branches in the region, and how it affects other areas and other regions — in the operational role, that is. Then we come back to the strategic role — my position on the board of Newey & Eyre — where we look at the future strategy of the company, what shape it will have and what product range it is going to move into. He is looking at the prosperity of the branch, and I am also looking at the shape of the company.

Questioned about the source of the expansive ideas of the sort which might move the company on to a new track, which might lead to fundamental changes in its product range for example, or, in other ways, shape it in the future, Mr. Hickman sketched the entrepreneurial character:

You asked me where the ideas start from. They have to start from the top of any department or company. Gordon Yardley can switch from thinking American, to thinking electronics wholesaling, to thinking about me! He has that ability. I don't know how he contains every train of thought that he has going into his head to run a company of this size. Pat Meaney is a very similar type.

I do not say that strategy is made by the man at the top. The ideas which are generated are discussed at the board of Newey & Eyre, and we then thrash them around and perhaps come up with some entirely new aspects, or confirm where we wish to proceed.

Mr. Hickman was quite ready to use the word 'entrepreneur' when speaking on this topic. He has been quoted elsewhere as saying that the 'entrepreneurial spirit' cannot be prevented from entering into a business, unless the organisational form is so thoughtlessly designed as to thwart it. The proper abode of this entrepreneurial spirit, he seemed to be saying, is at the top of any organisation, large or small.

The spark is lit — and I believe this applies to the branch, area, region or company — by the men at the top. If the top man hasn't got the spark in him, the branch, the company, whatever it is, does not succeed. That is my experience. I know if I go into a branch I can judge the atmosphere and success of that branch as soon as I walk into the manager's office and talk to him. I don't need to look anywhere else. I do look elsewhere for confirmatory details, or details which the manager himself has overlooked, but it is in the man himself first.

He enlarged his comments when he spoke of an exchange in which some ideas come from the top and also in which there was a 'feedback' — and it was in the use of this phrase that he seemed to be suggesting that there could be found, somewhere in the transmission, a source of new ideas. But there was clearly a qualification implied in his remarks.

There could be new ideas. If you think of Tilling, they have very definite areas of operation and they very rarely move outside those areas. We in Newey & Eyre have a very definite area of operation, which is distribution. We would not go into manufacturing, for instance. We don't know enough about manufacturing to do it. Any new ideas which we gain in distribution may be talked about, for instance, at Tillings, and then Pat Meaney may say: 'That's a good idea, Graham Building Services, our sister company, could use that idea.' I don't know whether that often happens, but I doubt it. It could happen. But there is no way in which a new idea from Newey & Eyre could be of benefit to Pretty Polly making nylon tights and stockings. So I think that most of the generation of new ideas starts at the top of individual companies and works its way down through the system.

The company has accepted the strategic constraint which it imposed on itself, that it operates within the field of distribution. Gordon Yardley said of his company that: 'My strength is sticking to distribution − I would not move away from sticking to my last.' Paul Hickman said the same with equal assurance: 'The shape must be something allied to distribution.' Distribution, said Yardley, did not necessarily mean electrical distribution. 'Sticking to my last' means sticking to the pattern of trade. Hickman said:

> If the shape is going to change it could be internationally (as we have gone into America), it could be a different set of products − but if it is a different set of products, we always look for a similar pattern of customers, we do not like to move out of our range of customers. We would not want to distribute eggs − we are not in touch with the egg market − but we may want to extend further if it is electronics or electronic wholesaling, or electrical tools, anything allied to our present structure of customers. I believe that our structure of customers could be enlarged, but not basically altered. But the products distributed can vary, can increase.

The Strategic Decisions of Newey & Eyre

One of the aims of this sub-study of Newey & Eyre was to examine how far the holding company influences, directly or indirectly, the strategic deliberations of the subsidiary. When Newey & Eyre moved into the business of distributing electronic components in the late 1970s, the company analysed the strategic implications from its own specialist knowledge and experience, and the part which Tilling played in it was that of a fully informed ally. But, at about the same time, Newey & Eyre was making a strategic decision on a move which had even more far-reaching consequences and on which Tilling themselves had, and were known to have, a strategic view. This was the decision by Newey & Eyre to move into the USA market.

As the earlier extracts from Sir Patrick's observations show, Tilling had seen an opportunity in the mid-1970s of investing in the US market. Paul Hickman suggests that the attitude in Tilling towards investment in the USA being known in the subsidiaries, Newey & Eyre may have been following a lead from Tilling. But he keeps it open whether the thought may have been arrived at independently by Newey & Eyre. Gordon Yardley said that policy in Newey & Eyre in the 1970s was to invest overseas and to diversify. The company's first ideas were towards investment in Europe and the Middle East but subsequently it became aware of the significance of the USA. 'We were stimulated', said Yardley, 'but not driven by Tilling.' Hickman points at the stimulus which Tilling may have applied:

> Tilling, at one point in their history maybe said: 'We have some money to invest and we would prefer that money to be invested in America, or Australia or South Africa. If *you* want to expand and you come to us with a good idea for America, we shall listen to you very carefully. But if you come with a good idea for expanding in Timbuctoo, the case has to be very much firmer'.

Hickman concludes that in this case, the idea of America might have originated at the top, but the decision was Newey & Eyre's. The company, in the 1970s, was concerned with two totally different aspects of diversification.

> One was the UK diversification into electronics and the other was our intention to diversify elsewhere in the world. We explored many areas and eventually came back to where Tilling wanted to expand, which was the USA, and we turned our sights in that direction — having failed in other directions. We had explored France and Australia, and we failed for various reasons. So, at that point of time, Tilling having expressed themselves as having money ready to invest in America, we moved in that direction.

The final decision of Newey & Eyre to invest in America, said Hickman, was a company decision, and it was largely due to the chief executive. 'He did', said Hickman, 'a lot of the spade work.' But prior to the decision to move into the USA, Newey & Eyre made some structural changes, by forming a group board. 'The decision to form the group board was fully discussed at the Newey & Eyre Limited board, and it was agreed that it was necessary — the whole of the company board could not be involved in something overseas.'

The group was a layer off the company board. It is composed of the chief executive, the managing director and the administrative director of Newey & Eyre Limited, together with the Tilling representative. 'So the line between Newey & Eyre Limited and Thomas Tilling takes one step back – the group board gets between them.'

At the time that the decision to form the group board was made, the strategy being considered was a general one of international expansion. In retrospect it may be impossible to identify the point at which the decision to go into the USA was made. In Hickman's view the chief executive plays a predominant part in the initiation of ideas such as these and, though he continues to influence the policy as it develops, this development draws more on the talents and energy of the team of top executives as a whole. So it may not be clear at what time a firm decision was formed in the mind of the chief executive that it was his objective that the company would invest in the USA. 'The chief executive both initiates and influences, but I think he plays a bigger part in the initiating of those ideas. The way we plan it or operate it then is discussed within the Newey & Eyre board.'

The development of a policy, planning and operating it, is a major function of the board, which will spend 'as long as is necessary' on it. 'It [the development of a policy] could be over a series of board meetings. Then there are breakaway meetings on the financial side. It could be developed over a period of weeks or months, even a year or more.' So all the time when this policy is being developed, everybody who is on the board is really a party a party to it, and the views of one board member would be merged into the general stream of thinking. It may be the case that a person himself, though he were party to the whole thing, would not know how much he had influenced a particular policy, and this would apply to everybody else. He used an example to show how, in setting up a policy in detail, continuous consideration of the board as a whole may be required.

When we have decided to develop electronics, say, or Newey & Eyre International, the first thing which we have to do is to find the man to head it up. And that is not going to be a quick procedure. It would take up to six months before you have identified and selected a man and maybe another two months before he is free to come. During that period of selection the whole of the board take a view of that person or persons who are applying for the job, who are shortlisted.

Reorganisation of the Domestic Appliances Business

The two Newey & Eyre strategies which have been mentioned in the discussion with Mr. Hickman were both strategies of change brought about by venturing into new fields. The strategy of investing in America was an aggressive strategy, supported and 'stimulated' by the holding company as part of their overall strategy. Entry into distributing electronic components, though fully entrepreneurial, was partly, if not largely, a defensive strategy, and was from its inception, entirely due to Newey & Eyre.

While Newey & Eyre were pursuing these major strategies the company decided on an internal change in the way in which a part of its business was conducted. Acting under the pressure of market change the company instituted an organisational reform of the Domestic Appliances distribution business — a business which amounted to some one-fifth of their total business at the time.

In the earlier study of this company this reorganisation was taken as an example to indicate the way in which the philosophy of autonomy worked in practice. Here it can be seen as a strategy — an internal defensive strategy — developed in response to an external assault on this part of the company's market. Here again the reorganisation is described as a responsibility which was shared by the commercial director and the regional managing directors, with Mr. Hickman acting as regional directors' spokesman in the dialogue. Hickman describes it as 'an evolution within our industry which took place.' Newey & Eyre was aware of the evolution of the method of marketing domestic appliances which was being brought about by the appearance of large, high-risk, discount outlets in this market and of the implications of this for Newey & Eyre in this sector of their business. But the company determined firmly against following the change in the pattern of business due to these new forms of distribution because, although it might have been tactically profitable, it would have been against the general strategic deployment which the company had achieved. In fact, the company was 'neglectful', said Hickman, in delaying its response to the market change for a decade or more. 'We did not sit down and say: What is happening in the domestic appliance world and should we be doing something about it — because the motivation of our business is profitability and we say that the profit was being diminished to a level at which we were not able to operate.'

In answer to the question why Newey & Eyre shunned 'discount' marketing and why it delayed its response, Hickman explained the thinking to which the company held:

Because that is taking us away from our business — our business is dealing with trade customers and not dealing with user customers. What I am saying is that during the 1960s, the domestic appliance business was virtually captured by the Comet type organisation and made, and as far as we were concerned, unprofitable. So our interest in it diminished. We were, if you like, neglectful and let the trade go to the Comets of this world, instead of doing something about it ourselves. Comet themselves, as an organisation, were depending on high risk factors for their success. We therefore let them get on with it, rightly or wrongly. It was only in the late 1970s that we observed the fact that manufacturers had capacity which they could not sell through the direct selling organisations and they also recognised that they had a great deal at risk in selling only to those organisations. That was also coupled with the fact that inflation and the increasing cost of distribution made those manufacturers say: Can we afford distributing ourselves any more to small outlets or to bigger outlets like Comet? Then they began to remember what they had recognised twenty years ago, that the wholesale trade was an ideal vehicle for distributing their products. They came back to the wholesale trade individually (one or two of them) and said: You have got something which we want — you have the organisation for distribution, how can we get together to make it work?

A complementary view of the mechanism of policy making on this issue was given by the commercial director. In the mid-1970s, Mr. Jon Brockett became commercial director, (previously he had been marketing manager), and the responsibilities of the commercial director were reviewed and enlarged. The functional responsibilities of his department included marketing and purchasing, the transport fleet and property, the company's pricing system and its profitability analysis and its UK central selling function. The department works in close co-ordination with line management, (which extends from branch manager through area director and up to the regional director and company managing director), and, as commercial director, Jon Brockett is responsible, in support of the line activity, for the efficient provision of the services which have just been listed.

'My functional responsibility here', said Brockett, 'is to employ professionals in their field. I can elicit from the expertise which exists here, information on which policies can be drawn up and which can be put forward for debate and acceptance.' His observations on the reorganisation of the domestic appliances sector in 1980 were put forward as an example of how the work of his department meshes with the activities of line management, and of the way in which co-ordination of line and function furthers the formulation and refinement of strategies. He outlined the problem which arose in the 1970s and he spoke about the way in which the strategy for dealing with it was considered in the company:

The domestic appliances distributors of ten or twelve years ago, (when retail price maintenance applied), stocked, invested in, domestic appliances, and sold domestic appliances at pre-determined, safeguarded margins. As a result, they were not price sensitive. Distributors were encouraged to invest in domestic appliances, not only in the depth of stock carried but in the width of stock. The traditional independent retail outlets which existed particularly at that time went to the electrical distributor and expected to be able to view a selection of products and we had many duplications of line as a result. We could be stocking — to give you an example — a range of Morphy Richards irons and also several competing ranges of products. The investment was justified because, as I said, the margin was safeguarded and the return was certainly adequate.

The traditionally smooth peformance of the domestic appliances sector of Newey & Eyre's business, shielded by the margin, was upset when retail maintenance had to be legally abandoned.

This is a market which has evolved very rapidly in recent years, [said Brockett, speaking of the 1970s], the strategic point being the abandonment of RPM in 1968. As a result of that, manufacturers of domestic appliances have tended to deal, rather than with the distributor who had been their traditional outlet, directly with the large purchasing outlets such as the Comet discount chain. Because of that our profitability in that sector fell. We tried (and I am speaking of distributors as a whole) to defend our market share, but it had fallen by 1979 from 20% to approximately 16% or 17% of our turnover. (This needs qualifying to some extent because our industrial and commercial turnover has grown proportionally).

Nevertheless, a new strategy has had to be developed if we are to put the capital which we invest in domestic appliances to a more worthwhile use. The marketing department here has evolved a new strategy which in their opinion, and in their qualified professional judgement, they feel is the way for Newey & Eyre to at least maintain its market share in the domestic appliances business and certainly to make it more profitable and possibly to make it grow. That policy was formulated and was taken to the main board for discussion — and obviously it was debated with me beforehand in this department. It has been subsequently agreed at main board level and, early in the new year, that particular policy will be debated with executives in line management and hopefully, subsequently, will be implemented. Clearly there may be some refinements to that policy as a result of that debate. But basically that is the policy which is taken through from here and implemented in the line.

7 CADBURY SCHWEPPES: THE NATURE OF STRATEGY

In two interviews with Sir Adrian Cadbury, attention was focused on two central groups of topics. The first was the nature of strategy, its identification with entrepreneurship, and the location of ultimate strategic responsibility: the second was the relationship between strategy and organisational form and the interplay between them in the formation of company strategy.

Sir Adrian started from the questions put to him: how did he conceive Cadbury Schweppes as a corporation, how did he see the corporate strategy, how did he envisage the firm? He began his reply by saying

> that is really the question which the strategy is addressed to — what sort of company do we wish to be . . .? It seems to me that you have business decisions and against them you have certain constraints, if you like, which are those of the nature of the company, the types of product we should be in, the way we do things and the rest of it, which clearly have some effect on the way the company develops. The question what sort of company we want to become has to start from what sort of company we are.

In referring to a paper which he had just produced 'for our internal consumption', Sir Adrian spoke of 'the character of the company, the values which I would like to see in the company'. In the broad approach to the company which is here employed, there is an indication that the concept of strategy includes both a choice of product-market scope in the way that Ansoff[1] defines it and a sense of values and style.

It is also clear that even in the earliest stages of conceptualisation of company strategy, Cadbury Schweppes faces the problem of harmonising conflicting pulls and pressures: 'the problem which we wrestle with is the problem of an organisational structure which of its nature must be geographically dictated . . . but on top of which we want to superimpose a business stream type of organisation.' There was clearly in mind here, what Sir Adrian regarded as

> the most difficult problem for us, both strategically and in terms of

the way we construct the business. By that, [he said], I mean that clearly from the point of view of our two main businesses which are confectionery and drinks, we want to develop these on an international basis, therefore we want to have a view of how Schweppes should be developed internationally — this has to be done in a relatively uniform way, such that wherever you come across Schweppes tonic in the market-place throughout the world, it will taste the same, it will be packaged in an identifiable form, it will be marketed in a broadly similar way. This requires some sort of direction . . . about the brand, what it means and how it should be developed.

But faced with a situation in which Schweppes will be marketed overseas by companies in which Cadbury Schweppes has only a majority (and in some cases a minority) shareholding, 'the question mark is how far can you, in fact, impose "uniformity" on the development of an international brand on a company which you own only in part, which is not solely in soft drinks but in other areas as well, so that they are going to have their own strategic plan, their own priorities, their own ideas as to how the business should be developed.'

Sir Adrian was here posing the question in the particular context of Cadbury Schweppes and the *modus operandi* by which it conducts the marketing of its products — he cited, particularly, the Australian operation. But the problem is the more general one of dealing with disparate strategies within the framework of global requirements: how, as he expressed it, 'to combine the development of plans and the strategies within a separate company with a separate corporate organisation with the global plans and strategies of the total business.' It concerns the crucial interaction between encouraging the separate companies to have long range plans of their own and securing 'a coherent view of how you would see the company as a whole developing'.

The strategic question is thus closely interwoven with the relationship between the centre and its plans and the separate parts of a group which constituted the main theme of the earlier parts of this study. The relationship is a difficult one: Sir Adrian touches directly on the topic which Alfred Sloan[2] evidently had in mind when he wrote:

Having . . . established techniques of control in the particular areas of appropriations, cash, inventory, and production, the general question remained: How could we exercise permanent control over the whole corporation in a way consistent with the decentralized scheme of organization? We never ceased to attack this paradox; indeed we could not avoid a solution of it without yielding both the actual decentralized structure of our business and our philosophy of approach to it.

Strategy is, then, as Sir Adrian sees it, the determination of business direction. But the strategic picture of the company is a shifting profile which is not universally to be defined in conventional terms of market scope. '. . . I would define the market', he said, 'as widely as possible, and I would say that if you really wanted an ultimate definition of the company, it may well be in terms of those consumer needs which are served through the main channels of distribution which we supply.' Thus, when he came into the business, the defining characteristic was the raw material employed – the cocoa bean. The firm then sold most of its products through confectioners, tobacconists and newsagents: now the bulk are sold through supermarkets which have themselves shifted from being purveyors of food to selling other goods too. Thus, 'that is why I do not think of the Jeyes element as being out of line with this development – it goes through the same channels of distribution. So the longer the view I take, the wider I extend the limits of the business.'

But where then are the strategic boundaries of Cadbury Schweppes to be drawn? When Sir Adrian made his comment about 'the limits of the business', he was asked whether he would limit it by the *stage* of manufacture in which the company was engaged and whether it was conceivable that they might want to go into distribution. His reply was explicit: 'No. I think I would limit it really on the basis of the things we know . . . I see us basically as a marketing company, not primarily as a manufacturing company, somewhere in between the raw materials at one end and the channels of distribution we have experience of at the other.'

The company does not have skills in distribution or in growing raw materials, does not have the understanding of property values which would be required for an entry into restaurants or the acquisition of distribution outlets. That is why Adrian Cadbury puts the boundary where he does – it utilises channels of distribution but that is the line where in Chandler-like[3] terms, it moves from the visible to an invisible hand. What is also of peculiar interest is the emphasis which he places on new geographical areas as well as products as an element in corporate strategy.

In sum, then, defining strategy for Cadbury Schweppes is a several-faceted matter.

One element of our strategy is the definition of the market. In fact, in our case, we have decided quite firmly that our strategy is to .compete internationally in the chocolate and soft drinks market, and that these are our priorities. That is a strategy. It means that you measure — by your plans, by your budgets, by all the proposals which are coming up — how they fit into your overall view of priorities.

But equally, geography is an element in the company's strategy: thus 'another strategic decision was in looking at the geographical balance of the company — it was quite clear to me when I became chairman that we did not have enough of our assets in North America' so there was '. . . the strategic decision that we wanted to shift from a position in which our largest overseas investment was in Australia to one where our largest overseas investment was in North America and primarily in the United States.' Then, as has already been seen, there is the element of position in relation to the customer as reflected in Sir Adrian's remarks about channels of distribution.

The common feature is the alteration in 'the balance of the business'. This, in Sir Adrian's view and terminology, is the essence of the strategic decision. It is clear also, that strategy is about numbers or coveys of strategic decisions — strategy is composed of decisions and sub-strategies.

The Market and the Pool of Assets

Sir Adrian was asked how he looked at the market and specifically: was it something which was there and to which the company went and filled a space in it: or was it something that was not latent in Kirzner's[4] sense but rather entrepreneurially created as Shackle[5] conceives the world: or did the company simply respond to the market? To this he gave what at first sight at least may seem a surprising answer.

I don't think that it is any of those — I don't think that is the way we look at it at all. The way in which I look at it is this. In our major brands, in confectionery and drinks, we have an asset, and our objective is to exploit that asset more effectively. So you simply look at all the opportunities which exist for the greater sale of those goods and then you have to act in the order of your priorities.

The point which emerged in pressing further in this context is the inadequacy of the rather simple categories in which it has been customary to discuss problems of strategy, market, organisation, and entrepreneurship. It seemed indeed in this aspect of the dialogue with Sir Adrian that it was the piecemeal, complex, interactive, overlapping nature of the strategic processes which caught his attention. On the question of responsiveness to market or entrepreneurial detecting or creation of opportunities, he said that the very difficulty of drawing a distinction was perhaps why it is 'such a fruitful source of argument'. Thus, he distinguished between recognising that there may be a gap in the market and finding something to fill it: 'I would say that it is totally clear to me that there is an enormous potential market for vegetable protein, an area which we are in, in a small way. Now that is an external view, because actually the market is not there. But it seems to me obvious that it is going to be there, but I have no idea in what form. So that's a marketing problem.'

In a singular passage of the conversation Sir Adrian referred to the idea that the trick was to turn an economic view into a marketable concept. He was talking at that point about the protein project and saying that because of all the factors tending towards making fish and meat more expensive '. . . sooner or later you are going to find a way of short-circuiting that process' (i.e. of producing fish and meat). This is what he sees as economic — whether or not it can be translated into marketable products is the problem: 'what we do is to get into the business; we sell a small amount of vegetable protein, almost on the side.' What this does for the company is to give it a feel of the market while R and D goes on to generate new ideas. The development of new products is complex: it is a process stimulated both internally and externally which may or may not result in a new product in the company's range.

But how flexible is it possible for the enterprise to be in determining and changing its strategic posture? In one sense Sir Adrian appeared to be saying that the capacity of the organisation was governed by the knowledge it had acquired through time and its fund of managerial experience. Yet later he said: 'I would have thought that you are totally at liberty to make a complete change of strategy, provided that you are a solvent business, and can retain the business which produces the cash while you move into the business which you think

you should be in.' If, for example, by analogy with the experience of
the tobacco business, the medical people were to declare cocoa a
health hazard and it were to be thought there was no future in the
chocolate confectionery business *'in the very long term'*, then 'it is
... totally open to me to use the cash flow which I have from the
business, not to invest in the continuance of chocolate business, but
in moving into selling teaching systems ...' Strategy would be defined
by the need to escape from the declining business, the speed of strategic
transfer would be constrained by a number of factors, but the choice
of direction would be totally free.

This is strikingly analogous with Professor Penrose's[6] concept of
the firm as a pool of assets which in the long-term has a virtually
unlimited plasticity of strategic choice: its output at any one time is,
as she describes it, but an incident in the time-distribution of its
behaviour. Nor, in Sir Adrian's view, is the firm's capacity to change
inhibited by its structure. Asked if the organisation of Cadbury
Schweppes with its attendant structure of information flows prescribed
the opportunities which could be perceived he agreed that there is an
on-going system which concentrates on existing areas of the business.
But here there arises precisely that difference between looking at the
business from top-down and bottom-up, respectively, which has been
extensively discussed elsewhere in this study. The plans of the separate
units in the company constitute 'a primary building block': assessment
of the implications of the aggregation of the plans is a matter for the
top. Movement into new areas of business is beyond the capacity of
the existing structure but it has always to be looked for and that is
the business of the centre. In Cadbury Schweppes it is the business
of Sir Adrian and his planning group to look at the overall planning
of the company.

> I would say, to avoid the constraints of your internal structure
> and information flows and so on, you either get outside consul-
> tancy help, or you form a team from inside with the same end in
> view, or you simply acquire a business. You decide what area —
> you may want to get into the electronic business, then you
> simply acquire a foothold in that business. Then you can work
> from there. That will change your information flows; they will
> have been changed by conscious decision.

Even allowing for the element of generalisation in this part of the
discussion, these are particularly illuminating comments: they are

considered in a wider framework in the overall analysis and conclusions to this part of the study. Here it may be said that they are in accord with the attitude taken by Sir Patrick Meaney since the ability to deal with diversity and the ability to change strategic direction clearly have something in common. That there is here, however, an ambiguity in Sir Adrian's view seems undoubted. Thus, for example, he was insistent at one point in this discussion when he was answering the question what is Cadbury Schweppes other than its parts, that 'you have history to take into account, you have a legacy of people, they have a legacy of experience . . .'. The clarification of the ambiguity lies in the passage of time, in the meaning of the phrase 'very long term' and in the fine balance between the incrementalism of particular changes and market testing and the wider strategic view which the centre alone is capable of taking for the company as a whole.

Looking at the picture of a complex process alters perception of the terms 'entrepreneur' and 'entrepreneurship'. The widely-understood coincidence of 'entrepreneurship' and 'strategic decision-making' was certainly acceptable to Sir Adrian though he thought the concept as it appears in, say, Marshall, a muddling one. 'It seems to me', he said, 'that what you have is a business problem which becomes confused with people — what you have are ideas and opportunities, and you are looking for ways of translating those ideas and opportunities into profitable openings for the business; what you are interested in is the linkage between them'. The business has a central core, those values to which Sir Adrian referred and it has its accumulated experience and structure: it does not rest on shifting sands. But the persistent search for 'a marketable concept' which is at the heart of strategic management, he describes not structurally, but as an interplay of ideas. 'So that is why it seems to me, that you can't pin this process down on any one person. You don't even know how the project is going to come out in the end . . . I would define the entrepreneurial role as the perception of business opportunities, profitable business opportunities at that'.

But this is only part of the story: there remains a whole period of tracking ideas around which may result eventually in a concept: and this may then have to be left aside until *perhaps* one day something may come of it. To this complex process through time in all its aspects and layers, Sir Adrian would not attach the term 'entrepreneurial function': indeed, he seemed to reserve 'entrepreneurial' to the element of perception but by this he seemed to mean, in turn, the transition from recognising that there was a market gap or opportunity to the translation of that recognition into an opportunity for the business.

Summing up the various strategic decisions in terms of product, market, and geography, and considering when strategic ideas can be said to have come to fruition or to have failed, Sir Adrian responded to the proposition that two factors were involved: time and organisational commitment. In general he thought of his own job as chairman as distinguished from that of the managing director partly by its more extended time-horizon, i.e. a ten-year rather than a five-year strategic outlook. Even where, however, the time between taking the decision and implementing it is relatively short, as was the case in the expansion in the North American market (where perhaps for that reason his own involvement was smaller), it will be seen as a major strategic decision if the balance of the company and the extent of organisational commitment are large.

Individual and Organisation in the Strategic Process

During the course of interview, Sir Adrian was asked about a phrase he had quoted from Emerson, that 'the organisation is the shadow of one man' and how he reconciled that with the emphasis he placed on the participative nature of organisation. He had been talking, he replied, about an analytical approach to organisations and organisational change and it seemed to him

> that you need a certain corrective at the end, because when you look at organisations, they are very influenced by one or two individuals and at the end of the day it isn't a specific kind of structure ... which is important – you can make a number of different structures work ... but what is clear is that someone who is used to one kind of structure finds it very difficult to work another.

In Cadbury Schweppes he believes that the pattern depends much less than it used to on particular individuals – partly as a result of splitting the chairman and chief executive jobs. Moreover, 'in a business of any size, or in the business into which I have come, you must be conscious of the multifarious influences and decisions which will limit those decisions [i.e. concerning business direction] which ... will decide what options will be presented to you and what options are practical.' The most fundamental issue for the Cadbury company was the merger — merge or not merge — and such a decision could not have been imposed. It required that a large number of people take the same kind of view. Thus, the strategic process, while it involves the peculiar function of the centre and of the central individual, is inseparable from the participatory element.

It does not follow from the argument that the organisational process is tidy and well-ordered. The point was put to Sir Adrian in this form: does the world present itself as tidy, and how far is that a tidiness which is not real but is imposed by his analysis? His reply was that the decision-maker never has all the information he needs nor can be measure one option against all the other available options.

> One of the untidinesses in the world is that you tend to be faced with decisions which have to be taken — as in the merger approaches made to us — and you cannot put them off and say: really what we should do is to make a search of all the possible options facing the company and then decide which is the optimum one. You are actually faced with a Yes or No decision, and you have to take that decision.

This arises from the familiar proposition that decisions have to be made with incomplete and inadequate information, within constraints of time which limit, also, the amount of consultation which can be undertaken, the need to proceed in secrecy, and so on. This, as he agreed, was the world of Simon, Lindblom, Cyert and March and the neatness and rationality of the strategic pattern is partly something imposed for the purpose of presenting the case. The ordered picture is a means of pulling out the salient issues and of trying to learn from experience, not a *description* of the decision situation as it actually is.

But how then, within this untidy situation, is the decision-agenda composed: what governs the areas of search in which the business embarks? Sir Adrian was asked to comment on this with reference to the question of merger. The picture of strategic thinking with which he responded was one in which 'you have a very wide conspectus of thoughts — a universe . . . of possible actions which are not really thought through, which are simply there in the background.' The possibility of a merger or of a bid from outside are instances in point. These things, he said, are always in the back of the mind with some sort of idea about the way you might react to them if they materialised: '. . . and then, I think, one can extract from that when the pressures are such that it actually appears on the agenda.' This is a function of the breadth of view which the decision-maker has been taking.

There are other levels of approach to which Sir Adrian drew attention. At the other end of what he classified as Mintzberg's spectrum is the threat to existing activities. There are the threats that disease might destroy the cocoa crop. But there is the threat of market definition which he explained in the following way: there is a market, not for chocolate confectionery but 'for pleasurable snacks of all kinds, and it just happens that a large part of these are covered with chocolate or are chocolate-flavoured. Therefore, you explore what action you ought to be taking to ensure that if there is shift in the snack market, that you are in a position in which you can cope with it. I have a planning group with which I meet and we kick it around.'

The definition of market with which the company is working is a mainspring in the formulation of its agenda since it governs the work which is put in on prospective developments and strategic shifts. But in addition, there is the interest which the company has in the way its products are distributed (dependence on a few large distributors). Hence, part of the thinking has to be about where snack foods are eaten and how the firm gets to the ultimate consumer.

Within the underlying framework of the firm as a marketing organisation and in a market defined as snack foods, important changes emerge from possibilities and problems which yield options which in turn lead to action. It is described as 'a sort of iterative process': it covers ongoing markets but does not make provision for electric changes, partly at least because in Sir Adrian's opinion 'in our kind of business, mainly dealing with food and drink, there have not been many Einsteins.' When major changes occur, moreover, Cadbury Schweppes will be involved in marketing rather than technology. 'We probably will not be involved in the technology, we will simply buy it in.'

The definition of the scope and character of the company are fundamental in that it provides the general area of search: to the extent that the firm is a pool of assets it does not wholly determine it in the very long-term but this seems to be a point of economic principle rather than of practical policy. But the actual process of strategic change is brought about incrementally. Moreover, recurring to the topic raised earlier about the ability of the company to make a total change in its strategy, it becomes clear that this is a matter of principle with very long-term implications, and there is genuine ambiguity in Sir Adrian's views. For asked whether he could envisage the firm in, say, a Tillings role in the long term, right outside its present areas, he replied, '. . . No, because you start with the area of *your management competence* (authors' italics). We have no competence to run a Tillings type of operation.' To attempt to do so would involve total *bouleversement* and 'then you would say, what reason have you to believe that having made all those changes that you would run the business better than any other company?' Since what is being sought is comparative advantage and hence to make the most of the assets (for Cadbury Schweppes these are brands and expertise), the company will need to keep its market reasonably fluid. Thus, the company will move in market terms, it will not remain stuck to one last, but will tend to do so within the concept of the business as defined by its managerial competence. 'We get a bit metaphysical discussing the nature of the business. You can argue that the other way of looking at changes in the business is that, in a sense, the business purpose has remained, but it has had to cope with changing external circumstances, so it finds itself moving into different patterns.'

A Comment on Profit and Objectives

The existence of business strategies implies that there are purposes which they are meant to serve. Conventional economic theory, treating the firm as a monolithic entity, characteristically assumes that 'it' seeks to maximise profits although economists are careful to note that this assumption is a device in modelling business behaviour. Managerial economists, interested in the behaviour of particular firms, and writers in the Simon, Cyert and March, Leibenstein, Lindblom framework have concentrated attention on the multiplicity of objectives and sometimes on profit as a 'required resultant' of meeting other objectives.

Sir Adrian, in reply to a question on this theme, made these points: a company will have an idea of what it is prepared to do any why it is in the businesses it has. It will aim, e.g., to be an efficient distributor of its set of products and it will have some measurable objectives of the kind that it wishes to cover a certain percentage of the market. The profit they achieve is a consequence of achieving their objectives. What is done is, moreover, 'the consequence of consensus decision; so you have got to say why those decisions have been taken. It is not an adequate explanation to say that they have been made to meet a particular target. That does not explain why some things were in and other things were out.'

Applying his general argument to the specific experience of Cadbury Schweppes, he instanced the company's withdrawal from distribution in which they were at one stage. Admittedly they had found it unprofitable, but his argument was that this was not inherent in distribution. The critical point was that they did not know how to manage shops: the opportunity cost of the resources engaged in distribution was too high. Recurring to his earlier remarks he said that 'it was better to put the resources somewhere where we had some real comparative advantage, which was basically in our core business.' The benchmark is in terms of increase in earnings per share — the opportunity cost is looked at in terms of 'the wide food and drink industry, and you say, in order to maintain our position at the top end of this, in the upper half of the group which we are looking at, this is the kind of earnings per share which we need to achieve.' This, with outside soundings from the brokers, gives the target. Thus, measurable targets are important but the structure of business strategies stems from the business and market concepts.

This attitude fits into the general picture of strategy which is rationally considered but within a bounded context and with a pattern of search which has a significant element of the haphazard. In as major an issue as a merger this is so: Schweppes approached Cadbury and one result of the subsequent merger was the entry of Cadbury into the manufacturing of confectionery in the United States (it was, of course, already selling its chocolate in the U.S.). This was because the combined concern had an administrative structure and cash flow in the United States which provided the means for putting up a Cadbury factory there: moreover, it provided a contact point which could negotiate with Peter Paul which Cadbury Schweppes acquired. This process which led to the emergence of North America as the company's biggest single operation outside the U.K., was a strategic one which met a strategic objective. Nevertheless, Sir Adrian remarks that 'it is impossible to say that this is an entirely logical operation in which you look at all the possibilities and then you choose the one which suits you best. You are faced with the decision and you have to decide where that lies on your range from optimum, through sub-optimum and so on.'

Looking back at the experience of concentration of business effort on the main businesses, the opening up of international branches and the shifting of geographical balance, and improved use of assets, Sir

Adrian concluded that it was not feasible to have more than a few (or a strictly limited number of) broad objectives. In an untidy environment with very many decisions to be taken, 'you are giving people a few guidelines against which they ought to measure whether they take this decision or that decision. I believe that this is as far as you can go.'

A Divisional Note

It was primarily the interviews with Sir Adrian Cadbury which dealt with strategy and this is in itself some reflection of the fundamental part played by the centre and central individuals in the formulation of policy and strategic purpose. But it is of course a matter of width of agenda: Sir Adrian thinks in terms of the enterprise as a whole. Within that context, the activities of the separate parts of Cadbury Schweppes may perhaps be envisaged as sub-strategies. There is at more than one level, however, a recognition that there is a form of thinking which is properly strategic as distinct from tactical. Thus, A.K. Slipper, managing director of Cadbury Typhoo Ltd. (the Tea and Foods division) which accounts (1980) for 10% of the profits of the group, is involved in major decisions about capital expenditure, personnel policy etc. Strategic thinking means looking

> 5, 10 years ahead into the future [to] decide where as a business we are going, what are the products we should be selling then, what will consumers be requiring then, what kind of management and employees should we be employing then. . . . . Longer term planning in my view is about ideas being floated upwards, downwards and across the various organisations. I do not believe any one area of a business can in isolation decide what the longer term strategy of any company is to be. It has emerged from debate, considered research and deep thinking prior to being put forward into plans.

Within his division, Slipper has product groups so that it is possible 'to cut across functional barriers and ensure that the various businesses are given priority as opposed to just the functions within those businesses.' He regards it as his job to think in long- as well as short-term ways even to the extent of initiating ideas about possible acquisitions – in this instance, however, he qualified his comment by saying that any such proposal would be related to the Tea and

Foods division. It was very improbable that a division would generate
ideas about acquisitions outside its own, more immediate context.

Notes

1. Ansoff H.I. *Corporate Strategy.*
   Op. cit., passim.
2. Sloan A.P. *My Years with General Motors.*
   Sidgwick and Jackson, London, 1965.
   Chapter 8, pp. 139-140
3. Chandler A. *The Visible Hand.*
   Op. cit.
4. Kirzner I.M. *Competition and Entrepreneurship.*
   Op. cit.
   Perception, Opportunity and Profit.
   University of Chicago Press, 1979.
5. Shackle G.L.S. For a fairly recent discussion, see:
   'Imagination, Formalism, and Choice.'
   In Rizzo M.J. (Ed.) *Time, Uncertainty, and Disequilibrium.*
   D.C. Heath and Co., Lexington, 1979.
   Chapter 2, pp. 19-31. In pp. 32-49 of the same chapter,
   S.C. Littlechild examines the Kirzner/Shackle theme
   under the title: 'Comment: Radical Subjectivism or
   Radical Subversion?'
6. Penrose E. *The Theory of the Growth of the Firm.*
   Op. cit., passim. But see, especially, Chapter VII,
   pp. 149-150.

8 MANGANESE BRONZE: A LATER VIEW

In the winter of 1979, the late Mr. John Neville was invited to give his views on the way in which strategic planning was arranged in his group of small companies, whose production includes building products, guns, sintered metal products, precision casting and bodies for the London taxi-cab. They are related in that they are all engineering companies but are diverse in their range of products.

A vice-chairman of an American company[1] has described control of such a group in these words:

> The real thing which we are contributing is generalised business knowledge and not expert knowledge about specific products and marketing. It is quite possible for people who have a good general knowledge of business to ask a lot of questions and to evaluate the answers that they get, even though they clearly could not answer the questions themselves. [Also we provide] an incentive and an enthusiasm in the operation of the business, along with a penalty for not doing better.

John Neville confirms this opinion but, as described in the earlier section on this company, he goes further in his emphasis on the need for a perpetual communication between levels of management designed to expose policy intentions in the arena of debate and to ensure that everybody has understood their significance.

He has described how this attitude of managing manifests itself in his company and the type of control which he exercises by emphasising that the management team of a subsidiary which has the responsibility of running the business must be given scope to achieve its ambitions. His understanding of the strategic process, as will be seen, is that the first steps of the process become possible only when the business environment of the executives of the companies is not restricted — only when they are 'given a free rein to do the job in the way they think is best.'

The use of the expression 'a free rein' requires particular comment here. There has to be some gravitational force which holds the group together and this means that the separate parts cannot be quite free. While the aim may be to grant as much freedom as possible, the freedom will be restricted for each part of the group by virtue of the fact that it is a part. This also must apply, incidentally, to the centre. Neville speaks of guidelines and rules in the same breath as freedom and he shows that he recognises that there must be a constitutional form to comprehend both ideas. Implicit in strategic process is the idea that this form is necessary because it is there to accommodate change.

What is common to the companies studied in Part Two is that the rules which are imposed incorporate a rolling plan over a period of years, i.e. the rules are constantly maintained. Manganese Bronze, like the other companies, base their plans on financial consideration and Poore (chief executive of the Manganese Bronze group since 1980) is quoted later to express the view with particular emphasis that a firm financial discipline is the best prescription for maintaining control without autocracy. The plan for each year in the group, as Neville described it, as it becomes current, is thorough and precise, and it gives the total requirement for finance, plant, equipment, building, labour and all the resources which the company needs or which it may have to call on. These company plans should be prepared in depth.

It would be quite wrong to treat the form which the group adopts in relation to the companies as a mere lever of control. On the contrary, it is used by the centre as a means of expanding their range of freedom. This comes about because in this task of the preparation of the annual plan the companies are compelled to give rational consideration to the choices which opportunity offers them, and they could be expected to emerge from the exercise with a more informed awareness of the possibilities on which strategic planning might be based. 'Thus many conglomerates make a determined effort to force the divisional manager to do more strategic planning for his division than was done for his company when it was independent. Indeed . . . it is not a case of doing better strategic planning, but of getting it done at all.'

Neville used the annual plan as a tool to 'educate' his company managements. He chairs the company boards. When a director puts forward a scheme at a company board meeting, Neville, as has been said, requires him to be prepared to present a brief explanatory paper. This requirement can now be seen as something which puts responsibility for the scheme and, necessarily, some of the control of its development, in the hands of the sponsoring director.

The Strategic Process

At the time Neville was speaking, Manganese Bronze was considering a shift towards investment in North America, Germany and possibly France. The company supplies components to the motor industry — one of the areas of manufacture in which it has some special ability. Towards the end of 1979 the opinion was forming in the group and in the subsidiary companies which were most concerned that the future in this line of manufacturing in this country was uncertain. 'Because, in my humble opinion', Neville said at that time, 'the number of motor cars made in this country will continue to decline for some time to come. It may decline to a point where the industry almost disappears.'

The proposed shift of policy towards international investment was bound, when implemented, to have substantial effects on work in the subsidiaries. Neville was asked whether this change was first suggested by the group centre and the Manganese Bronze board or whether the management in a subsidiary had had a part in forming this view. The fact was that the Manganese Bronze board had had experience of a sudden decline in a related field of manufacture since it had, a few years before, seen the disappearance of the British motor cycle industry at the time of the acquisition of the remnants of BSA Limited by their company. On the other hand, the Manganese Bronze subsidiary, Carbodies, was intimately associated with the main industrial groupings of the motor industry and its management and was constantly aware of the climate in which they operated. The centre and the subsidiaries had their own separate sources of information about the state of the motor industry, but a subsidiary like Carbodies, being closer to the ground, may have reached a more lively perception than the executive centre in London, of changes in the mood in the industry in which they dealt. Who then would be expected to initiate a change of policy such as this — the group's executive centre and the board, or the team of managers in the subsidiary?

Neville said that there would no general answer to the question, because of the different circumstances of different companies in the group. However,

In the case of components for motor vehicles the change in policy has emerged from successive discussions at the subsidiary company and these have made it clear that if we stay where we are we will face a progressive decline in our business. Therefore the recommendation has come from below and come up to the parent company which has endorsed the idea of buying and making overseas investment to manufacture components where the market, we believe, will expand.

Neville gave an illustration of the way in which a subsidiary, active in its special field, may gather information, the 'grass roots' information, the sort of material which may be drawn later into boardroom consideration of strategy. One of his subsidiaries was supplied with components by a large manufacturer and, through their trade relations, the two managements maintained constant personal contact. At a time when the industrial future of the supplier was reported to be uncertain, the management of the Manganese Bronze subsidiary, being aware of the difficulties which the supplier faced, became naturally concerned that they should keep an adequate stock of these components. Neville went to the subsidiary and was informed of the situation which he then described in this way:

> On the day I was there, our staff went to a certain plant owned by company X to discuss the position of supplies, to find that on the shop floor the men were organising life to run a new business, cutting out company X altogether, and our staff were welcomed with open arms as the first of the new customers who were going to get priority treatment. As far as they were concerned, to hell with company X, because they were scheduled to be closed down. So instead of being in a position where the management were told, 'I'm sorry, this week you can only have a very limited number of components', we finished that day with the whole of the stock.

That was the sort of direct, spontaneous information which Neville saw as one of the primary sources of strategic intelligence. Also Neville suggests, through this illustration, that this type of intelligence, which makes an impact, the information shock which opens the perceptive mind to impending change, is most readily gathered in the field of action.

There are many instances of dialogue in this study in which higher management acknowledges the debt due to lower management, the importance of the detailed awareness acquired in operational experience. This is a main reason why the principle of decentralisation is consistently adhered to. Sir Adrian Cadbury says that perceptive thinking is not to be seen as confined to higher executives, but 'it is a bit of everybody's job who has any kind of management responsibility.' Richard Bagnall of Tube Investments talks of the importance of 'decentralising the action . . . ' – by which he emphasises the active intention of the higher levels of management to unload responsibility throughout the company. It seems that the first spark which ignites the strategic train of thought could well be struck in the operational field. In a group of diverse companies like Manganese Bronze, each with its specialist management team, is it not reasonable to expect that the spark will be often struck in the companies rather than at the centre? Neville thought that it could be so. 'I think so, yes, – because they have the facts, they can see what is going on.'

Nevertheless, Neville's conception of the type of strategic planning which he would consider ideal in his company appears to be, not a form of procedure to be followed, but a part of a progressing group-company dialogue. 'New ideas do not come from a single source', he said, meaning essentially that the germinal idea, though it may come from the company, has to be fashioned in the dialogue before it attains significance. He has a view of the strategic process which he has tried to promote in his company in which the contributions from the companies and from the centre are each distinct and crucial. His statement: 'You have to recognise that there is an interplay between the two levels of boards', (the Manganese Bronze board and the company board), is a statement of principle about the strategic process as he prefers it.

In this process, he recognises the indispensable part which operational management plays. He starts from his conviction that the group centre cannot be expected to identify strategic possibilities without help from the operational subsidiaries. But neither would be expect that ability, that discernment, in the companies on their own without the help of the centre. There is a lack on both sides which makes each a complement of the other. In the case of the companies the lack is evident in the inexperience and the narrowness of vision of operational managers before they have been exposed to business problems in their entirety. That is why he had insisted that operational managers have to be trained to take part in useful deliberation. Many of them are 'totally unconditioned' to this aspect of their job until it is presented to them as an explicit demand of the boardroom business discussion in which, in time, rank or seniority might involve them. 'The blank looks gradually give way to the dawn of discovery as they realise that they should think about these things . . . One man bitterly resents being asked at a board meeting "why is it that we're not getting the business that we need?" '.

In the strategic process the operational managers have the indispensable role of gathering the root sources of information. The distinction of Neville's view is his explicit recognition and emphasis that, somewhere in the interplay between the two levels over which he presides, information becomes business intelligence. The idea which might have been said to emanate from the companies may not be more than the tissue from which growth can be cultivated. The cultivation of this growth is the first contribution which the executive centre gives to the strategic process.

Neville requires the company managements to be creative in the primary stages of strategic consideration. The original source of new business ideas should be in the companies, not because the higher management is devoid of creative ideas, but because the lower management, who are constantly immersed in the environment in which they are operators, should be able to add, from the beginning, a practical ingredient to the mix of strategic consideration. The centre is always there, and the subsidiaries would certainly expect ideas to be floated down to them by the parent company. But if the company managements do not understand the part which they have to play or if they are prepared to leave creative proposals entirely to the group executive management, the centre must force them to do what is required, urge them to bring forward ideas, ('I personally believe that if you can make people think, they will find that they have the ideas'), and force them to throw the weight of their specialists' experience into the scales. The centre will only make these requirements of the companies if it already respects the competence of their boards and is prepared to give them the freedom to risk error or misjudgement. Neville has been quoted earlier as saying that the company managements 'have got to learn that they have to be able to stand up and debate it, even if they've made a mistake.'

He illustrated, in an example which was briefly touched on earlier, his principle that a group executive who disregards grass-roots opinion and experience could easily go into error.

Perhaps I could tell you a story about BSA Guns. I'm very interested in the subject because all my life I have handled guns since I was about 'that high', shotguns, rifles, air-rifles, pistols, everthing you can think of and nothing to do with **BSA** Guns —

I had all these weapons at home long before I had anything to do with this particular company. I thought that BSA Guns should expand by manufacturing a shotgun, a good quality, medium price shotgun. And Alf Scott, whom you know well, and all his colleagues were totally and absolutely opposed to this proposal. However, I've a great respect for that board. I think they're very able men doing their job, so I did nothing of the sort and of course events have proved them absolutely right. Webley and Scott had to publicly announce that they're abandoning production of shotguns and indeed there are no longer any mass produced shotguns manufactured in the UK at all, fullstop. And so, some of the ideas at the top aren't very good ones, you never know, do you?

Neville's illustration has been expanded here because it does more than show the importance of grass-roots opinion. Although the centre has the ability and the right (and in some cases the duty) to initiate, there is an expectation that it is the subsidiary companies who (in the best circumstances), will bring forward information and examine it as a business possibility. Thereupon, the involvement of the centre could be immediate. It is at this early stage that a product or market possibility may graduate to a business idea, whose development may possibly lead to a business change. There is no formal analysis of the mechanics of entrepreneurial change which could be presented here, because there is no formal process. But there is a difference of responsibility corresponding to the difference in the two levels of management, and to the differences in their past experience and their present range of working. This difference of responsibility predisposes the subsidiary towards the role of initiation and the centre towards the role of review.

The function of the centre is in these circumstances to form a second tier in the strategic process by which the function of review or judgement is kept distinct from the scene of action. Neville's emphasis is that even when the idea has come from a company, the responsibility of the centre at the second stage remains. The executive centre and the group board must have knowledge enough to be able to review the intelligence which is brought before it and to judge its strategic significance. The board is chosen for its collected experience and general business knowledge. Its judgements must have the sense of impartiality (particularly important for a centre management of diverse subsidiaries) and the sense of reviewing evidence and offering qualified criticism. The Manganese Bronze board is predominantly

non-executive. At the time of which Neville was speaking, there was
only one executive director on the board other than himself. 'Otherwise they are all outside directors. Which in many ways is a very good
thing in my opinion. Outside directors cross-examine the executive
very ferociously indeed about what is going on.'

Strategies for Growth

When he was asked whether the general strategy which Manganese
Bronze had been following had growth as an element, Neville indicated
certain parameters within which the subject would have to be set.
The motivation of the firm was to optimise profits. In the business
conditions which prevailed at the time and in the circumstances in
which Manganese Bronze especially found itself, the first constraint
on profit maximisation which he encountered and recognised was the
availability of cash.

The motivation of everyone is to maximise the profits. First and
foremost. But as long as that is compatible with also maximising
the cash being generated in the business. Money is a very expensive
commodity today. I have recently been discussing with the bank
an additional facility for which the current rate of interest would
be 17%. There are not many engineering industries actually making
17% at all. On anything they do. So I encourage the concept that
the profit at the end of the year should be substantially expressed
in cash. You can then take a conscious decision whether to invest
it within the existing business, or by acquiring something else, or
by establishing a new business somewhere else. Or starting some
completely different activity possibly. Not very often that, but
possibly. I think those are the sort of motivations with which
we deal.

Allowing for the need for the generation of cash, expansion within
limits would not present a general problem to the organisational
structure of Manganese Bronze. 'If the business trebled in size by
doing the same things, with the same number of principal companies,
I do not think you would need to change the organisation at all.' But
as the group already had to contend with the problem of diversification, there would be a constraint on growth in the degree of diversification which would be tolerable.

The break point, I think, surely comes as you increase the number of activities. Because each one of them needs control. I think the criticism that people level at what we're doing now, is that I am trying to be involved in too many activities. This I am remedying to some extent by sub-grouping companies, so that, for example, you can see here that there are a number of companies, all of which are engaged in powder metallurgy. These three here. We have now grouped them effectively into one board, and I only concern myself with that board which is the policy point with these three companies and what they do. Equally here, Alpax, carries on everything in this zone, and that's been grouped.

There is a third constraint on a growth strategy in that the market for disinvestment may be, as at the present, restricted. An active policy of investment requires that when there is an advantage in selling a business it must be possible to do so.

Where the rub comes is that the buying and selling of businesses is excellent in theory, but in practice I would think you would find it very difficult to sell an engineering business at the present time. If you're a buyer, then start negotiations, if you like, on some of our less profitable activities. You can always buy things, it just depends on how deep your pocket is, but selling is a very difficult exercise.

A Later Perspective

The chairman of Manganese Bronze, Mr. R.D. Poore, took on also, the position of chief executive, following Mr. Neville's death in 1980. In an interview at the end of 1982, he was asked to comment on the ideas which had been followed in the past and to say whether there had been serious changes in the past two years in the way in which the group was managed. His answer was: 'No change at all. In fact, my views that it was the right way to proceed were very much confirmed.'

He expressed the same general view about the part which subsidiary companies must play in the strategic process. His immediate answer to the question whether it could be said that ideas, in the main, come from individual companies, was: 'Oh, entirely', but he qualified it by saying that ideas, of course, also came from the centre, from the chief executive for instance, who is in constant touch with the company managements. In making this qualification he tried to intimate the form of collaboration which is practised between the centre and the subsidiaries. 'This is a matter of degree rather than a black or white answer, but of course I have ideas but I do not − or I do my best not to − enforce them. I suggest them if I feel inclined, but they must be distilled at the units and they must understand why they want to do them and take responsibility for the result.'

Poore sets out the general distinction between the responsibility of the subsidiary and the responsibility of the centre which he and Neville had had in mind. Starting from the point that the subsidiary company must take responsibility for the result, he goes on:

> They have to tell me what they think they can do. I think it is fundamental, otherwise, if at the end we fail, they might say, 'Well I never thought we could do it anyway.' You must not get into that position and if you push them too hard they could well turn round and say, 'well come and run the damn thing yourself.' I have had that said to me many years ago. Not now − I have learned better. So they have to tell me what they can do and I tell them, say, that they are unduly pessimistic or this or the other, and I sometimes send them away to think again, but it always must be what their budgets, their budgets not my budgets, allow. I sometimes put what I call a prudency factor on them before adopting them − in fact we have done that this year, because in one case they were, I think, a bit over-optimistic. It is sometimes a matter of judgement of the market-place rather than a judgement of what they can do. But they do not know that I've done that. The budgets are still their budgets.

Financial Discipline

The principle that the management in the subsidiary should be expected to initiate is validated by the management practice that the budgets of the subsidiaries, after certain prescribed requirements of the centre have been met, are under their own control. This principle of self-financing for development was maintained even in the years when the group as a whole had funding problems. Poore recounted the difficulties of that period:

> Our history in the last decade has been totally dominated by this

fuss with the motor cycle industry. You know we invested £5 million in it jointly with the government, and of course the thing was torn apart by the following government who wished to do things as social experiments rather than aiming to make a profit. So that was a catastrophic period and at one time it appeared we might not even survive, because just to lose £5 million like that is a very serious thing for us. But the managing directors have rallied round very strongly and we have got over it all now and our balance sheets are beginning to look very much stronger and they have targets to achieve.

As in the years of exceptional financial stringency so, *a fortiori*, when 'normal' conditions have returned, the companies can be sure that the profits they earn will be available to finance their development plans. 'If anything', says Poore, 'I push this a bit further than John Neville did.' He described the management form which has been established in these words:

Each managing director is told at the beginning of the year how much money he's got to send up to head office to pay out head office expenses, the audit fees and the central interest, and to pay the dividend. He is told precisely how much money he has to supply and he puts that down in his own budget and he knows that if he can make more money than that, it is his for developing his business. Now this is a tremendous incentive. Nothing annoys people more than to have a good year and have someone ring up from head office and say, 'Look, send that £100,000 up quickly if you don't mind.' It destroys their initiative completely. I think that everybody in our group appreciates this point. They know precisely where they are at the beginning of the year and they build this into their budgets and, naturally, they send it up for approval with the main board. But normally they are expected to finance their own expansion. (It is only when we get a rather exceptional thing like the new taxi cab that the parent company enters into it — we couldn't have done it any other way, of course). But otherwise they are there. The main board indeed do consider whether we are right to have so many million pounds invested in that industry, but we would not on the whole seek to restrict the people in it.

Allowing, he added, that the board has the power to sell something if they chose and invest the money in some other way. 'That would be the ultimate. We have sold one or two things for various reasons during the recession, but mainly to get our cash position straight rather than for any other reason.'

Poore's exposition of the strategic process in Manganese Bronze together with the mechanical control set up to guide it, makes it clear that the subsidiary is under pressure to initiate, because the whole purpose of management in the subsidiary is manifestly to optimise the use of funds — their own funds. There is a congruence in the purposes for which planning control and financial freedom are designed. Just as earlier it was seen that the form of planning control which is exercised, (through Neville's guidelines and rules) leads to a higher freedom, so it can be seen that the form of financial freedom which is exercised is an imposition on the companies. They are forced to behave rationally. Planning control of the companies is the means through which they can expand their range of freedom and the financial freedom which they are allowed is the means by which they can be yoked to the burden of responsibility.

The financial freedom which the company allows is a residuum of a prior financial discipline. Poore underlined in a most emphatic way that financial discipline is a necessary ingredient in any autonomous structure whether the autonomy is in financial or in general policy making. He prefaced his remarks here by suggesting that a characteristic of people in this country, which has to be allowed for, is that they simply will not 'go along' with any attempts to do things by methods which are imposed on them against their agreement. In some places, people are much more used to discipline and being told to do things in a certain way,

> but English people, I have found, do not respond to that kind of treatment, they would much rather be given an objective and set to reach the objective in the way they want to, not the way you want them to. But, of course, the difference really is as to whether you have a financial objective or whether you have a departmental objective, and I mean you can still have a monolithic structure and not impose things on people.

Thus his business method of strong financial control is conditioned partly by his experience, partly by the logic which guides him and partly by his confirming social philosophy. Poore rates financial discipline so highly that, he says, it is not even essential to decentralise in order to have an autonomous structure, so long as management throughout its compass can be held accountable to financial objectives. The reason why the principle of management autonomy often cannot be logically followed in a centralised structure is simply

because you then have a sales department, a technical department or you name it, and the people who run those can do it their way but, of course, they are not responsible for the overall result which is left to the central administration — they themselves are merely responsible for running their part of it in the best way they see fit. I believe it's very difficult for them to do that because they have no financial yardstick as to whether what they are doing is worthwhile or not. You have got to have a financial objective, [Poore says], before you can achieve that and that is what the autonomous structure does as opposed to a monolithic structure.

A firm financial discipline is thus seen as the essential basis on which the managements at the companies can be made aware of the importance of their cash position as well as their responsibility for initiating and directing policies towards the future. When he became chief executive, Poore tightened control and he expressed the change and the reasoning which lay behind it in this way:

John was a bit looser on this, but he used to have rather more daily control over what they did, and if he thought that spending was too much he would say: 'Just hold up payments for a week or two — we're a bit tight at the minute'. He had more time than I had, of course, and I didn't think, for myself, that that was quite good enough. So people at the subsidiaries have a line drawn at the bank and they know that I am down on them like a ton of bricks if they overshoot it. They can't think that they can write a cheque for £50,000 just because they need it — they have got to wait until they have the money coming in, and this is very salutary. And as a result of that our cash position has dramatically improved. They chase up all the stocks in the corner that they were worried about, they realise if they don't get them out and sold they can't have that new piece of equipment they want. All this is, as I said, very salutary. They are right up against the financial results — and I think you have to do this — and it gives them a proper awareness. For some of them, when they start, it is a novel feeling, because they haven't had to do this before. But they all have a proper 'numbers man' as I call him, who feeds all the facts into them and this works very well, and

indeed I find that I don't have to worry. If people ask, what is your
cash flow programme? I say, 'What do you mean? I haven't got a
cash flow programme. I know what I am going to get and it is up
to them.' I mean, if they can't do what is required I'm not going
to put someone over them to do it. I'll get someone else who can
and they understand that and they accept it and they appreciate it.'

Strategy and Organisation

In the theatre of strategic action the characters who walk on in the
first scene may be drawn from the subsidiaries. But throughout the
play the centre has its part to play in various ways. The first indispensable way is that it has the duty to see that the strategy is 'organised'.
The business idea has to graduate into business action, the purpose
of which, as in all strategic intention, is to lead to change. The larger
the organising capacity which is available, the greater the potentialities
of change and greater the importance of organisation as an ingredient
of strategy.

Poore gave an example which showed that the business idea amounts
to nothing unless it can be designed into a piece of business action. He
was speaking about the manufacture of components for the automobile
industry in which he saw little future unless the component is made
in the same country as the car.

You see, we've found that we can't introduce a new technology
product into a car part if it is going into a French car because the
first thing they say is, 'Where can I get this in France. I'm not buying
it in England unless I can get it in France too.' So if you've got some
idea you can't use it, they'll design it out, design out of the need for
it unless they can get it in their own country. This doesn't apply to
British Leyland, but British Leyland make something like 800,000
vehicles now instead of the 2 million or so they were making ten
years ago, and that is one of the reasons why our automobile
components business has declined.

Poore regarded it as essential to a company in modern circumstances
that it should be continually scrutinising its product range, the product
possibilities which may appear and the uncertainties to which existing
production may be exposed. He made a survey of his subsidiary
companies in an attempt to define the changes to which Manganese

Bronze may have to adapt. This was thinking about strategy and Poore clearly identified it as a main responsibility of the centre.

I'm about to ask our managing directors, [he said], to tell me where they think they're going to be and what they're going to be doing in five years time and in ten years time. I'm about to do this. I think I know the answers and I'm forming an opinion of what we ought to be doing.

I don't think that industry in this country will survive unless it is high technology or speciality products and we are not in this nearly enough. We have to do this.

I can see where we're going with Carbodies, because I've had quite a lot to do with that one way or another — we've got quite a lot of ideas there. I'm not sure that I see where we are with anything else that we are doing.

In BSA Guns, if we could get into the defence industries, I think there is a future in that.

I'm sure that to make components for the automobile industries is not the thing for the future, for the simple reason that you have to be in the same country where they make the cars, otherwise you are a second or third supplier who is brought in only because you are cheaper. We have disposed of one unit to a company who were hopelessly tied in to the automobile industry — they were the only buyers with the volume needed to make that kind of plant pay. To some extent, I think, that with similar products we may find the same. I have actually had unofficial discussions with the chairman of GKN to find out whether they think that there should be some kind of amalgamation. These declining industries have to rationalise whether people like it or not. This is something that the Manganese Bronze board should now be turning their mind to.

Was this sort of thinking a special function of the centre? 'Absolutely', said Poore. 'You will never get the unit managing directors to come up with suggestions that what they are doing is a waste of time.'

Sir Adrian Cadbury pointed to the same direction once when he said: 'Almost by definition, it would be very unusual for somebody

who was actually working in the confectionery business to think up
ideas which envisage the elimination of his present business.' The
disposition of operational executives, quite naturally, is to provide
for the future of their own division, and their thinking cannot be
expected to encompass the strategic imperatives of the company
as a whole: 'If you simply add together the ideas for growth in the
existing divisions', Cadbury said, 'they don't usually add up to what
you want — so there is a gap in any case.' On the present occasion
Poore chose a different but equally revealing form to express the
distinction between the strategic roles of operational and centre
executives. 'You see', he said, 'they answer the question "how", but I
have to answer the question "why" — a very big difference.'

The 'centre' here would, of course, include the chief executive, but
Poore thought that it must also have have the vital participation of the
board. He considered that ideally 'we should have on the board a young
man — or two young men — who are interested in this kind of subject
and who can make a proper analysis of the sort of things we ought
to be doing', and who would add energy and general business and
industrial experience.

> They would not be expected to be able to cope with the managing
> directors of the units — those are the people who are supposed
> to have that kind of expertise. The people of the board should
> have general industrial experience, and particularly financial
> experience, which of course the units do not have — I find that
> most of my time assisting the units is spent on financial subjects.

Neville and Poore had described the strategic process as they see and
manage it, and had explained the role which the centre aims to play
in that process. Asked what business matters he found himself thinking
about mostly, how his working day was ordered, Poore replied:

> I suppose, to a self-analytical question of that kind one never really
> applies one's mind — , [but he went on to offer a three-point resúmé
> of his main, day to day, duties.]

> On the whole, at first, I am concerned that the units are achieving
> what they tell me they are going to achieve and I go round and
> deal with that.

> I then spend some time thinking about whether they're in the right

businesses anyway. I think this is particularly important nowadays because British industry won't survive if it thinks it is going to do the same as it did for the last fifty years. We have to do something different and so I spend time thinking about that and whether we should dispose of certain activities or invest more money in others.

And, thirdly, I suppose I am thinking about problems which are presented to me from the units, particularly those which cover areas which the units are not staffed to cope with — for example, major financial operations. A large part of my time ending about six months ago was spent financing our new taxi cab, because we had to raise a large sum of money to supply the tools and we had a lot of negotiating and arguing to go through. And so I would expect to have to play a sort of detailed executive part — functions which the units can't do.

He elaborated on the advantages and disadvantages which management of a company of the size, structure and style of Manganese Bronze entailed, where management is decentralised into units which are not themselves self-sufficient in higher management/business skills.

One of the disadvantages, (if that is a disadvantage), of having a very decentralised structure with units of our sizes, is that they cannot afford to have people who are knowledgeable about finance, international trade, or any of the sort of things that are outside the simple running of the factory and finding customers for your goods. In a centralised company like GKN they would have central departments for dealing with law suits, patent actions and whatever. In a decentralised affair that doesn't really work because responsibility rests lower down, and somehow, our headquarters staff have to cope with these things when they crop up.

Then there is the disadvantage that avenues for recruitment to higher management may be blocked and that a company could be starved of the higher abilities which it should itself be cultivating. There are signs of this problem arising even in a 'monolithic' or centralised company when it undergoes the first stages of decentralisation. Poore has given a lot of thought to this, believing with Neville in his own company and, for example, with Brockett in Newey & Eyre, that it is becoming a serious problem for British industrial management.

A further disadvantage which is beginning to emerge is that you don't, you can't, offer people a career structure. I'm beginning to think about this rather more seriously, because we are not taking on any young men in the way that you might expect. Our board is getting very old. I was asked only last week by one of the managing directors: 'What are the opportunities in this group — what chance have I — of getting on the main board?' I said to this man: This is something I'm thinking about, but my answer is, No, there is not much.

In the earlier section on this company it was suggested that this has the advantage that it defines the separate responsibilities of the two levels. But the corollary is that the centre accepts that the young man with outstanding talent would seek his career elsewhere. Neville, like Poore, recognised that and both say that they would not stand in the way of the progress of a young manager outside the group. Neville, in answer to a question, said: 'If we can't see an opportunity for them, we tell them that, and encourage them to go somewhere else. We encourage the man to go and very strong recommendations, if that is justified, go with him. And we have placed a number of people at great advantage to the individual concerned.'

Poore sees it as a growing problem for the group and he does not see a way through it yet. He wants none of the solution which 'seemed the natural thing to do', that the boards of semi-conglomerate, holding companies should be staffed by the managing directors of the units.

I know from experience that these people sit round a table and all they do is to argue their corner. They will not look at it from a group point of view, and in no way can they possibly argue that what they are doing is not the right policy for the group. They want whatever there is to be invested in the product that they are going to run. The board meetings, therefore, unless you have an extremely strong chairman who lays down the law and has the authority to enforce it, just resolve into hopeless argument. And, of course, there's no group strategy of any kind. I'm quite convinced that to have these people on the main board is disastrous unless they were rather exceptional people — I suppose one always has to make an exception like that — but, in the normal way they find it very difficult suddenly to divorce themselves from what they're doing and look at it from a purely investment standpoint.

The great advantage which decentralisation offers, Poore said, is the sort of 'keen, direct incentive that you get with our group'. But the problem of recruitment remains, and he could see some difficult questions which were becoming urgent and which had still not been answered. 'What kind of people do you want on the board if you don't have the unit managing directors? One can bring in some young men, but what are the young men actually going to do? What is their relationship going to be with the unit managing directors? For anybody interested in running groups in industry, I can see that this is a terrible problem.'

9 TARMAC: THE DEVELOPMENT OF STRATEGY

Introduction

The evidence from Tarmac is in two parts. The first is drawn from three papers which Mr. R.G. Martin, chairman and chief executive of the company, gave at the Industrial Seminar at Birmingham University between 1966 and 1975. This was followed by discussion with the authors in 1979, a few months after Mr. Martin had relinquished his appointments at Tarmac. The second part is drawn from discussion with Mr. E. Pountain, the present chief executive and his senior colleagues.

Tarmac was founded in 1903 at Wolverhampton as an offshoot of an iron and steel works which operated at Bilston, Staffordshire. Both companies were privately owned by the Hickman family of Wolverhampton until 1913, when the Tarmac offshoot went public. There was a simple relation between the two companies. The primary road laying material which Tarmac used was the slag which the iron and steel works produced as a by-product.

R.G. Martin's father married into the Hickman family. He came into the firm after the First World War and became managing director in 1926. He retired from that position in 1958. R.G. Martin had just become managing director of the roadstone side of Tarmac, and soon after became managing director and, in 1971, chairman and chief executive of Tarmac. He therefore presided over the major expansion and diversification of the 1960s and the 1970s, when the company was transformed from a purely slag business into a much larger building materials, construction, and civil engineering group.

The experience of Tarmac over the past twenty five years encompasses a variety of features with which any examination of the modern corporation must be concerned. Martin's arrival at the head of the company is associated with major strategic change. It led in due course, moreover, though not immediately, to a more sophisticated approach to strategic questions and to a concept of corporate strategy. While it retained sceptical caution about the value of long-term numerical projections, the approach depended on a conscious attempt to define corporate purpose and strategy. Thus, Tarmac displays problems of growth and acquisition, the genesis of change, and the

influence of shifting managerial styles. The relation between the centre
of a business and its divisional components and the ways in which the
influence and authority of individuals at corporate headquarters are
exercised are shown through changing times and changing size and
form of the group.

Watershed of 1958

The sequence of written and spoken discussions with Mr. Martin
could be considered as a commentary on the managerial thinking on
the company which runs parallel to the development of the company
itself. He himself was well aware of this parallel development, and
seems to have regarded what he wrote or recorded as if it were a
set of extracts from a diary of his thoughts as he sat in the company
chair.

In the discussion at Birmingham University in the winter of 1979,
Mr. R.G. Martin described the years after 1958 as a period of change
in the fortunes of Tarmac and one which, in retrospect, seems to
represent a sudden and complete reversal of existing policies. But
in fact, as he says, the perception of a need for change in corporate
policy came about gradually. He recalls that he himself started at
the beginning of the War as a production supervisor and that only
when he had moved higher up the hierarchy did he begin to understand the situation of the company and its problems.

This occurred about 1958, I should think, and then one perceived
that if Tarmac were to survive in the world in the future that it had
to get bigger, otherwise it would be gobbled up by somebody else.
What one thought at the time, (in an entrepreneurial way), was to
diversify the company away from its purely slag business, and to
go to tar and bitumen, and if we were going to get bigger, we had
to go into other sorts of stone. We had, in fact, to go into quarrying.
I think the big development of Tarmac, from about 1958-59
onwards, was perceived to be turning it into a much larger company
— anyway into a company dealing not only with slag, but stones
of all sorts, what we in the trade call 'aggregate'. This meant,
particularly, the enlarging of Tarmac through the purchases of other
people's quarries, by a series of acquisitions. In fact, I can't
remember a case in which we opened up a greenfield site — I think
we were always purchasing other people's. This has been a policy
for a very long time, and it took, or at any rate kept, Tarmac in the

'big league'. If you had the aggregate, if you had control of the stone reserves, you had a very scarce asset which other people had not got and that scarce asset was always scarcer if it happened to be in a scarce place. If you happened to have a quarry near the middle of Birmingham, such as Rowley Regis, then of course it became invaluable indeed. It was simply an acquisitive expansion — purchasing this scarce asset of stone and exploiting it — that got Tarmac into quite big company, because it made quite a lot of money out of stone and quarrying, and that, in fact, still remains its biggest side. So that is the way that the perception arose, that if you did not do this, somebody else would certainly take you over and do it. This method of expansion, putting it in a nutshell, was buying stone, buying assets, which very often were inefficiently managed. Tarmac, in fact, used to get the best of both worlds — it got the stone and it managed what it got rather better. It integrated its purchases into its own sphere, into its own aggregate business, and thereby became more efficient.

In making the shift from slag to stone, management's main concern was for the largest side of the business, which was road building. But even before the change in the source of supply was decided upon in 1958, consideration had been given to expansion into other uses of the materials. Thinking 'went on in one's mind regarding the other side of the business, the other smaller sides of the business', and this thinking had its roots earlier. These other sides of the business were diversifications into construction generally, and these had to be reconsidered at the time of the decision to move into stone — a material which was eminently usable for 'all sorts of building work, not only road building, but all types of things, railway ballast, for example, and concrete aggregate of every sort of description.' But the chief consideration remained road building. Mr. Martin himself entered the firm on the stone and quarrying side of the business, and it was from that standpoint that he viewed the changes which were needed in the late fifties.

The need for a careful reappraisal of corporate policy came on the agenda for discussion by higher management of the company as the result of changes in its management and of simultaneous changes in its market position.

It came to the forefront as a natural break in management. The management break brought the perception that the company had to expand quite rapidly, and I think that this occurred about 1958, when my father retired and the company was split into three. It had been divisionalised, but then it was split into companies, and it was much clearer after that who was doing what. It was much clearer that there was a roadstone side, there was a construction side and there was a vinculum side or a concrete side. I became managing director of the roadstone side — it was the biggest company.

I said that the break was in management but, of course, there was another reason for this break and that was the market. The market began to rise quite rapidly in the late 50s and early 60s, certainly up to about 1967-68, with the motorways. You had an extremely good market in roads in the very late 50s and up to three quarters of the way through the 60s, a better market than you ever had earlier in the 50s. The rather flat growth in the market coincided perhaps with the period of our elderly management, and the break point occurred at that time I think. I suspect that the market was not rising all that highly about 1958, but it certainly began to rise fairly rapidly soon afterwards.

The new, younger management, which took over in the late 1960s, 'perceived' that the company would have to grow. How far was this attitude, this evaluation of the need for expansion by acquisition, (an attitude which was common enough at that time) the result of strict analysis?

I think it is a very interesting question, [was Mr. Martin's reply], and I think that it was just a question, in those days, (and I think that one was fairly unsophisticated about the idea), of a type of empire building. I think the situation was perceived to be such that, if one bought this or that quarry, one would have considerably more power in the market and considerably bigger influence here, there and everywhere. I think the concept of earnings per share came a little later, but certainly by doing what we did we certainly increased earnings per share in those days. In some respects that is what it's all about, or at least what the financial side is all about.

Mr. Martin described the development of the new policies (the strategy for expansion, as it appears in retrospect), as entrepreneurial behaviour. It was not the result of any sophisticated analysis, it was rather off the top of one's head in those days, there wasn't a flow of sophisticated information, there was a flow of information but it was not really very sophisticated . . . We took the market and the opportunity as we found them . . . but there was no particular purpose or planning in Tarmac before 1958 and indeed not much after until 1965 or 1966, when it was beginning to put in corporate planning.

Initially, it seems the entrepreneurial behaviour was unconscious. What the management saw about 1958 was a combination of possibilities. The position of Tarmac, both on the side of supply of resources and the side of demand in the expanding market, combined to put a pressure on the company which the management may not have recognised but to which, nevertheless, they reacted. It was probably necessary to have a change in management.

I think there would have been considerable pressure to do something, yes — something much more than we were doing. I think there were some quite happy coincidences, but I would not like to say that the older management wouldn't have done something about it. My father was quite entrepreneurial in many ways, but he was seventy when he retired and he was cautious. There was no doubt that if there hadn't been a management change, there would have been stresses and strains.

Thirteen years before, in his paper of 1966, Martin had discussed in more detail the changes of the late 1950s:

1958 is thus a watershed as far as Tarmac's directorial organisation was concerned, but it was a watershed managerially also, especially on the Roadstone side. This business had been centrally managed from Wolverhampton in the past. Works managers, sales representatives and garage managers throughout the country had reported to general managers at Wolverhampton. The area representatives were not of high calibre and the general managers had to travel a good deal. The need for decentralising this organisation was becoming urgent . . .

So in 1958 the opportunity was taken to create three geographical Roadstone 'divisions', a movement towards decentralisation which followed the model which one of its recent acquisitions, Tarslag, had already introduced. But the other main department of Tarmac's activity, Civil Engineering, did not follow suit, and 'managerial strains developed.'

It may be helpful, [says the 1966 paper], to contrast the two activities – Roadstone manufacturing and Civil Engineering. Civil Engineering originated from laying roadstone, but it is a very different business. A civil engineering business has to depend almost entirely upon the quality of management for its success or fortune. It has no scarce commodity or raw material to exploit, except its own management. Top management in this profession is likely to be individualistic and may become even a little military in its strict chain of command. This was a fault in those days, because there was no desire to decentralise and the seeming absorption of the acquired company into one centralised organisation was individually highly discouraging.

In later acquisitions and mergers, [the paper goes on], this aspect was to receive considerable attention. It was recognised that individuals have their own horizons and loyalties, these having a close relationship with the conditions under which individuals worked before the acquisitions. To destroy these horizons was to confuse aims and loyalties. If integration had to be carried out in the interests of efficiency, it was best carried out slowly, otherwise efficiency was more likely to be lost for some time. In practice few difficulties have occurred latterly because of these changed policies.

The decentralisation of the Roadstone division which started in 1958 went quickly, and in a year or two the only centralised activities left were the secretarial and accounting departments, but even these activities began to move outwards. It was not until after 1963 that much progress was achieved on the Civil Engineering side. The philosophy of structural change on which Tarmac acted in that time is set out in the words of the 1966 paper:

As a company grows its management structure has to grow and the problem is to prevent the number of people reporting to any one individual increasing beyond a certain level. When this gets too high, it is time to consider further delegation and the creation of new tiers of management. In an expanding company this is a never-ceasing exercise. The company will not expand if the necessary management pyramid is not being constructed at the same time.

Management in the 1960s

The 1966 paper describes the experience of an expanding firm which is growing out of the old style of management based on family connections and is taking up a more professional style.

In companies dominated or managed by family interests it seems often the case that somewhat prudent financial policies usually prevail. These take the form of an abhorrence of bank overdrafts, debentures or other forms of debt finance and go towards cautious capital programmes governed by the amount of money in the bank. That Tarmac's financial policies were somewhat on these lines during earlier years is fairly clear. However, latterly it has been recognised that to spend 'other people's money' within reason is a quicker way to progress. Tarmac have at present a £3 million debenture, and bank borrowings to facilitate expenditure have been the rule in recent years.

Investment in the past was decided upon for somewhat arbitrary reasons, generally because the managing director had a hunch and there was enough money in the bank to back it. If money was insufficient and the hunch was considered a really good one, funds might be raised by the issue of preference shares or a rights issue. If a company is to expand, however, it cannot work in this *ad hoc* way. It has to work out its investment programme scientifically so that it knows what its cash flow is likely to be and then it has to adjust, if necessary, so that it can work within its borrowing limits. It cannot be concerned only with one year but must project its programme over a longer period, such as five years. This must be a rolling programme, and, as one year goes by, another year is added with appropriate modification to the plan. It would be optimistic to say that we have perfected this in Tarmac today, but a start has been made to obtain rolling five-year plans from each group or subsidiary so that they can be blended into an overall plan.

Reviewing in 1979 the changes of the 1960s, Martin says that the corporate planning which was instituted at that time was a facility which had to be devised by the company itself.

It was really a facility which was started by me and it made all the mistakes that everybody made, such as number crunching for five years ahead, which I think was an error that people fall into. You cannot put accurate numbers to something you think you are going to do about five years from now. You can be reasonably precise on the directions and certainly try and be as precise as possible about the numbers, but I think probably only for a year or two on the numbers. That's as far as Tarmac are concerned. I think other companies have some longer horizons in front of them and would be more precise about the numbers further ahead.

The Strategic View

The thoughts which are developed in the interview are in contrast with those of the paper of 1966. Entrepreneurial thinking in the 1950s was centred on the managing director or the chief executive aided, as he wished, by some of his colleagues. He was the unsophisticated but thinking head of a company which was essentially structurally centralised. The changes of the 1960s were to have the effect of spreading entrepreneurial responsibility and of decentralising the structure. The character of entrepreneurship was changed. Investment in the 1950s was, as noted above, 'decided upon for arbitrary reasons, generally because the managing director had a hunch and there was enough money in the bank', but now it was being progressively subjected to strict analysis of investment possibilities and being informed by continuous strategic reviews. The Tarmac papers in succession trace the development of a strategic view of the company over a period of a decade.

The 1966 paper offers thoughts on the method of expansion:

Business can be developed in other ways than geographical expansion, and vertical integration is usually a well-worn path. This path of diversification can be carried out in three principal ways, each of which is linked to the main business as follows:

(a)   Integration towards the customer
(b)   Integration towards the source of raw materials
(c)   Development of by-product based on the original business.

This paper goes on to analyse the ways in which the three types of diversification which lead from vertical integration were achieved in Tarmac.

The 1972 paper turns again to the need to diversify and, taking further the suggestion of the previous paper, it traces 'Tarmac's thought processes which lead to specific consideration in this direction.' The paper asks:

What sort of diversification? The 1966 paper was very much taken up with the way in which Tarmac had developed. There had been a fairly logical sequence of events – doing the same thing in new areas and doing different things allied to the original business, described in the 1966 paper as vertical integration. Vertical integration in many instances was in fact an over-simplification of what occurred. The new business produced products the original business used but a type of diversification known as concentric usually occurred afterwards in the new business, and new markets or new technologies grew from the vertically integrated activity ... Also the apparent faith in vertical integration seems now misplaced ... Unless there are other factors a true vertical integration adds to the main features of the original markets ... However there could still be opportunities for vertical integration and the resulting business may show, through substitution or other factors, a higher growth rate than the parent business. Concentric diversification arising from vertical integration probably offers better growth opportunities.

The paper also discussed the possibilities of the other route to expansion, namely geographical expansion, and decided that this was hardly open to Tarmac any more: 'Doing the same thing in new areas has nearly come to an end in the UK because of the predominant position which Tarmac has in many of its markets. Unless market share can be further increased, the basic market growth must be the main criterion.' But the paper makes two exceptions. One is the construction industry. 'This market is so diverse and enormous and market shares of each competitor so small that there is considerable flexibility to the extent that market shares in many segments can be changed rapidly ... In this respect our present Construction division has been consistently successful since 1963.' The other exception is geographical expansion outside the UK, where the company may possibly improve market share and also participate in the growth rate of the country concerned.

In about 1970, during the period when a wave of interest in the strategy of diversification was affecting much of British industry, Tarmac began to pursue possibilities of diversification more actively for itself. Tarmac's thoughts on unrelated diversification were set out in the 1972 paper:

The principal drawback of expanding the existing business vertically or geographically is that the expansion is liable to assume growth patterns similar to the original business. Even concentric diversification arising from the original businesses is likely to have this drawback. If these growth patterns are unfavourable, it is hard to avoid the conclusion that unrelated diversification may be the only answer.

We are probably all familiar with the arguments against unrelated diversification. It has been called conglomerate diversification and the word 'conglomerate' appears to have an emotive context now. If Tarmac were to attempt it, some rules would have to be followed. The business would have to be acquired, since the knowhow would take too long to get and the growth rate effect would then be very small. The acquired business must be:

(a)   high growth;
(b)   dominant or potentially dominant in its market segments;
(c)   compatible;
(d)   capable of being funded after purchase.

Taking these factors in turn, (a) is fairly obvious. Tarmac would not be looking for a business with lower growth characteristics than its own. Past growth, however, would not be enough and quite a deep examination would be required to assure us that future growth at worthwhile rates is probable.

(b) has to be analysed carefully. It is now quite clear that we have to know a good deal more about the market segment than the growth rate. We have to know, especially, the share of the market each company has in it. A small market share with large competitors would make for a doubtful purchase unless the competitors were 'soft'. Market share brings accumulated experience, and the larger the market share, the greater the experience. This experience is eventually reflected in lower costs. Tarmac should not buy a business which is vulnerable to large and powerful competitors.

(c) is not easy to define. What does Tarmac find compatible? Perhaps it is best to ask the opposite. Certainly Tarmac is not trained in businesses having a high technological content involving R and D. Also consumer businesses which reach the general public do not seem generally in its line, though in the construction and sale of houses Tarmac does reach the public at one point. Probably businesses concerned with the manufacture and distribution of high volume products are suitable, but engineering and manufacturing other than high technological products would appear appropriate.

(d) Ability to fund the acquisition afterwards is important. If the business is high growth, it is unlikely to enjoy a return on assets which will enable it to finance its own investment. Tarmac must find the difference and must avoid investing too heavily in its lower growth businesses, otherwise the necessary funds will not be available. Too large an acquisition must be avoided because subsequent funding of its growth would be difficult. Tarmac's available funds have therefore to be gauged to match the acquisition.

In the following paper, (1975), Tarmac's strategy was summed up as follows:

The strategy therefore became the twin one of seeking to acquire a new compatible busness of sufficient size and growth characteristics which could have a significant influence upon Tarmac's future growth rate, together with disposal of all those businesses whose influence or growth rates were likely to be minimal. These were generally businesses whose market shares were small and dominated by much larger competitors, and the engineering companies were some of them. At the same time the mainstream businesses were developed as far as they could be, commensurate with the high market shares in two of them.

Compatible Diversifications

Central to the characteristics of the acquisitions which Tarmac sought is the idea of 'compatibility'. In the autumn of 1972, Tarmac made a bid for Wolseley-Hughes, in the course of which the motives on which Tarmac acted were expressed in terms of this idea.

Wolseley-Hughes had just the characteristics . . . The main business of Wolseley-Hughes was in the central heating market, where they are both manufacturers and suppliers of oil and gas burners in their own right and specialists builders' merchants for all types of heating equipment. In both business they had a dominating market share and the market was growing rapidly. They also had a number of other businesses in the engineering and agricultural field, the markets of which they also dominated very largely. The growth of Wolseley-Hughes itself showed at the time a 20% increase in profits before tax over a long period. Their earnings per share increase was lower because in order to finance growth, they had had to make recourse to some rights issues. The main business was compatible with that of Tarmac in that it was allied to the construction industry.

Wolseley-Hughes resisted the bid which was dropped when the matter was referred to the Monopolies Commission. But reflecting on the bid in 1979, Martin found no reason to alter his views: 'Wolseley-Hughes thought it was very incompatible, they thought it had nothing to do with Tarmac whatsoever. We thought it was reasonably compatible, it had an affinity towards the building industry and it seemed to us to be something which could come under Tarmac's mantle.'

When again putting forward, in the interview of 1979, the idea that diversification would be 'useful only if it was compatible', he recognised that the idea presented some difficulties.

Compatibility is a rather difficult thing to judge, but I think a compatible business obviously is quarrying as against slag, building houses and building generally as against civil engineering. They are, in fact, step outs. They are diversifications. They don't change everything but they change some factors, and as long as you don't change all the factors and go and open betting shops instead or something like that, so that the whole lot changes, you can probably master the change — or you have a better chance of mastering the change.

The perception of 'what the company wanted to do' became more sophisticated as it grew through acquisitions.

The acquisitions that we achieved brought in a number of different activities which we had never seen before. For example, the takeover of Derbyshire Stone brought in some engineering businesses, Baird and Tatlock, and one or two others, and some of these new businesses were seen to be not much good because they had such a small market share. Unless you put a great deal of energy and resource and money into them, they were going to be overshadowed by some very big brothers, and as it was not your main business anyway, you were not going to have that resource to do it. So it was very clear, in some of these areas, that they should be disposed of, they were not commercially useful. Coming further ahead from there it was perceived in the early 1970s that Tarmac's main business would not supply Tarmac with the necessary growth that it wanted in the future. The thing really that was required was diversification into some other businesses, into compatible businesses of the type which you can understand.

In the interview in 1979, Martin went further towards a definition of the idea of compatibility.

I myself think that the word 'compatible' is perhaps a trap which people possibly fall into — in which we, maybe, could have fallen into. There was an instance, for example, where we bought, not so very long ago, a company called Arnott Young, in steel scrap processing and knocking ships down and getting the scrap out of it and getting rid of it. This sort of business was described as compatible with Tarmac's rather rough and ready methods of banging things about and hauling things around and conveying things and selling things in rather rough markets. In fact, material handling of a rough nature, such as the quarrying and so on, bulk handling, was described as compatible, but it was compatible only perhaps, in that sense. When you have had it a year you realise it is an entirely different kind of individuals managing Arnott Young than a quarry.

The sense in which this diversification was compatible was that the two production processes (of Tarmac and Arnott Young), were similar. The appropriate term here, he said, is that the two processes were 'related'. It is possible to find the managerial skills required for the production process and the technology but yet be short of the managerial skills, experience and expertise in some other area such as marketing or finance or administration. If you had all the necessary skills, there would be no barriers to wider diversification. But if you lacked skills in one area it could be that an acquisition which depended on these skills might lead you to an unreasonable diversion of your efforts.

I think that if you had the managerial and marketing expertise, that would amount to a compatibility. But when I say compatibility is a trap, you have got to look at both sides of the equation. That is, you must be production orientated in your compatibility analysis, and in the case I have been describing in Arnott Young, there was a production orientated compatibility equation, whereas in fact, what people failed to realise was that the marketing was quite incompatible.

Structure and Organisation

From the time in the early 1960s that the company set out on a course of growth by diversification, there were — had to be — changes in the internal management and more thought had to be given to the functions and to the organisation appropriate to each stage of the expansion. Though there were problems, Mr. Martin did not recall that the company encountered 'tremendous difficulties'.

Certainly there had to be a growth in internal staff, there had to be a personnel dimension. There had to be a planning functional dimension. When you are a smaller company your finance side is the one function, the one centralised function, that determines a great deal, but as you get bigger you discover that you have got to have some industrial relations advisers, that you have got to have, certainly, planning people. I think it was in the area of the personnel and planning that changes had to be made and one had to think them out. In a smaller company you don't get that kind of thing. It has to grow with the company, it has to come in with it, and certainly in this case it did. We didn't have to do any planning, then we began to plan.

In the process of this expansion of the functions, the central staff in the head office necessarily grew. 'In the year up to 1958, the head office was a one storey building, then it became two storeys, then it became four storeys, and then after that it diversified outwards and some of the people that were in head office went to the other buildings in Wolverhampton.' The strength of the head office staff grew to about three hundred and fifty, and then, sometime in the late 1970s, it began to be seen as becoming top-heavy, and there was a drastic reversal of the situation. 'I don't think it necessarily needed consultants to tell us, but we did have consultants to tell us, that several of the functions that head office was doing were superfluous and that they could be done in the divisions, or that several of the functions of the divisions were superfluous and should be done in the head office, and that they shouldn't be done twice over and you shouldn't have tier upon tier of functions.'

There was a considerable paring down of the head office staff in 1978 and Mr. Martin, recalling it, thinks that it was done too abruptly. 'It caused a lot of alarm and despondency, and looking back at it now I should have thought that one would have preferred to have saved it a bit.'

He suggested that if one could find a file of organisation charts which recorded the broad changes in the structure of a company in its period of growth, it might offer many points of interest. 'It would tell you a great deal. It could tell you of the growth of functions and it could raise points on the legal functions, the insurance functions, the personnel functions, and then it could lead you to realise that some of these things had to be decentralised again and go into divisions so that it collapses again.'

A main problem which had to be resolved is which functions should be decentralised and, if so, whether some part of them should be retained at the centre. He thought that this problem was bound to arise simply as a consequence of growth.

The difficult point is to know precisely, and you never know, what size your personnel function, shall we say, should be at head office, and what size your personnel function should be in the divisions. Should each division have a personnel manager, a planning manager, a publicity manager? This is a function of size because in the end what happens is that each division does become, tends to become, its own company, having its own personnel and so on. But in the centre there are people who merely administer guidelines or who are saying that we must have some general rules and here they are. This goes for many functions. It does not go for the publicity function – there is a central function there which has to be done by head office – and, of course, the finance function – the main finance function – has to be centralised. But there are several other functions of which the question arises: should they be done at head office or should they be done in the divisions? And as the divisions grow they want to do it themselves and they usually do. The trouble we had for a time was they were being done by both and there were rather too many overheads. [He summed it up by saying] : You have to retain the group financial controls at the very centre, you have to retain group publicity at the very centre, publicity in terms of the group, though each division has its own publicity. You have to retain overall strategic planning at the centre, but the rest, legal, perhaps, insurance, a great many other services can all be devolved if necessary.

Was there a danger that the divisions, growing in size and becoming largely autonomous except for strategic and financial planning, could go into conflict with the centre or between themselves? Were there conflicts of objectives between divisions, and if so, how were they resolved?

If you divisionalise successfully, that is to say that your divisions are doing something entirely different, then you do not have to worry about conflict except insofar as resources are concerned, insofar as there is competition for scarce resources. But if your company has grown, not as a conglomerate but as a related series of divisions, it is inevitable that some divisions will use the products or services of other divisions and in those sort of cases conflict can very often arise and does arise because one company of the group thinks that, in order to get an advantage over its competitors, it should be offered a lower price from another company of the group who supplies its commodity. That is to say that it wants subsidising in order to obtain work. It feels that it wants an edge and this is the way it gets the edge. The particular conflict that used to afflict Tarmac was the one between the construction side and the road-stone side, where if construction was tendering for a road job, it always wanted to get special treatment from the roadstone side from the point of view of asphalt laying and/or the supply of aggregates or whatever. This would not necessarily suit the roadstone side who, from their own point of view, might be able to sell their aggregates or asphalts to somebody else or some other contractor at a better price. It could happen, although Tarmac Civil Engineering Limited got advantageous prices from the Roadstone division, it did not get the road job, so it could mean that Tarmac Roadstone was deprived of supplying, at a better price, somebody else who actually got the job. Certainly there was conflict in that area — a very difficult one to resolve as a matter of fact, and I do not think it ever did get resolved. The point was made that whatever the roadstone companies supplied, or the services involved were, it only amounted to about 10% of the whole tender, and even if that were advantageously put forward, it would only make perhaps a very small difference to the price, but each division should attempt to be reasonably free to deal with each other at arm's length. Nevertheless, the feeling on the construction side was always: I want to get the best I possibly can from one of our companies in the group and they ought to favour me. And the other would say: If we favour you we may do ourselves some damage or we may not be able to sell to anybody if you don't get this job.

This was one of those problems which head office was strangely unable to resolve and the reason for that may have been that the conflicting parties did not want a resolution.

It was something to which in fact I never did get the precise answer, I think one must plead possibly being too busy but it did need an answer. One of the curious reasons was that it very rarely got up to higher authority, that people didn't like to bring it up. They thought they could settle it lower down, they didn't want the chairman or somebody else being brought in and they disliked somebody from head office being brought in as an arbiter of the problem. There was a great reluctance to bring the thing out and to have it settled and they almost would have preferred to have the thing festering along and disagreeing with each other rather than have the thing settled by head office.

The other sort of conflict which could arise, that is to say, conflict between divisions for resources of the group, gave little trouble.

They may not have been happy with the resolution, but if it was explained to them and so on and so forth, that was that. The system was such that decisions about allocations had to be made. They might not have been happy about it, at least those who didn't get what they wanted, but there we are, it had to be made. There was machinery to deal with it, but there was no machinery that really seemed to work that dealt with the other one (subsidy pricing).

Even so, there was, over the period of expansion, a change in the character of control from the top. It became less easy to define or locate precisely where the decisions were made because the decisions were the consequence of the information and data which were presented. In time the collection and passage of the greater quantity of data which was coming through became an influential factor in the decision process. In the early days of the expansion – the late 1950s and the 1960s – decision-making was a shared responsibility but with the final word clearly coming from the top.

> The company was divided into subsidiaries in those days and each had a board meeting and people discussed at the board meetings certain things which they wanted. But the ultimate decisions on what we should acquire, this or that or the other, tended I think certainly to rest with me in the final analysis, although of course in the final analysis it rested with the board. But if I thought that something required to be done and should be done or should be bought, then it usually was. There was a certain amount of bottom-up ideas coming up and indeed, as the company got bigger and bigger, I became less and less immersed in the detail and away from it. In Tarmac itself, and in the subsidiary companies when they became larger, there was much more information coming up from the bottom as to what they themselves wanted and what they wanted to do – often more than what I felt I wanted them to do. In fact, as the company got bigger it was their ideas and not mine which tended to occur in the 1970s or the later 1970s.

One organisational problem which Tarmac found troublesome was to find the structure best suited to the company's international ventures.

> If the roadstone market is widened to countries outside the UK, a different situation does arise. Tarmac may well have saturated the UK market but in Germany, for instance, where it has a small market share in asphalt and coated macadam operations, it may be possible to improve its share and also participate in the growth rate of the country concerned. In theory, this will be a continuation of the UK expansion but on a European or even world scale.

When in the early 1960s, Tarmac started to expand internationally, in Germany, France and South Africa, it experimented structurally with international divisions, but it experienced problems of finance in addition to the 'usual difficulties of language, customs and management', and by 1970, Tarmac had come to the view that the organisational problems of overseas business are not best solved in that form:

> The bad showing of many of the overseas businesses gave rise to the feeling that the activity abroad should not be launched unless it was part of the division in the UK carrying out the same function. Partly the cause of the South African and French difficulties was the original structure which made overseas activities divisions in their own right. This might be correct for mature businesses but the idea was evidently wrong for those in their infancy. One original difficulty was that the UK division which should have had the responsibility for the particular overseas operation was reluctant to part with good staff to manage it. Having eventually the responsibility, the management then had to be found.

Strategy and Structure

Mr. Martin was asked whether he could recognise a direct relationship between the organisational changes and the changes in strategy which had come about after 1958. How far were the structural forms which had been devised, consciously intended to implement the strategy which had started from the management break and the market break of about 1958 and which became the strategy of expansion by acquisition and diversification?

> The questions you have to ask yourself are where am I going, how do I get there? Those are the primary questions that you have to ask yourself but you are not going to get very far or get as far as you want without having a planning department. You are not going to get very far in relations with the city stockbroker, for instance, unless you start taking up publicity on a much more structured basis. The same goes for personnel. As a company gets larger it gets more complicated. You have got to look after more people, and unless we have departments looking after people, with relations with the outside world, relations internally, the planning of where you think you are going and so on, you do not grow, you remain as a small company. The strategic direction of Tarmac — the general strategy — was, I think, correct, but you cannot carry out a general strategy unless you have the people to go with it and unless you have

the organisation to go with it.

In response to a question on the converse relationship — whether a new structure when established partly determines the subsequent strategy — Mr. Martin gave a qualified answer. 'I think the answer to that is it didn't determine the strategy that followed but it certainly determined the ideas.' The modification of the organisational form to suit the needs of the expanded company affected the channels of information, the information itself, and the ways in which ideas were presented. All this had an effect on the way the decisions were reached, so it had its effect on strategic thinking. 'It certainly determined what information came up. Put simply, I think the difference between the thing is that in the 60s I would think on a quarry to acquire, which I happened to know about or whose owner I happened to know or something, and I would do that. In the 70s, I probably would not know who to acquire any more but a lot of people underneath would and they would be dealing with it.'

Is it the case, as this example may imply, that as the organisation grows, control from the top — real control — is reduced? Or is that going too far? Mr. Martin said that this danger is present unless the organisational machinery is continually adapted to meet the problems as they arise. 'It does reduce the knowledge of the business in terms of the top people. Certainly Tarmac lost its way on the construction side and it was allowed to make decisions and do things which were dangerous and shouldn't have happened. There is a constant problem as you grow that you do lose control unless you keep on reviewing your formal machinery.'

He went on to cite a case in which control from the top was extremely difficult, because there was considerable difficulty in getting the organisational machinery to change.

I think it was especially difficult on the civil engineering side and especially overseas civil engineering. The problem was who made the decision and at what point? For example, to go into a £100 million contract to go into Saudi Arabia, at what point did you actually say, I agree to do this and on who does it? The argument, of course, is that it's a very difficult thing for top management to keep their finger on because the conditions for going into that £100 million contract are going to change as negotiations change. Top management are not in charge of that negotiation but they know if somebody makes a slip on it or something like that, that

£100 million contract will go very sour indeed and bring a great deal of loss to the group. So that it's very difficult for top management to keep a finger on something like that.

Policy at the Top

R.G. Martin became chairman and chief executive of Tarmac Limited in 1971 and relinquished that appointment in 1979. This period and the period just before, when he had been managing director was, as has been seen, a time of general expansion in the company. The Construction division and the Roadstone division expanded greatly in the 1970s, and this expansion brought in new businesses like the Building Products division.

Mr. Martin was able to shed light on the problems of choosing and balancing a team of top management, able to cope with the problems of the company in its new size. 'I was chairman and chief executive, which some people say is not a very good thing to be, though I think at certain times and at a certain age it possibly fits. But I felt myself that I would rather revert to being an executive chairman and have a managing director as soon as convenient. The question is, who should be the managing director? '

Thoughts on these lines were partly influenced by one or two business setbacks in this period. A venture by Roadstone into Germany was a failure and a venture into Nigeria even more so, and it could not be certain how far responsibility for these failures should be attributed to the centre and how far to the divisions. Clearly the relations between the head office and the divisions, and the degree of control, required examination. Mr. Martin accelerated the talks on control and on the reform of the top organisation and brought in McKinsey & Co. as consultants.

We asked the question what is the role of the centre, what is it doing? Really at the back of my mind was the intention to avoid disasters again such as Nigeria, because clearly the centre was culpable on that one. It shouldn't have happened, the thing should have been looked at a great deal more carefully, but it happened. Anyway, we went through the exercise with McKinsey and I think they were very useful in many ways. They said we needed a new finance director and a new planning director. I still wanted a managing director, to which they said: 'You get your finance

director and your new planning director' [leaving the further decision until that had been done] .

He went on to say, however, that 'looking back at it now, they
obviously did not carry – they might have carried me – they obviously
didn't carry some other members of the board with them. If you bring
in new people into a company, (and we did), and talk about future
managing directors, the people whom you have will not necessarily
share the McKinsey view.'

Quite soon Tarmac began to recover from the Nigerian debacle, the
company appointed a new finance director and a new planning director
and its position improved. But the measures which were brought in by
the chief executive, and particularly the changes in responsibilities
which they required, did not carry the confidence of all the members,
and especially the executive members, of the board. In his account of
those changes in the position at the top, the importance of inter-
personal relationships, and the difficulties of achieving a balance, Mr.
Martin comments on the circumstances which led to his decision to
relinquish his appointment.

'A lot of controls were tightened up, especially on overseas contracting and so on, and yet the people who were there, the top people,
began to feel very uncertain . . . . . that was very clear.' The position
he had been taking up led to the reaction among a number of his
colleagues in April 1979, that he should go. 'It is not much good if
you have not got the confidence of the executive directors and so
I departed.'

Martin distinguishes, in the light of his experience, between what
he thinks of as 'a good job in improving the controls of the company,
financial controls etc.', and the uncertainty which, unfortunately, was
generated among some of the top management people.

'I did not know the way they felt – that is to say the top management – nor did the other directors, the non-executive directors, and
it was a considerable surprise to discover it rather belatedly.'

As Mr. Martin saw things at the time of the discussion, the company
was, in his words, 'on a fairly good tack. They have had the benefit
of McKinsey's advice,' and some of the people who had felt the
uncertainty to which he had referred 'have positions with which they
are satisfied and probably getting better job satisfaction out of it with
the new managing director.'

He did not think that the crisis of confidence was on the matter of
the general handling of the company's business. Certainly there were

doubts about the type of diversification pursued in the 1970s — particularly the channelling of resources into construction overseas. But the crisis was not due to a disagreement on the general strategy or a loss of morale arising from that. He thought, looking back at these events, that as chairman and chief executive — 'the boss who runs everything . . . .' — he might have relied too much on discussions with too few people. He made an observation on the position of the chairman in relation to this:

It depends on what sort of chairman he is. If he is a non-executive chairman, he is merely a presider, a tentative presider at board meetings and a sounding board. He can influence things but he does not necessarily enter into the burden and the heat of the day. If he is an executive chairman or managing director, which I think quite a number of chairmen are, he does enter into the burden and the heat of the day a bit, but of course the managing director does rather more. If he is what he was with me, chairman and chief executive, he runs the show still. As such I was too encouraged to make decisions having discussed the matter with too few people. One had discussed the matter with McKinsey and worked it out rather logically, then one had discussed it with one or two directors and one or two non-executives, but did not discuss some of the things with the directors as a whole.

That, he thought, had not been liked. Martin referred to 'the crux of my departure,' locating it in disagreement of most of the executive directors over the managing directorship of international division. But from the point of view of the wider analysis here, the chain of events suggests interesting points about balance and the functions of the most senior management in an enterprise.

The Idea of Strategy

The development of Tarmac over the whole of Mr. Martin's period as chief executive had been governed by a sense of corporate strategy and planning. There may be reservations about the extent to which a corporate plan was consistently pursued: thus, for example, the unsuccessful attempt to acquire Wolseley-Hughes might be seen, perhaps, as more a search for a growth opportunity than an acquisition which met the criterion of 'compatibility' which Mr. Martin had emphasised. Nevertheless, the central direction of the company was imbued with an intellectual sense of corporate strategy and design.

In 1983, in an extended discussion on recent years in the business, Mr. Eric Pountain, at that time deputy chairman and chief executive, Mr. Bryan Baker, the assistant managing director, and Mr. Graham Odgers, group finance director, gave their views on the formation of strategy in Tarmac. These three men, based at group headquarters in Ettingshall near Wolverhampton, are the executive core of the company (the chairman then being part-time and the term chief executive the equivalent of managing director).[1] Pountain came in initially when he brought his own company into the group: Baker had been with Tarmac for many years: Odgers had come from GEC four years previously.

Changing circumstances, different personalities and managerial styles frequently go together and without necessarily implying that a past approach was inappropriate, generate the opportunity for a change in outlook and direction. This part of the study afforded the prospect of a dialogue which was both a postscript to one era in the style of the company and a signpost to its subsequent outlook. In terms of perception of the company there was much in common with the past. As Pountain expressed it when asked how he envisaged Tarmac:

> . . we're basically a building materials group, that's what we see ourselves as; and of course then, we go on and additionally we're

a construction group, we have these quite separate; we're a house-building group and we've got an international flavour to the group. [Baker reinforced this view when he added that he saw the company also as] an owner and acquirer of mineral resources and an exploiter of those into primary building products associated with aggregate and their end uses, on certainly a national scale and slowly maybe more for the future, on an international scale.

The sense of a corporate identity is no transient matter: as Pountain put it, 'we see our quarrying division as being the sheet anchor of the group and I can't see . . . that in the foreseeable future that will really change. The basic balance of the business will be heavily on to the building, the aggregate side of our business.' Balance and continuity, understood parameters of action, are as clear in this approach as with Adrian Cadbury and his emphasis on balance and organisational commitment. There is a reminiscent reference to Mr. Martin's emphasis on compatibility when Odgers remarks that 'the concept of diversification doesn't really appeal to us in itself but the idea of building on to our existing strengths, our existing businesses, means that there could be a broader range of products, a broader range of activities in the longer term.'

But how is this interpreted in terms of the formation of strategy? It was here that the philosophy of the present executives was made quite explicit and reflected a disenchantment with the concept of 'grand strategy designs'. Pountain, commenting on the earlier attitude of the company, said 'we never by a mile, hit our five year plans. . . people extrapolated the numbers but we were miles out and then I think the centre lost some credibility . . .'. This is in part a kind of conventional scepticism about numbers and the risks attached to being wedded to a spurious precision: in part it reflects a determined pragmatism in response to the unknowability of the future. Such an attitude is by no means simplistic: as Odgers puts it, since nobody can foretell the future and the longer ahead the more that is so, 'what you must make sure is that each one of your operating businesses is the best it can possibly be.' By analogy with an athlete, a company needs to be 'in prime condition': in those circumstances it will have the resources and the credibility (an important word to the Tarmac men) to produce good ongoing results, can tackle the problems thrown at it, and is 'in a position to seize the opportunities.'

Thus strategy for Tarmac as it is perceived by the present executive heads of the firm is not designed as a long-term rolling forward plan.

In colloquial terms Odgers expressed scepticism about written planning documents when he said that 'if you say, let's look at the peaks, five years, ten years ahead, and that's your concentration, you lose sight of where your feet are going in the potholes just around you.' But, continuing the analogy of the athlete, 'if . . . you're really in fine condition, surely you'll be seeing those peaks over there as possible opportunities but you'll also see your way, how to get through the mire just immediately ahead and if you're moving better and faster than your competitors it's amazing how many more opportunities open themselves up . . .'. The peaks are there, albeit changing ones, but they are attained through effective competition and adaptation in the present. Forward strategy is a matter of being ahead of the market as far as the operating divisions are concerned.

Being ahead of the market is, however, a matter of persistent monitoring of trends and of control at the centre: formation of strategy is an ongoing rather than either a spasmodic activity or centrally planned process. Mr. Pountain gave two specific related examples when he said, firstly, that Tarmac monitored their sales on a week by week basis and 'you do suddenly think to yourself, well, our sales are not going as quickly as some of our competitors.' He went on to say that

> Barratt who was quite small at one time, now the largest producer by a mile, and you've seen a company like Wimpey's who had the key spot were building 13-14,000 houses five years ago, now building only 7,000. So you can see that Laurie Barratt has taken his market — he hasn't taken ours because we've kept our momentum up. But there you've got a good situation where they've said 'Laurie Barratt's going to fall on his face, it isn't right to put carpets in, it isn't right to do television advertising, he's going to fail', and in fact all the time Rome was burning, they were fiddling as it were, not being too concerned and suddenly, hey presto, he's got twice as much market share than they had and obviously they didn't react quickly enough to the market conditions. We would have done . . . .

Secondly, when Odgers pointed out that the Housing division would be constantly on to how developments were going, for instance in relation to timber-framed houses, Pountain intervened to say that 'there we did take a view outside most of our major competitors: we didn't go over to timber frame . . . we did do timber frame within the company, then we got caught out a bit. You know most of our timber for houses is imported and we got caught out by timber rocketing . . . .' Even there, the company gained some relevant knowledge which helped to keep construction time relatively good.

The approach to strategy expressed in these statements is thus a blend of attitudes which are more fully explored elsewhere in this study. It does not abjure the long-run: in the Quarry division, for example, Tarmac has in the nature of things to look some twenty years ahead. But it sees strategic progress within a framework of competition as rivalry: opportunities arise and are perceived in the process of competitive activity: the firm looks ahead but does not devise a strategic grand master-plan. On the one hand, as Baker put it, 'most of the decisions we take have a futurity of anything up to twenty-five years . . . . Every quarry we open . . . it's going to be there and the decision that led to it is a decision in the futurity of the event we're taking now.' On the other hand, Pountain emphasised that 'strategy is something that develops . . . . We don't put it down . . . no, it isn't so formalised.'

One point which was emphasised was that strategy depends on opportunities: excessive addiction to the reverse view would be regarded as a dangerous restriction. For instance, Quarry Products division had for a long time been 'stalking' Hoveringham but had been unable to acquire it because it was family-controlled and the family was unwilling to sell. When it suddenly became available the decision became a real one: did Tarmac genuinely want to make the acquisition? It did and hence it took the opportunity: 'suddenly there is an opportunity' Mr. Odgers said, 'and Tarmac is a different group now with Hoveringham, than what it was before Hoveringham.' This may seem a curiously reactive stance for a company which has grown substantially in recent years (to a £1,000 million turnover), very unlike Ansoff's entrepreneurial enterprise. None of the three Tarmac executives, however, would interpret their behaviour in that way. They see Tarmac, rather, as persistently monitoring market trends, acquiring and considering normal market intelligence, looking at companies of which there are always some in which Tarmac is quite interested, and being alert to opportunities when they are truly feasible.

What Pountain, Baker and Odgers all perceive as critical, therefore, is not the formulation of an overall corporate plan but adherence to a distinctive, deliberate management style.

It's wrong for the centre [according to Odgers], to have ideas about what it can do, which are inappropriate to it or to its particular type of business: we try and restrict absolutely to the minimum those things which we can do and do properly. We keep these very tight controls on all the essentials but we don't take the view that we really know how the operating divisions can develop their own business in detail.

One consequence of this view, which all three (including Pountain) ascribe to him, is that the total central staff of Tarmac is just under a hundred. That includes everybody — accounts, treasury, taxation, secretarial, pensions, chauffeurs, and is, they say, much smaller a centre than the rest of the construction industry. This number compares with over 300, perhaps 350 or more, at about the time that Mr. Robin Martin left the company and was clearly related in their minds, to their philosophy of management and their concept of the role of the centre. Mr. Pountain had run the public company which he brought into Tarmac in the same way so that for him the thread ran back a long way: Mr. Baker thought along the same lines, Mr. Odgers had come from GEC which had something of the same style. This feature of like-mindedness and propinquity at headquarters was clearly regarded as important. Even in a large and dispersed enterprise, with the appurtenances of governance which have been emphasised in this study, it would be misleading to underrate the critical influence of the executive core and of the informal contact and discussion which take place between men working in neighbouring offices.

Is strategy conceived in the framework of clear and unambiguous objectives? Mr. Martin thought in terms of multiple objectives but he took as a central objective, as a kind of acid test, the idea of maximising earnings per share. This was something to which at first hearing, Mr. Baker instinctively responded with consent but which was extended by Mr. Odgers in this way:

we see the absolute level of profits as being something that is very important to the three of us, and indeed to people throughout the group. You know, we're a £50mn. company and we want to become a £100mn. company so growth is very much an objective; no question about that. But we particularly at the centre, say that it must not be at the expense of the growth in earnings per share and then the dividends per share that count above everything else.

But Mr. Pountain added that 'there's a lot of pride in being, which we are now, the biggest construction materials group in the UK.'

This hint of an anthropomorphic view of Tarmac is made more explicit in the idea that the group is more than the shareholders, (largely the institutions), important though they are. It includes them but as Odgers said 'it's the activities, it's the individuals'. The three executives are themselves all shareholders, the chief executive with a very large holding: this adds to their sense of personal identification and there is also a certain pride in the name of Tarmac.

The Strategic Flow within the Company

The idea of strategy as an ongoing activity is intimately associated with the explicit philosophy of management and hence with the relationship between the centre and the operating divisions. This relationship forms a main theme of the first part of the study and it merits equal attention in Tarmac particularly in the light of the centre's insistence that 'centrally we don't have any grand strategies; we don't think . . . that we can see more than the people at the sharp end of the business see.'

Mr. Pountain's reply to a question about the general strategy of the group and the role of the board suggested that he envisaged a mixture of a number of elements. One was the absolutely crucial role of the core executive, 'the three of us at the centre': a second was the close relationship between himself as group chief executive and the divisional chief executives of the seven divisions which Tarmac run. It is essential that this be based on mutual trust (an echo of the Meaney/Yardley terminology) with 'the very strong commitment to a budget, to a strategy, which we endorse at the centre' for 'a lot of these things are sponsored from the division to the centre, so you've really got a bit of a bottom up rather than a top down'. A third element is that the businesses are independently managed but there is a tight rein of control: indeed, all three executives were explicit about the combination of autonomy with firm control from the centre based on a regular supply of very detailed information and of regular, rigorous monthly meetings of each divisional board with the three group executives. Thus, although the use of the word 'endorse' was emphasised because each of Tarmac's divisions is seen as a major business in its own right, there is clearly a continuing dialogue between the centre and the divisions which not only ensures that the strategy generated within a decentralised system cannot be implemented arbitrarily, but also develops a context of shared experience, perception and outlook.

Baker put this last point very distinctly when he said:

> We haven't got a pre-set thing that says let's put 25% of our invest-
> ment over the next three years into the States, i.e. that Tillings
> are reported to have said some time ago — I'm not commenting
> whether it's good or bad. We don't do things like that but each
> division . . . through the framework of the control mechanism or
> one part of it, the regular rigorous monthly meeting, one develops
> with each division a series of things that they know are ones that
> we should share in terms of aspiration, theirs and ours.

And while it is evident that the edifice rests on the strength and cohesiveness of the small central core and its pervasive presence in the divisional boards, it would be a facile cynicism to underestimate the genuine importance which the executive attributes to divisional autonomy. Odgers gives a formidable instance of this in respect of the major issue of acquisition in a lengthy statement which follows the comment on the role of the centre as an endorser of strategy.

> . . . if we at the centre tell a particular division that they ought to
> go for a particular acquisition, it causes all kinds of problems in
> control in the longer term in the sense that if people are told what
> to do, the baby is not their baby, it's our baby. How do you then
> get the commitment to the operation of that particular acquisition,
> to the achievement of the particular targets or criteria, financial
> criteria, that have been set? But if, on the other hand, you have a
> division like Quarry Products, say you want to acquire Hoveringham,
> and they put forward the proposals to us at the centre saying 'this
> is what we want to do, this is what we think we ought to pay for
> it, these are the kinds of levels of profit achievement that we reckon
> we can get in years one, two or three'. And they come to us, one,
> with a very strong record of achievement themselves so that there's
> a high level of credibility, and secondly, with a set of criteria which
> to us seems a reasonable return on investment, a reasonable payback
> period. And thirdly, there's this tremendous commitment . . . this
> is what they want to do and if we turn it down it'd be terrible.

Ultimately, moreover, 'you've got the control from the centre:' thus, if things go ill, it is clear who is sponsoring the scheme, if they go well the division has the achievement. 'If we have sponsored it from the centre and told them this is what they must do, then if the thing goes wrong, well they say, you forced this on us.'

This is a matter of general philosophy rather than a commentary on specific examples although it appears to have been influenced by a reaction against what were seen as some unsatisfactory decisions in the past. That philosophy sees the centre, standing for the group as a whole, as the banker, and like a good central banker, 'we've got control of the cash' as Pountain put it, 'and as far as we're concerned, that normally follows the credibility of the management and the performance of the management.' In other words, this philosophy of divisional autonomy and initiative is tempered by the judgement of an executive core which forms a view of the capacity of divisions to carry out projects. For as Pountain went on to say, 'in some instances somebody might come forward with a very good proposal that one could approve, but then we might be slightly unsure that was too big for that particular management or maybe that's where we didn't really want to invest any of our money.'

There are two streams in this presentation of Tarmac's position on the flow of ideas within the company in the formation of strategy. The emphasis on 'bottom-up' is clear since the centre holds that the divisions know best how to operate their businesses. At the same time, however, the centre believes in a tight control once it has defined what it regards as essential for that purpose. Its control is both formal and informal, based, as already noted, on closely-monitored performance of divisions expressed in detailed reporting and regular meetings and on a judgemental element of assessment of management capabilities. It is not a function of cash limitations: 'We've never had a situation' according to Odgers, 'where there is, in a sense, a competition for limited cash resources between the operating divisions.' Whereas this might have been happening at the beginning, i.e. when the present centre group had acquired responsibility, it did not do so now. For 'it is our duty at the centre to make sure that the cash is available for legitimate projects if we want to go ahead.' Inadequacy in cash resources will not happen if 'we ensure that the ongoing performance of the group is good.'

In these phrases the executives at the heart of Tarmac express what they see as their critical responsibility — the overall performance of the group and the provision of cash for development. The purse strings will be opened if the centre is satisfied as to the legitimacy of projects in terms of market direction and returns, underpinned by the centre's own judgement *that the particular management is capable of handling the task.* That judgement is no trifling matter since ultimately it can lead to the removal of the managing director of a division. One feature which emerges as much in Tarmac with its £ one billion sales and the very much smaller company Manganese Bronze is the extent to which a few individuals seek to maintain control by personal presence, by seeing and being seen. John Neville emphasised this point and it was borne out by Mr. Poore. Tarmac see it partly as a question of personal knowledge and contact and not (annual audit apart) according to Odgers through 'an internal audit operation which extensively goes into the operating divisions and checks on what they're doing: we expect the managements of those divisions to be highly professional in their own right' and capable, therefore, of providing top-rate financial information. But the centre, specifically Eric Pountain, will be well-informed on key variables in each of the key businesses within the group, such as housing starts, average price of the houses Tarmac and competitors are building, and so on. And then there is the fundamental control that the managing director in each division is appointed by the centre. The key people in the group – the heads of the operating divisions and the one or two levels below them – come within the purview of the chief executive of Tarmac and the centre approves promotions within that senior management. It is this element of control which is crucial: this is the mechanism at the apex of the pyramid.

Odgers elaborated the story in this way:

> It's an odd thing, in a way it's a light touch . . . but, on the other hand, people would regard the Tarmac group as being one of the most tightly controlled groups, managerially speaking, in the country. And it's right, it is very tightly controlled, but the control mechanisms are in terms of relationships and personal commitments, and standards of performance and monitoring that goes on.

All three executives clearly believe the management style to be related to their personalities and particularly to Pountain and the way he managed his earlier company: they are convinced that it is well-accepted and liked within Tarmac as a whole: they see it as depending on trust with the ultimate sanction of the central control. Lastly, they consider it as related to their kind of business: the requirement for autonomy stems from diversity: as Odgers said, '. . . Tarmac . . . is a highly diversified operation' even though it is within construction, so that the centre cannot 'make those detailed decisions or would want to, but within individual operating divisions the thing is going to change dramatically from one kind of business to another.'

These views are part and parcel of the attitude towards the idea of comprehensive corporate strategy (a corporate planning staff numbering only two) and detailed quantitative plans. When Baker said that 'The easiest thing you can have in big companies is to confuse everything' he was expressing what all three wish to express as, so to speak, their brand of conventional wisdom. Hence, paradoxically, Mr. Odgers with his experience of the Harvard Business School felt constrained to put 'the latest techniques from the business schools' into a relatively limited perspective since 'when it comes down to it we'll say, who is sponsoring this project, what does the project look like in relation to that sponsor, what do the returns look like in terms of the profitability and cash flow over the next few years? How quickly are we going to get our money back and how committed is the management?'

Once again the discussion with the executive centre of the group illustrates the combination of organisational processes and powerful individuals which leads to choices of courses of action in a large enterprise. In Tarmac there are three men at headquarters who try to ensure that the movement of the group is within certain defined boundaries: they are the custodians of the direction of the enterprise. Quis custodiet custodies? The board is there to monitor the performance of the central executives: 'there are issues, and certainly acquisitions go to the main board over a certain size, and it has to have their thumb print ... '. In the last resort, the board is sovereign with the role of the non-executive directors 'there to sack the chief executives' if so gloomy a situation should ever arise. But so long as the executives get it right, they can continue largely untrammelled by constraints. In this respect, the three senior executives spoke less in terms of a constitutional structure than some of their counterparts in other firms studied here. They operate, nevertheless, within the framework of an organisation: given the tight control mechanisms and the important part played by managerial commitment, the concept of divisional autonomy as the source of ideas and development projects was made quite explicit.

A Note on the Reverse Process

This discussion of Tarmac, in common with other studies of divisionally-organised firms, has considered the formation of strategy primarily in terms of the attitude of the central system towards the constituent members of the group. There is, of course, the reverse question: what do the divisions get out of being part of the group over and above what they would have if they were businesses wholly on their own? Odgers responded to this question by citing the instance of the small property division, employing only 28 people and the example though not unusual, indeed a copybook case, is interesting for its very specificity. What this division does

> is not to invest in property but to put property deals together and that means they find a piece of land or property that's going on the market, they find somebody who wants an office or a factory, they find somebody who wants to build a factory . . . They find an institution or a pension fund that wants to fund it. And you've got all these things put together before you commit yourself to any financial money at all. The result is that these . . . people produce returns on capital of anything up to 50 and 100%.

Why then do they not abandon Tarmac and go off and do it themselves? Because, he says, 'Tarmac gives them a credibility; the people they're dealing with know that Tarmac is a fine performer . . . And the same is true of our Construction division. People know the strength that we've now got so it all flows.'

Pountain underlined the advantage of group strength from another point of view when he claimed as one of its important functions, that of 'talking to our institutional shareholders and talking to the brokers, and to give them a better understanding.' In the mid-1970s the company had made some bad decisions and was very reluctant to talk to anybody from outside: this, he said had now very much changed.

It would be a heroic argument to say that the backing of a group is an essential condition for every one of the developments which Tarmac has undertaken but there is a case for arguing that certain strategies only become feasible for the subsidiary units because of their membership of the group. It need not be synergy in Ansoff's sense: nor is it only the traditional benefits of bulk purchase, massed financial resources, and so on. It is that managerial perceptions may be stimulated because of the freedom given by the knowledge of Tarmac backing and because energies can be directed to tasks without the distraction of seeking for resources.

The concept of a group style is clearly of particular importance when there is an acquisition. Asked what steps are taken in those circumstances to build the acquired company into the Tarmac style, Pountain replied: 'Well, that's immediate. That's almost a prerequisite.' Odgers cited the Hoveringham business which, 'within a matter of months . . . was completely integrated into our Quarry Products division and the results started coming through almost immediately.' In practical terms, Baker underlined this when he said: 'With the standards required, you must see stuff in a consistent form. You can't look at one form, a set of presentation of data in one hand in one week from a profit centre and see different from another, it just doesn't work. You'd never synthesise and distil it if that were the case.'

A Note on Incrementalism and International Investment

It has been seen that the executives at Ettingshall eschew the notion of a grand corporate design although they have an image of corporate development as a whole. The small centre of the company is powerful but the management process is a symbiosis of offering and demanding managerial commitment from the senior levels of the divisions. The pattern was interestingly exemplified in reply to a question about Tarmac's investment overseas, where to the usual uncertainties of business policy are added differences of custom, managerial style, and other factors. '. . . . As a generalisation' Mr. Odgers remarked '. . . a number of companies in the U.K. in the past, and this has included Tarmac . . . have felt that the grass has been greener on the other side of the fence and have been prepared to take risks and go in on a scale.' Indeed, Mr. Pountain added, he was astounded by the willingness of people to 'do things overseas that they'd never do at home, in terms of taking on contracts, buying businesses and all the rest of it.'

Tarmac's approach, according to the three senior executives, is cautious and conservative. Just as with Sir Adrian Cadbury, there is a feeling about the balance of business, the feeling that the present 15-20% of Tarmac turnover being overseas is reasonably satisfactory: similarly that not all seven divisions can take off at once but that there will be a balance of ups and downs. What, however, the group will not do is to be wedded to the percentage and to say, in Odger's words, that 'because our percentage share of overseas is such and such at the moment and that we feel this may be a little on the low side, therefore we're going to go for a very big acquisition in the United States.' Tarmac's method in their investment in the United States was in fact of the 'toe in the water variety' reinforced by sticking to their business philosophy and dealing with like-minded people.

Baker emphasised that all three of them felt that they would move further in the United States, particularly in lines of aggregate, concrete or black, and this was something he described as intuitive. But it is not a question of anybody saying 'it's about time you started getting cracking in the States'. It would be a 'stage by stage approach to further investment there' in a climate in which any division wishing to move in that direction would be aware that the company climate was sympathetic if the project was promising and, once again, the sense of commitment was strong.

Tarmac has an international contracting division and, according to Mr. Pountain, after a period in which there has not been great success, is now in a position in which the company does not feel compelled to do overseas contracting but will do so if the terms are right. The right terms have to be 'slightly better than we'd get a job in the U.K.' In this area as throughout Tarmac as the core executive conceive the process, there is an interplay between the centre and the divisions. Thus, the big investments overseas have been in Quarry Products division: the ideas may very well have come from the operating divisions, but the centre will determine whether or not the moment is ripe. This was so in the case of Quarry Products division, for example, when in the case of a particular proposal for a very substantial investment in the United States, the centre doubted that the time was apt 'in terms of their (the division's) own credibility abroad, in terms of the risks involved in this particular situation.'

Notes

1. As already briefly noted, Mr. Pountain subsequently became (full-time) chairman of the company: he does not now use the title chief executive. Mr. Baker, Mr. Odgers, (and Mr. Kettle), became group managing directors.

11 CONCEPT AND FORMULATION OF STRATEGY: A SUMMING-UP

Introduction

Part One of this book was concerned with problems of managerial initiative and control, with managerial discretion and the diffusion of entrepreneurship within the modern corporation, and with some implicit questions of centralisation and decentralisation. In the seminar in which the work originated, the visiting industrialists, in discussing the development of their companies, referred frequently in one way or another, to decisions about policy and strategy. Their companies had experienced major changes. When the late Sir Frederick Hooper had come to the seminar, he had done so as managing director of Schweppes which had been transformed from being 'a gentleman's drink for gentlemen' into a modern format as a soft drinks company. Some years later, when Sir Adrian Cadbury came, it was as deputy chairman (he is now chairman) of Cadbury Schweppes, the resultant of a merger of the two companies. Until the later 1950s Tarmac was a roadstone company: in the period over which Mr. R.G. Martin presided as chief executive it became basically a building materials and construction company. Similar experiences have characterised the other companies considered in this study.

In Part Two, consequently, attention was focused on the meaning of strategy and its formulation: once again it was based on a dialogue with the companies which is designed to allow the executives to speak for themselves in a kind of annotated commentary. The firms considered were as before except that for TI was substituted Tarmac, where the authors had available extensive papers and discussions with Mr. Martin reinforced by discussion with Mr. Eric Pountain, Mr. Bryan Baker, and Mr. Graham Odgers. In the case of Manganese Bronze, the material was substantially extended through an interview with Mr. R.D. Poore, chairman of the company.

In his book *Strategies for Change: Logical Incrementalism,* Professor Quinn[1] gives the following quotation from an executive in General Motors Corporation:

When I was younger I always conceived of a room where all those [strategic] concepts were worked out for the whole company. Later I didn't find any such room ... The strategy [of the company] may not even exist in the mind of one man. I certainly don't know where it is written down. It is simply transmitted in the series of decisions made.

Quinn himself remarks at the outset of his book that it appeared to him that

most strategic decisions seemed to be made outside the formal planning structure, even in organizations with well-accepted planning cultures. This tendency was especially marked in entrepreneurial and smaller enterprises. As I observed my client companies over long time periods, however, it became increasingly apparent that this was also a characteristic of good management in large organizations and not an abrogation of some immutable management principle.

The concept of strategy is embodied in a certain class of decisions and what the strategies of the corporation actually are is revealed to light only in the decisions and their outcomes. The study of strategy is thus logically inseparable from the management process and is intricately interwoven with the examination of managerial initiative and control with which the earlier sections are concerned.

That is one central topic. Another is the question of how strategic questions come on to the agenda. As Kenneth Arrow[2] expresses it, whereas in classical maximising theory 'all variables are .... *agenda* of the organization, that is, their values have always to be chosen,' in reality the matter of getting something to be considered may be much greater a problem than that of assigning a value to it.

For Arrow, therefore, innovation in the firm is a question of getting a matter on to its agenda ahead of other firms. What then determines the agenda of firms, how wide should it be, who determines the strategic view?

There is, further, the mechanism by which strategic change is generated and made effective. Elting Morison[3] comments on the persistent wish of human beings to avoid the pain of changing conditions. Yet, he writes, 'As Ecclesiastes glumly pointed out, men persist in disordering their settled ways and beliefs by seeking out many inventions.'

Strategy and Strategic Decisions

The conventional treatment of strategy is concentrated on those decisions which are conceived as determinants of the general direction of an enterprise. Quinn[4] defines a strategy as 'the *pattern* or *plan* that integrates an organization's *major* goals, policies, and action sequences into a *cohesive* whole' and strategic decisions as 'those that determine the overall direction of an enterprise and its ultimate viability in light of the predictable, the unpredictable, and the unknowable changes that may occur in its most important surrounding environments.' He adds the important converse statement that 'They intricately shape the true goals of the enterprise.' These statements, though perhaps rather sweeping, are in line with other writers such as Ansoff and with industrialists' own perceptions whenever these are made explicit.

The components of strategy as they are perceived by the senior figures in the companies considered here are not always, perhaps not often, overtly stated[5] except in very general terms. Ansoff[5] remarks that business enterprises are often slow to recognise the problem of strategy and that they give periodic rather than continuous attention to it. This certainly varies from firm to firm and what is perhaps probable is that many industrialists are less disposed than academic investigators or even management consultants, to academic introspection or to conceptualising what to them appear as needs to respond to a variety of pressures. In another context, it is interesting to reflect on Mr. Poore's reply when he was asked to what matters he addressed his mind and how he used his working day. 'I suppose to a self-analytical question of that kind one never really applies one's mind.' The executives at Tarmac similarly responded to the nature of the prolonged interview with a sense of having explored in some depth what was normally for them part of a continuing series of commitments and responses to a persisting pattern of requirements.

When, however, they did pause to consider the nature of those commitments, they had no difficulty in specifying what they conceived to be their obligations as individuals and as the centre of their enterprises. The first and perhaps most obvious element in the central disposition of strategic forces is concern with the organisation as a whole. The strategic task of the centre is to determine, control or monitor the distribution of resources between the divisions and to minimise the likelihood and consequences of 'organisationally perverse decisions.' Wedded though they are to the notion of bottom-up rather than top-down approaches to the government of their firms, the senior men are all clear as to the inability of the divisions to take a wide enough view. Strategy for the group is ultimately made or at the least authorised at the centre, not only because it governs direction, but because the managers at divisional or subsidiary level cannot be expected to envisage the wider picture. In any case, they are unlikely to initiate decisions which significantly shrink their own areas of activity. In some instances, the existence of the group in itself provides a facility which frees the divisions from having to consider certain kinds of option: Gordon Yardley made this point when he said that he left diversification to Tilling although had Newey and Eyre been a wholly independent concern he might have found himself thinking about it.

The second, and related component is in respect of the balance of the group both in terms of product-market scope and of geographical dispersion. Sir Adrian Cadbury put this particularly explicitly in the example cited of the extension of Cadbury Schweppes' interests in the United States. No single division or subsidiary company can of itself arrive at a conclusion about the product and territorial spread of the group. Similarly, it is the responsibility of the board and of the executive core of Tarmac at Ettingshall, to set the parameters of product scope and international expansion though they may do so in response to projects originating in the divisions. Mr. Poore saw the corollary of this in his perception of the chief executive's role in Manganese Bronze as that of concerning himself with the relations between the separate business units. He has also to concern himself with the long-term future, with basic decisions on investment and disinvestment. Moreover, the decentralisation of decision-making rests on the ability of the divisional senior management to deliver the goods. Both Tarmac, which is a billion pound business, and Manganese Bronze, which has a turnover perhaps five per cent of that size, make the same point: there is an ultimate sanction which reposes in the centre to ensure that what it sees as the right men are appointed and retained in the senior jobs. Autonomy clearly could not imply an arbitrary power: on the contrary, it rests on methods of control, formal and informal.

The evidence of the dialogue in all the companies is that there is a flow of strategic thinking from division or subsidiary to group and that the business units are invested with an entrepreneurial responsibility. There is no obscure paradox in this: the units are expected to contribute to the strategic process but only at the centre can the balance of the group as a whole be assessed. Sir Patrick Meaney's views on the nature of the management process, matched by Adrian Cadbury's propositions on consensus and consent are held both normatively and descriptively.

Salancik and Pfeffer[6] argue that 'power is shared' (in organizations) 'because no one person controls all the desired activities in the organization.' In their 'strategic-contingency model of power,' they go on to say that 'Because power derives from activities rather than individuals, an individual's or sub-group's power is never absolute and derives ultimately from the context of the situation. The amount of power an individual has at any one time depends, not only on the activities he or she controls, but on the existence of other persons or means by which the activities can be achieved and on those who determine what ends are desired and, hence, on what activities are desired and critical for the organization.'

Both Meaney and Cadbury might be said, on the evidence of the interviews, to share this view. Meaney insists, for example, that a business must be run on a basis of trust; Cadbury emphasises the need to carry management along with the central decisions and believes that this implies a participative element in the strategic process. At Tarmac, Odgers made the point that managerial commitment was a critical factor in business projects: for this reason he held that strategic ideas should stem from the divisions and that the centre should consciously avoid imposing itself on the units in this respect. The late John Neville's example of his reluctance to press a new development against the judgement of the BSA Guns management is another instance of much the same attitude. All these senior men, however, combine this sense of a symbiotic flow in the strategic process, an intuitively favourable reaction both to the idea of diffused entrepreneurship and that of incrementalism, with a sense of their own authority and that of the centre of the organisation. It is a matter of balance: in another context Kenneth Arrow[7] wrote that 'There is plenty of reason to suppose that individual talents count a good deal more than the firm as an organization.'

The wider implications of these points for the analysis of power and authority within organisational contexts are further discussed below: at this stage they serve to emphasise the fundamentally subjective character of strategy formulation. It lies within the minds and perceptions of the executives and within that group particular individuals at the centre play a major part in setting the parameters of policy i.e. the general values and goals of the company and its strategy. This study has emphasised the nature of business as a system of governance but of course there is no virtue in throwing out the heroes with the hero worship.

So far, the elements which have been distinguished are those of the marshalling of the major forces of the organisation to move in terms of general strategy and responsibility for the balance of the organisation as between its constituent parts. There is a third feature of strategic concern, namely, the design of the corporate structure. The choice of product-market scope is not the whole of the strategic concept. It is certainly the stage on which the activity of the business is played out: but *corporate* strategy extends beyond market strategy and entrepreneurship consists also in the determination of the overall organisational system. This has two aspects: there is the selection of those factors which are retained within the control of the centre, which will stem from the basic decisions about centralisation and decentralisation and the specific structural forms designed to achieve the desired balance between them. Thus, in all the cases considered here, finance and the appointment and promotion of top personnel are within the competence of the centre. This is well understood in the literature on centralisation and decentralisation and it is emphasised by the industrialists from two points of view. On the one hand, as Tilling and Tarmac specifically indicated, they hold that their scale and credibility make it easier to provide the funds required for major developments in the business. On the other hand, they see themselves as having a commitment to the business units: there was a very marked comment on this from Mr. Odgers who said that he would regard it as a serious shortcoming if the centre ever had to refuse funds for a worthwhile project emanating from a division.

Similarly, the organisational relationships both formal and informal, the structure of governance and its conventions, clearly exercise the attention of the senior executives at the centre. Moreover, this is mirrored within the major separate units. Meaney clearly thinks in these terms for Tilling but so, for example, does Hickman for Newey and Eyre when he says that he has to think tactically 'in the operational role' but also strategically because of his position on the board of Newey and Eyre. When he speaks of the strategy of that company he is looking at 'what shape it will have and into what product range it is going to move.' Hickman was not necessarily using 'shape' in the literal sense of organisational pattern. Nevertheless, it is interesting that he should employ the term. Similarly, in Cadbury's remark about Kenco cited earlier in this study, a concern with structure is quite explicit.

To sum up this part of the argument, it can be said that even within the complex and perhaps bureaucratic design of the large modern corporation, the sense of alertness to opportunities as the hallmark of entrepreneurship is not lost. Nor is entrepreneurship purely a matter of organisation: it is exercised by individuals albeit through organisational procedures and processes. These individuals at various levels of the enterprise and with different degrees of authority and power are engaged in the strategic process. At the centre of the organisation overall strategic mission is defined and overall control asserted. Pfeffer[8] points out

> that decisions are, in large measure, determined by the premises used in making them. As Simon (1964) discussed when he described organizational goals as systems of constraints, if a given party can determine the constraints, then they can in effect determine the decision. Similarly, decisions can be affected by the goals, norms and rules that are advanced and then accepted by those participating in the decision making situation. Therefore, those social actors who either have or can acquire influence over the constraints and the values and norms employed in the decision making process can substantially affect the decision outcome.

Pfeffer's statement is part of his much more extensive analysis and it would go beyond the evidence of the dialogues presented here to generalise too widely about the multifarious influences and circumstances which, as Cadbury put it, play on the ultimate outcome. He thought that the influence of single individuals had diminished but at the same time it seems clear that small numbers of persons bear a particular weight in setting the values and parameters within which action is permitted. The Tarmac executives undoubtedly regarded it as a matter for them, as the centre of the group, to determine whether or not major projects in the divisions should go forward and they did so if those projects fell within their concept of the nature of the business. Thus, Quinn is right in presenting strategy as something which emerges 'in the series of decisions made' and in his implied assent to the proposition that 'it may not even exist in the mind of one man.' What he says is within the same kind of framework as Lindblom and Alford but it may run the risk of understating the function of senior individuals and of their perceptions.

Strategy and the Agenda

Two of the most striking points made by Sir Adrian Cadbury are his description of the selection of options which Cadbury Schweppes chooses to consider and his complementary view that 'you are giving people a few guidelines against which they ought to measure whether they take this deecision or that decision. I believe that this is as far as you can go.'

It is clear from this approach, which is repeated in the experience of other companies, that strategic behaviour is as much a matter of deciding what to do and where to go as of how successful the firm is in doing it. Arrow's penetrating remarks rightly direct attention to the fact that firms do not operate with a given agenda: they recall Simon's pioneering emphasis on the function of the executives in choosing the balance of objectives and in designing alternatives. A similar pre-occupation is reflected in Loasby's[9] discussion of the width of the business agenda: it requires to be wide enough to take into account the relevant interdependencies, not so wide as to incur excessive diseconomies in organisational communications and inertia.

Sometimes the agenda of the business enterprise and changes in it may be determined by major changes in the external environment. Thomas Tilling is of course an acute example since the company's situation was radically altered by the legislative programme of the 1945 Government. Mr. Martin describes the changed configuration of Tarmac after the late 1950s partly in terms of perceived changes in the environment, notably the expansion of the road-building programme. It need not be sudden shock: indeed, the experience of some companies which have made inadequate responses or even succumbed to such shock is frequently the record of failure to recognise the fundamental character of individual changes in the environment or even to notice them. Martin stressed the gradual nature of the change in corporate policy: in retrospect, he noted, the picture is one of abrupt and total reversal of what had gone before. But while that may be true of what occurred, it does not accurately describe the process by which it came about. This was much more a melding of changed perceptions in the mind of new management in the light of a changing environment. Viewed *ex post,* it has been pointed out[10], strategies always look like 'patterns in streams of decisions.' But *ex ante* they are 'causes which mould streams of decisions into patterns.' More generally, 'Strategies are the more or less well integrated sets of ideas and constructs through which problems are spotted and interpreted and in the light of which actions are invented and selected.'

Mr. Martin's remarks draw attention to an aspect of change which once stated seems perfectly obvious but which is not for that reason always observed. The ability of a firm to create, perceive and respond to opportunities depends on the internal receptivity of the organisation. The movement of a business is not along a predetermined groove which must be followed like the maximising firm with perfect knowledge in the neo-classical model. Observation and discussion suggest, not only that different firms pursue different strategies within the same external environment: they may not even focus on the same set of options.

How that receptivity is engendered, how in other words, the company creates its agenda is clearly fundamental but it admits of no simple answer. In the companies considered in Part 2 of this book (and earlier in Tube Investments) a critical part is played by a modest number of dominant individuals located at the group centre and *mutatis mutandis* at the top of major subsidiaries or divisions. Meaney and Yardley are instances of the two levels in Tilling and this is perceived by other executives in the group: Poore puts it explicitly when he places business direction, investment and divestment in the forefront of his pre-occupations. Bagnall saw this as the function of the centre in TI − to think out policy and strategic direction. Even in the managerial bureaucracy of the modern corporation, these are the heirs of the classical entrepreneur, insofar as the creative recognition of opportunity is concerned.

None of these men see themselves, however, in the classical mould in the sense of the nineteenth century captain who initiated the business, since they are at one and the same time both the products of the organised corporation and the actors inside it. They have a peculiar importance which stems in part from 'the power to define what is critical,' (Salancik and Pfeffer) since for them as for sub-units in an organisation, power *is* a matter of determining what *are* the critical organisational problems. But they exercise that power through the processes and procedures of organisation: moreover, although it is the case that ideas frequently originate in the centre, leading the enterprise on 'the path of discovery' as John Neville expressed it, the agenda is not wholly determined in this way. As has been repeatedly emphasised, the subsidiaries are also required to play a part in the determination of the strategic agenda.

In business enterprise as in all activity there is an element of serendipity and to that extent what comes up for consideration and the place which any item occupies on the agenda are not predetermined by the existing structure and background of the managers. But no organisation is a pure *tabula rasa* and in large, continuing systems, the expertise which has been built up through time and the forms which have been established, influence the directions of thought. A very widespread impression which is received is that what eventually emerge as major departures, innovations in products, markets, and corporate organisation, are the outcome of a quite elaborate though not wholly formal process. Ideas are in the atmosphere, floated in response to a variety of internal and external considerations and pressures and in exchanges among individuals. Thus, at Tarmac, the senior executives at the centre emphasised the importance of propinquity: this is not a matter of abstraction but of persons who meet and discuss matters frequently with their colleagues in 'the next door office.'

It is of course true that devastatingly new ideas occur to entrepreneurial individuals: Kirzner and Shackle-type men are to be seen at the origins of major firms and in their continuing development. The key factor is their ability to perceive and to develop profitable business opportunities and this is pertinent both in the relatively small, owner-managed enterprise of which Marshall was thinking and in the large modern corporation. Adrian Cadbury thought that 'managers divide into those who have this perception and those (the majority) who have precisely the same map of the market but cannot see how to exploit it in an original way.' In the discussions with him about entrepreneurship, Cadbury said that he found it difficult to see what was meant by the term 'entrepreneurial function' in a large company such as his own 'owned by institutions and professionally managed.' But he himself provides a large part of the answer precisely when he interprets the function as the capacity to exploit possibilities. Of course in the large modern corporation the formulation of strategy is a complex, interactive process and the provenance of ideas cannot be located solely in one spot nor can their progress through the company be traced along only one thread. In large organisations, moreover,the element of consent based on shared realities, is extremely important as Adrian Cadbury emphasised in the context of even so major a decision as a merger. But this emphasis on organisational behaviour does not mean that organisations are, so to speak, blind beasts: the decisions are made by individuals within them, albeit within the organisational framework.

An example of the balance between individual and organisation is afforded by Quinn[11] who quotes an executive as follows:

Typically you start with general concerns, vaguely felt. Next you roll an issue around in your mind till you think you have a conclusion that makes sense for the company. You then go out and sort of post the idea without being too wedded to its details. You then start hearing the arguments pro and con, and some very good refinements of the idea usually emerge. Then you pull the idea in and put some resources together to study it so that it can be put forward as more of a formal presentation. You wait for 'stimuli occurrences' or 'crises', and launch pieces of the idea to help in these situations. But they lead you toward your ultimate aim. You know where you want to get. You'd like to get there in six months. But it may take three years, or you may not get there. And when you do get there, you don't know whether it was originally your own idea — or somebody else had reached the same conclusion before you and just got you on board for it. You never know. The president would follow the same basic process, but he could drive it much faster than an executive lower in the organization.

The extent to which this step-by-step, incremental process is a valid picture of the genesis and progress of change in the large modern corporation i.e. how far it may be regarded as a legitimate generalisation, is a matter for continued research. Indeed, as Leibenstein[12] remarks: 'The question of how individuals in multiperson firms influence firm decisions seems like such a natural question to ask that it is amazing that it is not part of the formal agenda of economists as a profession .... In other words, micro-microeconomics has never become an established field.' But the description is both intuitively attractive and readily recognisable in the experience of anybody who has been in a managerial role in a large organisation, and emerged frequently in the companies here studied. At the same time, the final sentence in the quotation lays emphasis on the differential powers of executives in a hierarchy and on the initiatory part played by top men: hence, for example, Yardley's attribution of an entrepreneurial function to Meaney, Poore's sense of his responsibility for scanning the more distant horizon, the emphasis placed by John Neville and Pountain on their own personal contact with the key figures in the divisions.

A Concluding Comment

In his study 'Gunfire at Sea' which was referred to earlier, Morison[13] showed how a resistance to change was inherent in the attachment of men to their existing habits of mind and how this was breached by a direct appeal to the highest authority, in this instance the President of the United States. At the same time, Morison's remark quoted above about the persistence of men in 'seeking out many inventions' is verified in the extent of business innovation in products, methods and managerial structures.

The evidence of the cases considered here is that the formulation of strategy may be expressed in Simon's[14] words about decisions in general. 'A decision', he says, 'is not a simple, unitary event, but the product of a complex social process generally extending over a considerable period of time .... decision making includes attention-directing or intelligence processes that determine the occasion of decision, processes for discovering and designing possible courses of action, and processes for evaluating alternatives and choosing among them.' And again, Witte[15] depicts decision-making by saying that 'a complex innovative decision is a multi-operational, multi-temporal process; a complex decision-making process consists of a plurality of sub-decisions.'

The first instance expresses in rather dramatic form, the importance of the top man in cutting through customary procedures and conventions: the second emphasises the complexity of decision-making in organisations which are systems of governance. The views of Cadbury and Pountain illustrate the role of the centre in setting the guidelines within which particular strategies are formed. R.G. Martin illustrates the close connection between strategy in the market and the creation of corporate structure when he speaks of the 'never-ceasing exercise' of creating 'new tiers of management' in a growing company. In all, the interviews which constitute the substance of this book exemplify the interplay of individuals and organisational processes out of which the activities of firms emerge.

Notes

1. Quinn J.B. *Strategies for Change: Logical Incrementalism*
   Richard D. Irwin Inc., Homewood, Illinois, 1980, Chapter 2, p. 13 and Preface p. ix.
2. Arrow K.J. *The Limits of Organization*
   W.W. Norton, New York, 1974.

Part 3. The Agenda of Organizations, p.47.

3. Morison E. 'Gunfire at Sea: A Case Study of Innovation'
In: *Readings in the Management of Innovation*
Tushman M.L. and Moore W.L. (Eds.) Pitman, London, 1982.
Section 1, Chapter 1, p. 84.

4. Quinn J.B. *Op. cit.,* p. 7 and p. 8.

5. Ansoff H.I. *Corporate Strategy*
McGraw-Hill, 1965.
See, especially, Chapter 1, pp. 5-10. See, also, his paper
'Towards a Strategic Theory of the Firm.'
In: *Business Strategy,* Ansoff H.I. (Ed.), Penguin,
Harmondsworth, 1969, pp. 15-21.

6. Salancik G.R. and Pfeffer J. 'Who Gets Power – And How They Hold on
to It: A Strategic-Contingency Model of
Power.'
In: *Readings in the Management of Innovation Op. cit.,* Section II, Chapter 4, p. 227
and pp. 227-228.

7. Arrow K.J. In: *The Rational Direction of Inventive Activity: Economic
and Social Factors.* Nelson R. (Ed.) Princeton University
Press, Princeton, 1962, p. 624.

8. Pfeffer J. *Power in Organizations*
Pitman, 1981.
Chapter 4, p. 116.
The reference is to Simon's paper 'On the Concept of
Organizational Goals', *Administrative Science Quarterly* 9:
1-22, 1964.

9. Loasby B.J. *Choice, Complexity and Ignorance*
Cambridge University Press 1976.
See, particularly, Chapter 5.

10. Naslund B. and Sellstedt B.

11. Quinn J.B. *Op. cit.,* p. 102.

12. Leibenstein H. 'A Branch of Economics is Missing: Micro-Micro
Theory.' *Journal of Economic Literature,* Vol. XVII,
June 1979, pp. 477-502.

13. Morison E. *Op. cit.*

14. Simon H.A. 'Administrative Decision Making.'
Public Administration Review, Vol. XXV, No. 1, March
1965.
Reprinted as Reprint No. 189, Graduate School of
Industrial Administration, Carnegie Institute of
Technology, 1965.

15. Witte E. 'Field Research on Complex Decision – Making Processess –
The Phase Theorem.'
International Studies of Management and Organization,
Vol. II, No. 2, Summer 1972.
p. 177 and pp. 156-182 *passim*.

INDEX